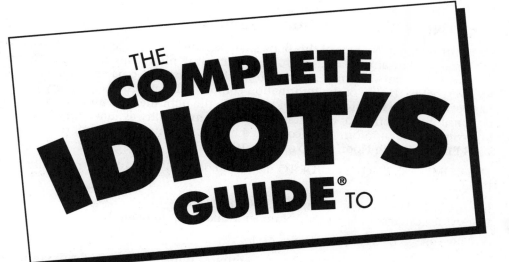

THE COMPLETE IDIOT'S GUIDE® TO

Learning Italian on Your Own

by Gabrielle Euvino

alpha books

A Division of Macmillan General Reference
A Simon & Schuster Macmillan Company
1633 Broadway, New York, NY 10019

Alpha Development Team

Publisher
Kathy Nebenhaus

Editorial Director
Gary M. Krebs

Managing Editor
Bob Shuman

Marketing Brand Manager
Felice Primeau

Senior Editor
Nancy Mikhail

Development Editors
Phil Kitchel
Jennifer Perillo
Amy Zavatto

Editorial Assistant
Maureen Horn

Development Editor
Amy Zavatto

Production Team

Production Editor
Stephanie Mohler

Copy Editor
Kris Simmons

Cover Designer
Mike Freeland

Photo Editor
Richard H. Fox

Illustrator
Jody P. Schaeffer

Designer
Glenn Larsen

Indexer
Nadia Ibrahim

Layout/Proofreading
Jeanne Clark
Christy Lemasters
Sossity Smith
Heather Stephenson

Contents at a Glance

Contents

Introduction

Reading can transport you to an entirely different dimension. A historical novel allows you to leave the present and revisit the past; science fiction enables you to jump into the future. When you read a good travelogue, you feel as though you are visiting that place. When you read an autobiography, you learn about someone—what they feel and how they think. When you read a language book, you expect to learn a new language. How does this process occur?

Much has been written on the theory of second language acquisition, which might be regarded as a separate process from learning a language. When you *acquire* a language, you are essentially absorbing the language, a primarily subconscious endeavor. When you *learn* something, you are consciously processing information, which you then use to achieve a stated goal.

Researchers intrigued by the process involved with language learning have gained a few insights:

1. **Grammar**. An understanding of grammar, verbs, and vocabulary is essential. Rules help the student make sense of an otherwise chaotic subject that has no real significance unless interpreted. However, research indicates that the more self-conscious the student, the more concentrated he or she is on form, *the less* that student is operating on the subconscious level, which is where real communication takes place.

2. **Exposure to a language**. It doesn't have to be all drills and memorization. When you expose yourself to Italian through books, films, music, and art, you are creating a context within which the language can emerge. It's no longer a bunch of words and sounds, but a vital, living organism. Without that input, the language remains one-dimensional and without purpose.

3. **Availability**. If you're open, your chances are much better at learning a new language. This sounds obvious, but if you have an idea of yourself as "lingually challenged" or without "an ear" for language, then you'll most likely live up (or down) to that expectation of yourself. Forget that C you got in high school or the last time you took a language course. You probably formed an idea of yourself based on someone else's projections. Deciding that one *will* accomplish a goal is half the battle.

4. **The Silent Period**. You're going to experience peaks and valleys. Expect them, embrace them, and be patient with yourself. If you find yourself retreating back to what you know, namely your first language, don't beat yourself up. You're digging for information that hasn't been planted. In many respects, you are reduced to a child-like status. Growth often occurs in mysterious, almost imperceptible ways. Give yourself space to breathe.

5. **Age**. Children are considered more adept at acquiring a second language largely because they are simply more open than adults. They're not afraid of making a mistake or sounding like a fool. On the other hand, adults have the advantage of being able to read; they have mastered their primary language and are more skillful at expressing when they do not understand. Many adults have high expectations of themselves and are uncomfortable with not having the ability to express their basic needs and thoughts. This is an emotional issue that is not about verbs, grammar, and vocabulary.

6. **Immersion**. Naturally, the best way to learn a language is to immerse yourself. You've got to get your feet wet if you want to swim. Where there is no other recourse but to negotiate through a second language, you're thereby forced to rely on your innate capacity to process the information presented. Not everyone can take leave of their life and move to a Tuscan village, however. Investing in a good immersion program for a day or a weekend might be the best way to take your language skills to a deeper level. Where English is not given as an option, you'll either sink or swim.

Learning or Acquiring: What's the Difference?

Intuitively, you understand much more than you realize. According to Noam Chomsky, a leader in the fields of linguistics and political science, we are all born with what is called a *language acquisition device* (LAD). Regardless of how we best learn, Chomsky's theory presumes we all have similar mechanisms in place at the time of birth that allow us to "absorb" language, and the constant chirping of Mamma and Pappa serves as input that we then process. All babies are born with this ability, and except in cases of autism, deafness, or other physiological disorders, whether the language is Chinese, English, or Italian, you somehow "pick up" what is communicated to you without one iota of grammar.

This has a lot to do with exposure. The child who is exposed to a language hears the same thing repeated over and over again, and slowly he begins to understand what is said. Later in school, that same child may analyze the language, but this is only after he has already learned how to comprehend and express himself.

How Important Are Rules?

You study rules until you're blue in the face, yet you're still quite a distance from fluency in Italian. This book is intended to give you an outline of the most important aspects of verbs, grammar, and idiomatic expressions, but these things alone are not enough. You need to hear Italian every chance you get. And don't be surprised if the first thing that comes to mind is French or Spanish or whatever the last language was that you studied. Your brain is a living computer and whenever it hears a foreign word, it goes to the foreign language section and pulls out whatever "comes to mind."

As you go deeper into Italian, continue to review the things you have already studied. Do it in a way that isn't overly critical. If you need to constantly return to Chapter 9, "Working the Crowd," to remember your verbs, do so. Language is not like mathematics in that you need to learn to count before you can multiply. Many things are learned out of sequence. You may remember how to use the future tense better than the past or vice versa. It doesn't matter, as long as you keep with it. Ultimately, you're not an idiot, or you wouldn't be reading this book.

How to Use This Book

Part 1, "The Basics," gives you the basics of the language, bringing you through in-depth definitions and explanations of key grammatical forms, verbs, and structure. You'll learn about cognates—how to make associations, or bridges, between English and Italian that your brain can recognize, helping you to retain your new language. The spoken poetry of slang and idiomatic expressions is also introduced.

Part 2, "You're Off and Running," gives you the vocabulary necessary for a variety of situations. You'll learn how to introduce you and your family, how to catch a taxi or bus, and how to make your way from the airport and get yourself set up in a hotel. It's a practical section you'll find indispensable while traveling.

Part 3, "Fun and Games." Do you love chocolate? Are you a clothes hound? Whether you're attending the opera or visiting a museum, this section offers you the vocabulary you need to enjoy the things that make Italy so special. It also gives you a more detailed understanding of irregular verbs.

Part 4, "Trouble in Paradise," prepares you for the inevitable challenges that are a part of the human experience. You'll learn how to describe the different aches and pains in your body to a doctor, how to ask a pharmacist for the right cure, where to go to get your glasses fixed, and how to find a good dry cleaner. Included in this section is a helpful list of terms used in banking and real estate for those of you interested in taking your love of Italy to a deeper level. It also introduces new verb tenses you need to achieve your goal of fluency.

Appendix A, "Answer Key," gives you the answers to the exercises offered throughout the book so you can check your progress.

Appendix B, "Verb Tables," contains charts for you to use to practice conjugating verbs, and will also serve as a convenient reference.

Appendix C, "Glossary," is a helpful resource, with English to Italian and Italian to English listings.

Appendix D, "Map of Italy," shows you the regions of Italy.

Extras

Throughout the book, you'll see interesting sidebars that highlight relevant aspects of the language and culture. You'll see the following icons:

As a Rule

As a Rule sidebars highlight or expand on some aspect of Italian grammar that has been touched on in the text.

Attenzione!

Attenzione boxes highlight particularly ambiguous or irregular elements of the Italian language.

What's What

What's What gives you definitions of grammatical terms.

Did You Know?

Did You Know? provides cultural and historical facts about interesting facets of life in Italy.

Acknowledgments

I've been waiting a long time to write one of these pages. One does not get anywhere without help, and that certainly applies to this book. There have been so many people whose acts of kindness have bettered this planet that I'd like to take a moment to thank some of them for their consistency and reliability.

For my parents, Louis and Lorrie, whose encouragement and wisdom left their imprint. In their memory the love stays alive.

To my students, whose energy feeds me, whose curiosity propels me, whose questions teach me, I devote this book especially to you.

Special thanks to my technical editors, the writer and journalist Stefano Spadoni, and author Anna Maria Pellegrino, for patiently checking my work and answering my endless questions at any time of day or night. As foreigners in a big city like New York, they have proven that vision combined with hard work equals success.

A big *grazie* to:

Gary Krebs, my acquiring editor, an angel with a great tie collection.

Amy Zavatto, my development editor, a kindred spirit with the patience and understanding of a saint.

My family: my baby brother Robert (a.k.a. Reptile Rob); Uncle Herby, "aunty" Sandy and TL; Andrea Euvino, Anthony and "poops," Rose Canino, Virgil Householder; my "cuzins" Barbara, Steve, and Miriam Peterson, and Shelly Friedland, who share my love of Italy.

To H. S. Ellison, without whom this book may never have been written and whose shoulders allowed me to peek over life's hedges.

To all the people who in one form or another have guided me through the dark times or have been there to celebrate the light: Sascha Ascher, Anne Bianchi, Rosemary Sava-Colao, Michael DeSimone, Giovanni Destillo, Laurie DiBenedetto, the Ellison family, Nick Fucci, Kilian Ganly, Elaine and Jen Grossman, Kim and Andrew Malcolm, Mario Mannone, the McFaul family, Jessica Mezyk, Marissa Palmisano, Trish Palumbo, Mags, Tony and Mark Salamone, Donna Sillan, Hege Steen, Elpi Stefanakis, Carl Stormer, and Beth Walden, Leslie Williams, and God help me, anyone else whose name has escaped me for the moment—thank you!

To Devorah Serafini and my friends at SSF&G—you kept a hungry writer from starving and helped groom me for the enormous effort of preparing this book.

To the following organizations: Alitalia, The Italian Tourist Board, The Italian Academy at Colombia, the College at New Paltz, New York University, The Film Society at Lincoln Center.

And finally, a message to the universe: I hear you hear me. Thank you.

Part 1
The Basics

You're ready to go. You've purchased this book and have taken the first step to learning Italian. Some of you have studied another foreign language and have a sense of what is involved with learning a second (or third) language. For others, it's completely uncharted territory.

Part 1 gives you the fundamentals of Italian. It focuses on important parts of grammar, verbs, and pronunciation. It shows you cognates (similar sounding words) and how you can use these to link Italian with English. It explains the tools to language learning and how you can begin practicing your new skills immediately. Finally, it shows you how to pronounce the Italian you are reading.

Don't be intimidated by the grammar or get hung up on what you think you should know. When you undertake learning a new language, you are like a child again—so much to learn! Be like a child and proceed without ego or expectation. Play, live, learn.

Keep your eyes on the prize and stick with your dream. Anyone *can learn Italian. Just put one foot in front of the other and* prima o poi *(sooner or later), you'll get to the end of the rainbow.*

Chapter 1

Why You Should Study Italian

In This Chapter

➤ The many virtues of the Italian language

➤ Where you can use Italian

➤ Developing a learning strategy

➤ There's no reason to be afraid!

It's recognizable immediately: the gentle cadence of words as beautiful as music, the sexy rolling of Rs, the soothing, sensual lilt of voices that move you as does an opera, a poem, or a beautiful work of art. It's the Italian language, and there's nothing quite like it.

You've always wanted to learn Italian. Until now, it's been a dream, something you wished you could do but never dared. Maybe you took a high school Italian class because you needed the credits, and you remember the word spaghetti but not much else. Perhaps you come from an Italian background and feel a desire to satisfy a primordial urge. You get weak-kneed when you hear an opera. You're an incurable romantic and want to murmur sweet nothings to your lover in Italian. You love traveling and want to follow in the tradition of the great writers, from Shakespeare to Henry James to Goethe. Could it be that you want to learn the language because it will connect you to something wonderfully mysterious, ancient, and rich? Whatever your reason, that small peninsula in the center of the Mediterranean has been affecting the lives of people, both great and ordinary, for as long as our calendar has existed and then some, and you want to be a part of it.

If you still need to ask, "Why learn Italian?" read on for a few more reasons.

You Love Life

The Complete Idiot's Guide to Learning Italian is a book written for you. You sense this as soon as you pull it off the shelf. You can feel it almost vibrate with potential. Yes, this time you're going to stick to your promise to learn Italian. You're not going to procrastinate any longer; you've been wanting this for a very long time and life is too short to spend wishing you had done something fully within your powers to do. The time is right, the time is now, and with this book, you will be one large step closer to making a dream come true.

Remember: Every great accomplishment starts as an idea. Imagine the reality of speaking Italian. You'll be able to:

> **Did You Know?**
> Italy's population is almost 58 million. According to one myth, a vestal virgin gave birth to the twin boys, Remus and Romulus. Saved from drowning by a she-wolf who suckled the children until they were old enough to go out on their own, Romulus later killed his brother and founded Rome, sometime around 753 B.C. Another myth involves the Trojan Aeneas, who came to Italy after escaping Troy. The great Latin poet Virgil used this as the basis for the *Aeneid*, unquestionably the single greatest epic poem of classical literature.

➤ Order your favorite dish in the local Italian *ristorante*, the one with the great food.

➤ Watch Fellini films without reading the subtitles.

➤ Quit pretending you know Italian by adding a vowel to the end of every word and *really* tell the taxi driver which direction you want to go.

➤ Understand what your in-laws are saying about you while they smile and wipe the tomato sauce off their chins.

➤ Go beyond feeling the passion of one of Puccini's operas, and genuinely understand Mimì's tortured heart in *La Bohème*.

➤ Read the soccer scores from the Italian newspapers.

➤ Understand the labels on those discount designer clothes you'll be able to buy because the nice Italian *signora* at the register told you about a sample sale down the street.

➤ Sound sexy.

➤ Sound smart.

Get Real

Now, get down to some *real* reasons to speak Italian:

➤ Leonardo da Vinci, Michelangelo, Giotto, Galileo, San Francesco, and Dante (to name just a few) did.

➤ You're studying art history. So far, the closest you've actually been to the masterpieces is the slide projector in the back of the auditorium. You're thinking of spending a semester in Florence to study the works of the great Renaissance artists—including Botticelli, Raffaello, Caravaggio, Pisano, Masaccio, and Ghirlandaio—and you want to follow the lectures offered in the local *università*.

➤ Ever since you discovered there were forms of music other than rock and roll, you can't get enough opera. You're planning to spend your honeymoon in Italy and you're buying tickets to see an opera in Milan.

➤ You love Italian food and can boil a mean pot of water. You're ready to take the next step and learn about what really happens in the kitchen. You've found an adorable school tucked away in the Tuscan countryside among the silvery leaves of olive trees. It feels like a time capsule where you've just jumped back three or four centuries, and if you never saw another telephone in your life, you wouldn't be sorry.

➤ You are an amateur wine connoisseur and plan to spend your next vacation visiting all the major vineyards where you can sample wines for your collection.

➤ Gardens! You've been dallying with various plant forms and flowers in your back yard and now you're ready to take it a little further—see how the pros have been doing it for centuries. There isn't a province in Italy that doesn't have a villa tucked away somewhere, where it's hard not to envision young, giggling maidens dancing among the rose bushes, their dashing suitors hiding discreetly behind the hedges.

➤ You're fascinated by ancient burial rituals and you want to visit the catacombs. You're not afraid of dark, moldy tunnels, you love the sound of bats, and you have always been intrigued by bones, skulls, and preserved body parts. You've been assured you won't get lost in the labyrinth of secret passages and chambers that once held the remains of early Christian martyrs and on a hot day, it's a great way to cool off.

➤ You love driving. There's only one car named Ferrari and you know there's nothing practical about driving a car made for speed, but wouldn't it be fun to do something just because? You want leather gloves that stretch tight over your knuckles, sunglasses that look like goggles, and a supermodel in the passenger seat. Okay, even if it's your best buddy sitting beside you, you still wouldn't mind driving along the Amalfi coast, the sunlight sparkling off the emerald waters as opera music blares from the stereo.

➤ You love walking. You decide to leave your sneakers in your room and pull out the loafers you bought on sale at the small leather shop in Florence. You want to amble through the winding *vie* (streets) of Siena, stroll past the limpid waters of Venice's canals, hike along the Appian way, and meander the ruins of Pompeii where, in 79 A.D., Mt. Vesuvius buried 2000 people under a layer of dust, lava, and stone. You'll walk so much you won't feel a twinge of guilt when the delicious food starts coming, and you'll say yes to dessert every time.

➤ You want to learn the secret that Italians have known for centuries—the healing elements of mud and mineral baths. You won't believe how something so stinky (the hot springs often smell like sulfur) could make your body feel so alive, so fresh, so pure. Your entire body covered in mud, you leave the camera in the car for this one.

➤ You are considering becoming a photojournalist. You want to wear khaki and carry several cameras around your neck as you search for that candid shot. You want to fill a book with images of old women hanging the laundry or their husbands sitting at the local bar down the street playing chess. You want to catch images of a bunch of stray tomcats eating leftover spaghetti from a piece of newspaper or young couples sitting along the Ponte Vecchio embracing.

➤ Pinocchio was Italian. You're writing a dissertation on the implications of his nose and you need to do some primary research.

Getting Wet

Whatever your reason is for wanting to learn Italian, you need to begin somewhere. You'll never learn to swim if you don't get wet; the same principle applies to learning a language. Before you even get to Italy, your journey begins with your intent. You've already made a great start by picking up this book. However, you also might want to consider some of the following tips.

Immerse Yourself—Literally!

Get used to the language by reading it. When you buy books of Italian poetry or a copy of Pirandello's plays, for example, buy the versions where the Italian translation is given alongside the English so that your eyes can move back and forth between the two. This saves you the effort of looking up every word you don't understand and gives you a general idea of what is being communicated.

Speaking of books, inspiration often comes from the unexpected. Go to your bookstore and leaf through several books in the Italian language section. See what interests you. Barrons has a terrific book that concentrates exclusively on verbs, aptly called *501 Italian Verbs*. Children's books are another fun way of building vocabulary. If you're in Italy, visit the *libreria* (bookstore) and pick up a few.

Italian publications, especially magazines, are usually quite entertaining, full of glossy, color ads and interesting facts. Fashion, travel, and food are three popular topics. Pick up a copy and figure out the contents by studying the titles. *La Cucina*, *L'Espresso*, *Oggi*, *Panorama*, and *Vogue Italia* are but a few. Italian newspapers include *La Repubblica*, *Il Corriere della Sera*, and *La Stampa*. Also, the next time a friend takes a trip to Italy, ask him or her to bring back the in-flight magazine if it has both the Italian and English. Alitalia produces a wonderful publication that has the Italian and the English side-by-side. You'll be surprised at how much you can pick up.

Become a Class Act

Call your local university and investigate whether it has an Italian department. Find out if it has a mailing list for events and make a point of meeting other "Italophiles."

Hang Out with Sophia

Rent Italian movies! Every week, make it a ritual to sit in front of your television (for educational purposes, naturally). Needless to say, you want the subtitled versions (stay away from anything dubbed—a character is his voice). Listen to the actors, read the words, and just enjoy. You will absorb far more if you are relaxed and having fun. Try to make out the different words within each sentence. Isolate words that are repeated. Make it a game to see how many words you understand.

Get the Right Tools

Invest in a good bilingual dictionary, preferably one printed in Italy. (Garzanti or Zanichelli are both excellent.)

Flash cards are also a good resource. You can pick up a box of flash cards at any bookstore, or you can make your own. That unused box of business cards from your old job or unused pages from your last address book are perfect. Punch holes in them and put 10 or 20 on a key ring so you can put them in your pocket or bag for "study quickies." Five minutes stolen here and there, waiting in line at the post office, at the bank, or in a traffic jam, can add up to more than you imagine.

Tune In!

Find out what station has Italian news. RAI, the Italian television and radio network, airs programs every day. Even though it will sound as though they are speaking a million miles a minute, exposing your ears to the language will evolve into understanding it.

Read the Fine Print

Keep the owner's manual to any appliances, electronics, or cameras that include multi-lingual instructions. This is a great way to learn technical terms, and once more, you don't need to pick up a dictionary; the English translation is probably already there.

Find Birds of a Feather

Study the language with a friend. There's nothing like having a partner to keep you motivated and on your toes. Practice together, and maybe invest in a private tutor to meet with you every couple of weeks. The cost is usually reasonable considering the kind of attention you will receive, and it will be good incentive to keep up with your studies.

While you're at it, make some Italian friends—or better yet, an Italian lover (assuming you don't already have one, that is). There's nothing like a good conversation (or quarrel) to hone your skills.

Play It Again, Salvatore

Make tapes of yourself speaking Italian and then play these tapes to a native Italian speaker (your new friends, the waiter in the local restaurant, your grandmother, or anyone who will listen). Ask them to evaluate your linguistic strengths and weaknesses.

There's Nothing to Fear

Learning a language does not occur overnight. As with all new projects, you will be hard-working and organized during the initial period, until such time that it requires real effort and discipline. Being aware of this can help you surpass the inevitable dip in your enthusiasm and persevere. You can learn Italian; it does not have to remain a dream. There is nothing to stop you from obtaining this goal. At times, your progress will be obvious; other times, you will wonder what, if anything, is being accomplished. The process of learning a language can be likened to watching a morning glory open. You can stare at it for hours and never see the gentle movement of its petal. Remember, it's the journey that counts, not just the destination. The following list outlines a few things to keep in mind that will make your journey a little smoother:

➤ *Set realistic goals.* Whether you devote 10 minutes a day, every day, or 2 hours a week on Sundays, stick to your program. If you can't do it one week, no guilt trips. Make it up the next week.

➤ *Grammar isn't for geeks.* Grammar is simply a tool for learning a language. You figured out how to communicate your needs and understand what your mother was telling you long before you could identify an adjective, noun, or verb. It probably started with a simple word, such as cookie, which you mispronounced as "coo-coo." As you matured, you began expressing your likes and dislikes with words such as "No!" or "Me!" Your mother did not follow you around saying, "That's a noun!" or "What a great verb you used!" She responded to your needs as best she could, based on your ability to communicate. Grammar is simply the vocabulary, as any trade will have, used in language learning. Fear not.

➤ *Make mistakes.* Lots of them. You never know what mistake might end up being a discovery. Did the great Renaissance man Leonardo da Vinci draw the Mona Lisa (entitled *La Gioconda* in Italian) the first time he picked up a pen? Would we know Christopher Columbus if he had made it to India? Hello! Get it? Make mistakes. It's the only way to learn.

➤ *Don't be intimidated.* The Italians are among the most warm, hospitable, fun-loving, open people you could ever meet. Your attempt to speak their language, even in the most basic of ways, will elicit nothing less than enthusiasm and good will toward you. Say *buon giorno* (good day) every time you walk into an establishment and watch the response. They are listening to what you are saying, not what mistakes you may have made. Put yourself in their shoes and remember the last time someone speaking English as a second language impressed you with his command of the language, the whole time murmuring, "I don't speak so good." "Are you kidding?" you want to ask them. "You speak very well!"

➤ *Practice rolling your Rs in the shower.* Or anywhere that you feel less inhibited. Pretend you're a purring, happy cat sitting on someone's lap. RRRRRRR. There are only a couple of letter combinations that make sounds you won't find in English, and even then, as long as you get your message across, who's going to care?

Italian is an easy language to learn. It's another story to master the language, but you can cross that *ponte* (bridge) when you come to it. You start at the beginning. One step at a time, an entire continent can be traversed, step by step.

The Least You Need to Know

➤ There's no time like the present to learn Italian.

➤ Italian is an accessible language that anyone can learn.

➤ You can communicate even if your pronunciation and grammar are less than perfect. Remember that language is simply a means to communicate your thoughts to another person. If you can learn to speak one language, you can learn to speak another.

➤ You have nothing to fear. Whether it takes you three months or three years, one step in front of the other is the way you will achieve your goals. Find your pace. Stick with it.

Chapter 2

Immerse Yourself

In an increasingly international community, it seems Italian has permeated every aspect of our culture. Italian restaurants specializing in different regional tastes have cropped up in just about every town and city. Italian films have made us laugh so hard our sides hurt, yet we can never escape the theater without having dabbed at the corners of our eyes at least once.

Advertisers have hooked into the enormous appeal that Italy has for just about every product imaginable, and there is more than one commercial using the Italian language to make its point. Italian lingo (*ciao*, *bravo*, *ancor!*) has crept into English—an interesting twist because so much of the English language has its origins in Latin, Italian's *madre lingua* (mother tongue).

This chapter offers you a different eye on the Italian language and compares it with English. It also gives a summary of different parts of grammar and attempts to take away some of the intimidation factor that often accompanies learning a new language.

Latin Lovers

The history of the Italian language spans centuries and begins with classical Latin, the literary language of ancient *Roma* and the language used principally by the upper classes, the educated, and later the clergy. Hence the term Romance languages (of which French, Spanish, Portuguese, and Rumanian are also derived). These languages were once called Vulgar Latin because they were offshoots, or dialects, of Latin and spoken by the common people. Italian is the Romance language closest to Latin.

Languages are like seeds that are pulled from one area into another along an air current, germinating wherever there is ripe soil. Latin made its way into English during the seventh century when England converted to Christianity, and later during a revival in classical scholarship stemming from the Renaissance (*rinascimento*, literally meaning "rebirth"). During the sixteenth and seventeenth centuries, hundreds of Latin words were incorporated into English, resulting in much of today's legal and medical terminology.

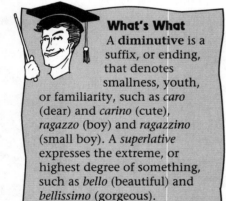

What's What
A **diminutive** is a suffix, or ending, that denotes smallness, youth, or familiarity, such as *caro* (dear) and *carino* (cute), *ragazzo* (boy) and *ragazzino* (small boy). A *superlative* expresses the extreme, or highest degree of something, such as *bello* (beautiful) and *bellissimo* (gorgeous).

As a result, many words in modern English have their origins in Latin, a hop from Italian. Chapter 4 gives you a more thorough listing of those similar words, or *cognates*. Keep in mind that English is a much broader language than Italian in terms of the sheer magnitude of words it possesses.

You will see that there is a great deal of "doubling up" on words in Italian, as well as the frequent use of *diminutives* and *superlatives* in Italian. For example, English has the pair *cat/kitten*. The word *kitten* is quite different from the word *cat*. In Italian, it's much easier to express a small cat: By adding the ending *-ino* to the word *gatto*, we create the word *gattino*. You're already familiar with the word *zucchini*, which comes from the Italian word *zucca* (pumpkin/squash). A commonly used superlative in English is *-est* which is attached to adjectives to describe the smallest, biggest, or best. In Italian, this would be expressed with the ending *-issimo*, as in the adjective *bellissimo* (very beautiful—gorgeous).

In spite of the fact that Italian has fewer words than English, the Italians have no difficulty expressing themselves, as you will find out for yourself.

Dialect

A dialect is a variation of a language, usually particular to a region and often quite different from the standard vernacular spoken. Due to its shape and long history of outside influences, Italy has hundreds of different dialects, many of which are still used today. Some dialects greatly resemble Italian, with particular colloquialisms and idiomatic expressions only understood by those familiar with the dialect. Other dialects are practically different languages. For example, up north in Lombardia, one hears a specifically German accent and a softening of the Rs, a result of the district having once been ruled by Austria. In the Piedmont region, one can hear the French influence. Down south near Napoli, Spanish, and French can be heard, whereas in Calabria, certain speech parts are quite clearly Greek (*kalimera* means literally "Good day" in modern Greek) or Albanian in nature. The islands of Sardegna and Sicilia also have their own languages.

Many Italian immigrants brought their dialects to the United States, where they were further influenced by factors such as culture, English, and other dialects. This explains, in part, why the Italian spoken by many immigrants often differs greatly from the Italian that is presented in this book and why you may still have difficulty communicating with your grandmother after having mastered the basics. There are many variations or dialects of Italian spoken around the world today, in such places as Switzerland and many parts of South America.

Tuscan Italian

In modern Italy, the standard language taught in schools and spoken on television is Tuscan Italian, primarily because this was the regional dialect used by the great medieval writers Dante, Petrarca, and Boccaccio, who used what was then only a spoken language. Modern Italian is often quite different from the Italian used during the Middle Ages, but, as when you compare modern English to Old English, there are many similarities. Look at an excerpt from Dante's *Inferno*:

> Nel mezzo del cammin di nostra vita
>
> mi ritrovai per una selva oscura,
>
> che la diritta via era smarrita.

Did You Know?
The poet Dante Alighieri (1265–1321) is to the Italian language what Shakespeare is to English. It was his poetry that essentially legitimized the Italian language as we know it today, since all of his predecessors wrote exclusively in Latin. His most famous work, the *Divina Commedia* is an epic poem depicting an imaginary journey through Hell, Purgatory, and Paradise, influenced by another of the world's greatest poets, Virgilio, who serves as Dante's guide both literally, as a writer, and figuratively.

Note the translation:

> In the middle of our life's journey
>
> I found myself in a dark wood,
>
> out of which the straight way was lost.

The Italian has a wonderful rhyme quality, the word *vita* working with the word *smarrita*, something which is lost in the translation. Not understanding the Italian, you can still get an idea of the musicality of the language. In fact, it's easy to rhyme in Italian because of the endings. The translation, however, still does not do justice to the flow and meaning of the poem. You can get a sense of what is being communicated, but it's not the same as the original. It's like looking at a photograph of a bright, sunny day where you can see the colors but you can't feel the warmth of the sun, experience the expanse of blue sky, or hear the wind.

How Much Italian Is Enough?

Understanding what your motives are for learning Italian is key to accomplishing your goals. It will help you to gloss over certain lessons that may be less relevant to your purpose while concentrating on those elements of the language more suited to fit your needs. Here are some examples:

➤ If you're learning Italian to pass your art history exam, or if literature is your thing and you want to be able to read Dante in the original, you might not need to spend a lot of time on idiomatic expressions, cognates, and helpful expressions. Instead, you should focus on verbs and their tenses, nouns, and adjectives.

➤ If you're learning Italian to be able to converse with your Italian business associates, you want to primarily develop an "ear" for the language. Here, pronunciation is essential and a knowledge of some common idiomatic expressions is helpful to help break the ice.

➤ If food and travel are your passions, a strong vocabulary is important. Developing a sizable repertoire of words related to your interests will make your trip that much more interesting as you seek new restaurants and hidden treasures. It's good to know a few verb infinitives just to get you pointed in the right direction, but it might not be necessary to spend too much time on the many tenses. The point is to be able to meet your needs and express your thoughts.

Knowing your destination will help you map out the journey without getting too lost in the meantime.

Your Dictionary Is Your Best Friend

Having a good bilingual dictionary is essential to learning a new language, whatever your purpose may be. Use your dictionary as an adventurer would use a map. Keep it handy, somewhere where you do most of your studying so that you don't have far to reach every time a new word pops up. You'll be amazed at how often you'll use it if you're not climbing a ladder to get to the top shelf of your bookcase whenever a need arises. Most good English/Italian dictionaries indicate what kind of word it is. You should understand the significance of the abbreviations used in the definitions. Table 2.1 lists a few of them.

Table 2.1   Dictionary Abbreviations

English Abbreviation	Italian Abbreviation	Meaning
adj.	agg.	Adjective
adv.	avv.	Adverb
—	f.	Singular feminine noun
—	m.	Singular masculine noun
s.	—	Singular noun
prep.	Prep.	Preposition
pron.	pron.	Pronoun
v.i.	v.i.	Intransitive verb
v.t.	v.t.	Transitive verb
—	v.rifl.	Reflexive verb
fam.	fam.	Familiar/colloquial

Speak Easy

Some of you may not remember seventh grade grammar as well as you would like. After all, at the time, you could see no practical purpose, you never envisioned you would actually choose to learn a language on your own, and you were much too busy writing notes to your best friend to pay attention to your teacher. You're older now, your hormones are in check, and you're a little wiser, so take a trip down memory lane and review some of those parts of speech.

Descriptively Speaking

Adjectives describe nouns. They are big, little, pretty, ugly, and all the colors of the rainbow. Unlike English, Italian adjectives agree in number and gender (sex) with the nouns they modify. If the noun is singular and masculine, as in *il libro* (the book), then the adjective must also be singular and masculine, as in *il libro piccolo* (the small book). Ditto for feminine nouns. In Italian, the adjective almost always comes after the noun it modifies, as in *la casa bianca* (the white house). You get a much clearer idea of how adjectives work in Chapter 9.

Adverbs describe verbs, adjectives, and other adverbs. They move us quickly and happily toward our goal of learning Italian. Most adverbs in English end in -ly. In Italian, many adverbs end in *-mente*, such as *rapidamente* and *allegramente*.

Person, Place, or Pasta

Did You Know?
Dating back to Medieval times, the *Palio* is a famous horse race that takes place in Siena every year. The entire city closes down to watch the various *contrade* (districts) vie for their own jockeys as the horses race around the town square. Afterwards, huge tables fill the streets and miles of spaghetti are cooked to feed the excited masses.

Nouns are people, places, things, and ideas. Poet, Pompei, pasta, and principle are all nouns. In Italian, all nouns have a gender: They are either masculine (m.) or feminine (f.). In addition, all nouns in Italian indicate number: They are either singular (s.) or plural (p.) You learn more about this in Chapter 6.

Pronouns substitute for nouns and refer to a person, place, thing, or idea. For example: We ate a lot of food in the restaurant, and *it* (the food) cost quite a penny. In Italian, pronouns are a little more complicated because they must, like nouns, reflect sex and number. There is no neuter *it* in Italian. There are several kinds of pronouns, of which the most important to remember are subject pronouns (he, she, and so on), direct object pronouns, and indirect object pronouns (it).

It's All Relative

Prepositions are words (such as above, along, beyond, before, through, in, on, at, to, for, and so on) that are placed before nouns to indicate a relationship to other words in a sentence. Prepositions are discussed in Chapter 10.

Where the Action Is

Verbs indicate action. An infinitive verb is a verb that has not been conjugated, as in **to be**, **to eat**, or **to travel.** A conjugated verb is simply a form of the verb that agrees with the subject. You conjugate verbs in English all the time when you say I am, you are, and he is. Verb conjugations are discussed in greater depth in Chapter 8.

Intransitive verbs can stand alone, without a direct object, as "sing" does in the sentence, "I sing." You can sing a song or just sing.

Transitive verbs can be followed by a direct object or require a reflexive pronoun, as in "We kissed *one another*," or "Robert is going to the party." You see, Robert can't just "go"; he must "go" somewhere.

It All Depends on How You Look at It

You don't have to be a rocket scientist to use a bilingual dictionary, but a little inside knowledge of grammar doesn't hurt. It's important to remember how versatile words can be, and you do that by looking at the entire sentence. This is essential to extrapolating the meaning of the text or even a word that you don't recognize. Look at the word *inside*. Watch how the meaning changes in the following sentences:

> The plane should arrive *inside* of an hour. (adverb)

> The *inside* walls of the church are covered with art. (adjective)

> It is very dark *inside* the tunnel. (preposition)

> The *inside* of the Coliseum was once quite beautiful. (noun)

Change *inside* to the plural and its meaning changes:

> She laughed until her *insides* hurt. (colloquial, noun)

As a Rule

If there's more than one translation listed in your dictionary for a given word, it's important to take your time and skim through the list. After you have found your word, if you are still not sure of whether it is the appropriate translation, look up the word you just chose in its opposite language. For example, if you are looking up the word *mean*, and you find the Italian verb *significare*, look up *significare* for the English translation. Do you want the adjective "mean" as in nasty, or the verb "to mean." This will help you make sure you are using the correct word.

The following is what a listing in a good Italian/English dictionary might look like:

> **inside,** [in'said] 1. *avv.* dentro, in casa, *within,* entro; 2. *agg.* interno, interiore; 3. *prep.* in, dentro; 4. *n.* interno, parte interna, *(fam.)* stomaco; informazioni riservate.

Practice Makes Perfetto

Using the Italian definitions just given, figure out the part of speech for *inside* in each of the following sentences, and complete the translated sentences in Italian:

1. We live inside the walls of the city.

   Abitiamo _____ le mura della città.

2. The woman's insides hurt.

   Alla donna fa male lo _____.

3. We will arrive home inside an hour.

   Arriviamo a casa _____ un'ora.

4. He has inside information on the *Palio.*

   Lui ha _____ sul *Palio.*

5. The inside of the church is dark.

   L' _____ della chiesa e scuro.

What's the Object; Who's the Subject?

Okay, let's go back to the seventh grade again. The sun is shining outside the school windows and the teacher is droning on about objects and subjects, and as she's speaking, you're on the verge of falling asleep. The room is too hot, you're bored, and you're thinking, "I'm never going to need this to do anything!"

Of course, in retrospect, you know better. But you still aren't quite sure what an object is, unless it's something unidentified and coming from parts unknown.

Use a sentence from your first grade book (just for the fun of it) to look at what an object is:

> Jack throws Jane a ball.

First things first. Take a minute to find the verb in this sentence. Remember, verbs are where the action is.

Did you figure out it was the verb *to throw*? Bravi! You're on your way. Next question: Who threw the ball? Jack did, that's who. That's your subject.

The million lire question now is what did Jack throw? Answer: The ball! That's the direct object. A direct object is the recipient of the verb's action.

In sentences with two nouns following the verb, the first is generally the indirect object, the word that tells to whom or for whom the action was done (Jane).

Let's continue with Jack and Jane. Jane, never one to say no to a challenge, decides to keep the ball rolling. Analyze the next sentence for its subject and object:

> She throws it back to him.

Did you figure out that "she" is the subject pronoun (the word "she" substituting for "Jane") and "it" (substituting for the word "ball") is the object pronoun? So you see, there's nothing to worry about. You know everything you need to get this ball rolling and learn the language you've always dreamed of knowing. What do you think is the indirect object pronoun in the sentence?

The Least You Need to Know

➤ Italian comes from Latin and is connected to a history steeped in tradition.

➤ You have no reason to be afraid of grammar. Understanding the different parts of speech takes away the mystery of second language learning.

➤ A bilingual dictionary is essential to language learning and can help you identify different parts of speech and understand common Italian expressions.

➤ Dante and Boccaccio are two of Italy's greatest writers.

Sound Like an Italian

You're committed to learning *la bella lingua* (the beautiful language) of Italian. The only way you're going to do this is to let go of the perfectionist within you and *make mistakes*. Have fun as you learn to pronounce the different letter combinations and sounds of the Italian language. Practice rolling your Rs in the shower as you sing your favorite opera; woo your partner with sweet nothings that sound so profound he or she has no idea you're simply reciting pasta dishes you read in a recipe book. And use your hands! The Italians know that communication doesn't just happen with the mouth—it's a whole body thing.

Italian is quite easy to pronounce because it is phonetic, meaning that what you see is pretty much what you say. In this respect, it's a lot easier than English with its silent letters and illogical letter combinations. Why is the word telephone written with a "ph" instead of an "f," and what is that silly "e" doing at the end of it anyway? A child just learning to string letters together will tell you it should be spelled "telefon" and the tot would be right. In Italian, the word is *telefono* and it is pronounced just like it is written. You'll find that the spelling of Italian is easy and, once you get the hang of it, the pronunciation is just as sensible. The later chapters will not have the pronunciation spelled out for you like earlier chapters; by then, you should have mastered how words are pronounced. Feel free, however, to go back to earlier chapters if you are not sure of how a word should be pronounced.

Don't Get Stressed Out

In Italian, knowing where to put the stress can sometimes be tricky (or stressful!). As a rule, most words are stressed on the next-to-last syllable, such as *giorno* (***joR**-noh*), *signorina* (*see-nyoh-**Ree**-nah*), and *minestrone* (*mee-neh-**stRoh**-neh*). Many words are stressed on the third-to-last syllable, such as *automobile* (*ow-toh-**moh**-bee-leh*) and *dialogo* (*dee-**ah**-loh-goh*). Stress should be placed on the last syllable when you see an accent mark at the end of a word, such as *città* (*chee-**tah***), *così* (*koh-**zee***), and *virtù* (*veeR-**too***).

As a Rule

Always remember to enunciate vowels clearly and not to slur your words. Say what you see.

Right now it seems like a lot of rules with just as many exceptions, but your brain will naturally pick up where to put the stress without a lot of headaches. This is the "fuzzy" period of language learning, much like having a box filled with puzzle pieces that haven't been fit together yet. At first, it's all just a jumble of sounds and letters and words, but slowly, almost imperceptibly, your confusion is replaced with understanding. Language learning is an intuitive process. Knowing this might help you overcome your initial frustration and confusion.

As a Rule

For the purposes of clarity, the pronunciation used in this text is designed to be read phonetically.

Rs are trilled and are capitalized to remind you of their importance.

Double *RRs* should be held and emphasized when trilled.

Double consonants should always be emphasized—however, not as separate sounds. They should be joined and slide into one another, as in the word *pizza* (*pee-tsah*).

Your ABCs

Like English, the Italian language uses the Latin alphabet. Unlike English, however, the Italian alphabet contains only 21 letters. If you've ever studied another Romance language, you'll have no problem with the pronunciation because the vowels are pronounced similarly. For first-time language learners, follow the rules as outlined in this chapter. Try not to overstress letters or syllables when you pronounce words; you'll end up sounding like someone trying to sound Italian instead of sounding like an Italian speaker. Keep your tongue and mouth alert; no lazy mouths please!

There are a few sounds in Italian that are not found in English, the most obvious being the rolled *R*. Some people can roll their *Rs* forever, but if you're not one of them, place the tip of your tongue so that it's touching the roof of your mouth just behind your front teeth. Now curl the tip of your tongue and exhale. You should get the beginning trill of a rolled *R*. If you're still not successful, do this while you're in the shower with the water running through your mouth. If that doesn't work, imagine you're a purring kitten happily kneading a pillow or an opera singer in Carnegie Hall. Whatever you do, keep trying. Even without a perfect *R*, however, you'll still be able to get your message across.

> **Attenzione!**
> Some sounds exist exclusively in Italian, or are seldom found in English. These sounds include the *gl* combination in words such as *figlio* (son) and pronounced *fee-lyoh*; *gli* (the), pronounced like the *ll* in the word million as in *ylee*; and the *gn* combination, seen in words like *gnocchi* (potato dumplings), pronounced *nyoh-kee*, and *bagno* (bathroom), pronounced like the *ny* sound in canyon or the *ni* sound in onion, as in *bah-nyoh*.

Vowels (Vocali)

The word for vowel in Italian (*vocale*) sounds just like the English word for vocal. Italian vowels are always pronounced clearly and are never slurred. If you can master the vowels, you're already halfway to the point of sounding Italian. Table 3.1 shows how the vowels are pronounced. Read aloud to practice.

Table 3.1 Pronouncing Vowels Properly

Vowel	Sound	Example	Pronunciation
a	ah	artista	*ahR-tee-stah*
e	eh	elefante	*eh-leh-fahn-teh*
i	ee	isola	*ee-zoh-lah*

continues

Table 3.1 Continued

Vowel	Sound	Example	Pronunciation
o	oh	opera	*oh-peh-Rah*
u	oo	uno	*oo-noh*

Now try a few words and focus just on the vowels.

A

Say *ah* as in "father":

madre	fila	canto	casa	strada	mela
mah-dReh	*fee-lah*	*kahn-toh*	*kah-zah*	*stRah-dah*	*meh-lah*
(mother)	(thread)	(song)	(home)	(street)	(apple)

E

Say *eh* as in "make" or "let":

padre	sera	festa	bene	età	pensione
pah-dReh	*seh-Rah*	*fes-stah*	*beh-neh*	*eh-tah*	*pen-see-oh-neh*
(father)	(evening)	(party)	(well)	(age)	(motel)

I

Say *ee* as in "feet":

idiota	piccolo	pulire	in	idea	turista
ee-dee-oh-tah	*pee-koh-loh*	*poo-lee-Reh*	*een*	*ee-deh-ah*	*too-Ree-stah*
(idiot)	(small)	(to clean)	(in)	(idea)	(tourist)

O

Say *oh* as in "note" or "for":

donna	bello	cosa	albero	gatto	uomo
doh-nah	*beh-loh*	*koh-zah*	*ahl-beh-Roh*	*gah-toh*	*woh-moh*
(woman)	(beautiful)	(thing)	(tree)	(cat)	(man)

u

Say *oo* as in "crude":

luna	una	cubo	lupo	tuo
loo-nah	*oo-nah*	*koo-boh*	*loo-poh*	*too-oh*
(moon)	(a)	(cube)	(wolf)	(your)

Did you notice any similarity between the words you just read and their English counterparts? You know more than you think! It's important to see how much the two languages share. Remember that a lot of English derives from Latin. It helps to make associations with familiar words. Each time you do this, you are creating a bridge from one shore to another. For example, the word *luna* (moon) comes from Latin as we see in the English word *lunatic*. It was once believed that "lunacy" came from the full moon. All sorts of associations can be made to "illuminate" (in Italian, *illuminare*) these connections.

Consonants

Table 3.2 contains a list of consonants and includes letters recognized in foreign languages. The *R* is capitalized to help remind you to trill. Roll on.

Table 3.2 Pronouncing Consonants Properly

Letter	Sound	Example	Pronunciation	Meaning
b	bee	bambino	*bahm-bee-noh*	child, m.
c + a,o, u	hard c (as in *cat*)	candela	*kahn-deh-lah*	candle
c + e, i	ch (as in *chest*)	centro	*chen-tRoh*	center/downtown
ch	hard c (as in *cat*)	Chianti	*kee-ahn-tee*	Chianti (a red wine)
d	dee	due	*doo-eh*	two
f	eff	frase	*fRah-zeh*	phrase
g + a, o, u	hard g (as in *go*)	gatto	*gah-toh*	cat
g + e, i	j (as in *jet*)	gentile	*jen-tee-leh*	kind
gli	ll (as in *million*)	figlio	*feel-yoh*	son
gn	nya (as in *onion*)	gnocchi	*nyoh-kee*	potato dumplings
h (called *acca*)	silent	hotel	*oh-tel*	hotel

continues

Table 3.2 Continued

Letter	Sound	Example	Pronunciation	Meaning
j* (called *ee-lunga*)	juh (hard j)	jazz	*jaz*	jazz
k* (called *kappa*)	kuh (hard k)	koala	*koh-ah-lah*	koala
l	ell	latte	*lah-teh*	milk
m	em	madre	*mahd-Reh*	mother
n	en	nonno	*noh-noh*	grandfather
p	pee	padre	*pahd-Reh*	father
q	kew	quanto	*kwahn-toh*	how much
r	err (slightly rolled)	Roberto	*Roh-beR-toh*	Robert
rr	errr (r rolled 2-3 times)	birra	*bee-Rah*	beer
s	ess (as in *see*)	serpente	*seR-pen-teh*	snake
s	zee (as in *busy*)	casa	*kah-zah*	home
sc + a, o	sk	scala	*skah-lah*	stair
sc + e, i	sh	scena	*sheh-nah*	scene
t	tee	tavola	*tah-voh-lah*	table
v	v	vino	*vee-noh*	wine
w* (called *doppia vu*)	wuh	Washington	*Wash-eeng-tohn*	Washington
x* (called *ics*)	ics	X-ray	*rah-jee-eeks*	X-ray
y* (called *ipsilon*)	yuh	yoga	*yoh-gah*	yoga
z	z	zebra	*zeh-bRah*	zebra
zz	ts	pazzo	*pah-tsoh*	crazy

* These letters are recognized in words of foreign origin.

Some letter combinations are more challenging than others because the rules change depending on what vowel is connected to what consonant. By remembering even one word's pronunciation that follows a given rule, you can always fall back on that word as a way of checking yourself:

Letter Combination		*Sound*	*Pronunciation Guide*	
c + a, o, u		k	Say *c* as in "camp"	
casa	amico		caro	bocca
kah-zah	*ah-mee-koh*		*kah-Roh*	*boh-kah*
(home)	(friend)		(expensive/dear)	(mouth)
colore	conto		cultura	giacca
koh-loh-Reh	*kohn-toh*		*kool-too-Rah*	*jah-kah*
(color)	(bill/check)		(culture)	(jacket)

Letter Combination		*Sound*	*Pronunciation Guide*	
c + h		k	Say *c* as in "camp"	
chiamare	occhio		perché	Machiavelli
kee-ah-mah-Reh	*oh-kee-yoh*		*peR-keh*	*mah-kee-ah-veh-lee*
(to call)	(eye)		(why)	(Machiavelli)
chiaro	amiche		macchina	ricchi
kee-ah-Roh	*ah-mee-keh*		*mah-kee-nah*	*Ree-kee*
(clear/light)	(friends, f.p.)		(car)	(rich, m.p.)

Letter Combination		*Sound*	*Pronunciation Guide*	
c + e, i		ch	Say *ch* as in "cherry"	
accento	cena		amici	ceramica
ah-chen-toh	*che-nah*		*ah-mee-chee*	*cheh-Rah-mee-kah*
(accent)	(dinner)		(friends)	(ceramic)
ciao	bacio		Francia	cioccolata
chow	*bah-choh*		*frahn-chah*	*choh-koh-lah-tah*
(hello/goodbye)	(kiss)		(France)	(chocolate)

Now let's look at the letter g:

Letter Combination		Sound	Pronunciation Guide
g + a, o, u		g	Say *g* as in "great"
gamba	lago	gufo	prego
gahm-bah	*lah-goh*	*goo-foh*	*preh-goh*
(leg)	(lake)	(owl)	(you're welcome)
gambero	mago	strega	gusto
gahm-beh-Roh	*mah-goh*	*stReh-gah*	*goo-stoh*
(shrimp)	(wizard)	(witch)	(taste)

The letter combination gh is also pronounced like the *g* in "go," as in *funghi* (mushrooms).

Letter Combination		Sound	Pronunciation Guide
g + e, i		j	Say *g* as in "gem"
gelato	giovane	giacca	viaggio
jeh-lah-toh	*joh-vah-neh*	*jah-kah*	*vee-ah-joh*
(ice cream)	(young)	(jacket)	(voyage)
formaggio	gente	giorno	maggio
foR-mah-joh	*jen-teh*	*joR-noh*	*mah-joh*
(cheese)	(people)	(day)	(May)

Letter Combination		Sound	Pronunciation Guide
g + n		ny	Say "onion"
lavagna	signore	legno	gnocchi
lah-vahn-yah	*see-nyoh-Reh*	*lehn-yoh*	*ynoh-kee*
(blackboard)	(sir, Mr.)	(wood)	(potato dumplings)
ragno	compagna	signora	guadagno
rahn-yoh	*kohm-pahn-yah*	*seen-yoh-Rah*	*gwah-dah-nyoh*
(spider)	(countryside)	(Mrs., Ms.)	(earnings)

Letter Combination		*Sound*	*Pronunciation Guide*	
sc + a, h, o, u		sk	Say *sk* as in "skin"	
sconto	scusa		scandalo	pesca
skohn-toh	*skoo-zah*		*skahn-dah-loh*	*pes-kah*
(discount)	(excuse)		(scandal)	(peach)
scuola	schifo		fiasco	schizzo
skwoh-lah	*skee-foh*		*fee-ah-skoh*	*skee-tsoh*
(school)	(disgust)		(fiasco)	(sketch)

Letter Combination		*Sound*	*Pronunciation Guide*	
sc + e, i		sh	Say *sh* as in "sheet"	
sci	pesce		scena	lasciare
shee	*peh-sheh*		*sheh-nah*	*lah-shah-Reh*
(skiing)	(fish)		(scene)	(to leave something)
sciroppo	sciocco		sciopero	scelto
shee-Roh-poh	*shee-oh-koh*		*shoh-peh-Roh*	*shel-toh*
(syrup)	(fool, fam.)		(strike)	(choice)

As a Rule

To ask someone how to say something in Italian, say, "Come si dice," and add whatever you want to learn.

Question: Come si dice *ice cream* in italiano? (How do you say ice cream in Italian?)

Answer: Si dice gelato. (You say *gelato*.)

Double Consonants

Anytime you see a double consonant, it is important to emphasize that consonant, or you may be misunderstood. Take a look at a few words whose meanings change when there is a double consonant. As you will see, you *definitely* want to emphasize those double consonants in some cases:

29

casa (house)/*cassa* (cash register)

ano (anus)/*anno* (year)

pena (pity)/*penna* (pen)

pene (penis)/*penne* (pens)

dona (he/she gives)/*donna* (woman)

sete (thirst)/*sette* (seven)

As a Rule

A single *s* is pronounced like "z" as in the name *Gaza* and the Italian word *casa* (house).

A double *ss* is pronounced like "s" as in the English word *tassel* and the Italian word *passo* (pass).

A single *z* is prounounced like "z" as in the word *zebra*.

A double *zz* is pronounced like "ts" as in the English word *cats* and the Italian word *piazza* (plaza).

Double consonants will not be highlighted in the pronunciation. It's up to you to emphasize them. Practice pronouncing the following words, remembering to slide the syllables together:

mamma	sorella	cappello	atto	pazzo	bocca	Anna
mah-mah	*soh-Reh-lah*	*kah-peh-loh*	*ah-toh*	*pah-tsoh*	*boh-kah*	*Ah-nah*
(mom)	(sister)	(hat)	(act)	(crazy)	(mouth)	(Ann)

Diphthongs

As you've probably already noticed (because you're a brilliant idiot), the Italian language is packed with vowels. Practically every noun, verb, and adjective ends in a vowel; in fact, it is the exception that does not end in a vowel. A diphthong is not a teeny-weeny-itsy-bitsy bikini (sorry, guys). The term *diphthong* refers to any pair of vowels that begins with one vowel sound and ends with a different vowel sound within the same syllable. You pronounce diphthongs all the time when you say the word for a young human male or "boy" where the *oy* is pronounced *oh-yee*, "about" where the *o* and *u* create the diphthong *ow*, and "feud" where the *e* and *u* create the sound *yoo*. The term literally means "two voices" (*di* = two; *thong* = tongue/voice) and originally comes from Greek. Perhaps you're wondering why you need to know this, and now you're questioning if you're really up to learning another language. It's not as complicated as it sounds.

Use the following examples to practice your diphthongs. Remember that Italian is a phonetic language, with no silent letters. By sliding the vowels together, you'll have the correct pronunciation. Keep in mind that diphthongs are pronounced as one sound.

Table 3.3   Italian Diphthongs

Diphthong	Sound	Example	Pronunciation	Meaning
ae	ah-eh	aereo	*ah-eh-Reh-oh*	airplane
ai	ay	aiuto	*ah-yoo-toh*	help
au	ow	aula	*ow-oo-lah*	classroom
ei	ey	sei	*sey*	six
eu	eh-yoo	Europa	*eh-yoo-Roh-pah*	Europe
ia	ee-yah	miseria	*mee-zeR-ee-yah*	poverty
ie	ee-eh	pietra	*pee-yeh-tRah*	stone
io	ee-yoh	olio	*oh-lyoh*	oil
iu	ee-yoo	giugno	*joon-yoh*	June
oi	oy	poi	*poy*	then
ua	wah	quanto	*kwahn-toh*	how much
ue	weh	due	*doo-weh*	two
ui	wee	guida	*gwee-dah*	guide
uo	oo-oh	può	*poo-oh*	he/she can

Anyone who has ever studied—or even heard someone studying—a new musical instrument knows that the first time you pick up a violin, you're not going to sound like a virtuoso (yet another Italian word). Fortunately, learning Italian is much easier than playing a violin. With a dash of patience, a dollop of dedication, and a pinch of practice, you'll be rolling your *R*s and sounding like a true Italian speaker. Keep renting films, listening to opera, and getting out there. Practice makes *perfetto*.

What's What
Diphthongs are combinations of vowels that begin with one vowel sound and end with a different vowel sound in the same syllable.

The Least You Need to Know

➤ Let your tongue do the talking. Tickle a single *R*, but rrrrrrroll your double *RRs*. Rev them up like an engine, purr like a cat, or growl like a bear.

➤ Don't slur. Enunciate vowels. But don't try too hard or your Italian will sound forced and unnatural.

➤ Fluidity is key, especially with double vowels, or *diphthongs*. Always slide your syllables together.

➤ Practice, practice, practice!

➤ Don't be afraid of sounding silly. Anything new is awkward at first, but eventually, you'll get the hang of it.

You Know More Than You Think

What if you were told that you were already halfway to speaking Italian? The fact is, you are. Remember that English came after Italian, which came from *Latino*. The list of Italian words you already know is longer than you can imagine. Some are virtually the same, whereas most are easily identified by their similarity to English. *Telefono, attenzione, università, automobile, studente*—the list goes on and on. Any words that are similar to and look the same as other words in a foreign language are called *cognates*, or in Italian, *parole simili* (literally, "similar words"). By the end of this chapter, you will be in the know for one of the mysteries of language learning, and with this key, many doors will be opened. *Andiamo!* (Let's go!)

Cognates: A Bridge Between Languages

You get off the *aeroplano* in *Roma* and push your way through customs. You hail a *tassì* and tell the driver you want to go to *centro* where an adorable *pensione* a friend recommended awaits your *arrivo*. As you race away from the chaos of the *aeroporto* and into the *traffico*, you are amazed by how *moderna* the highways are, in *contrasto* to what you had *imaginato*. Where are the cobblestone *strade*, the vendors hawking their wares, and the *cattedrali* you read about in your guidebook?

In the *distanza*, you see the silhouette of cypress trees against a bright, cloudless sky, fields of sunflowers turning their heads toward the light, remnants of the ancient Roman *acquedotti*, and the high arches that are testimony to the *creatività* that was the Roman legacy. The driver of the *tassì* asks if this is your "prima volta" in *Italia*. You smile and nod your head *sì*. You look up the word "prima" in your Italian *dizionario* and read that it means "first," like the word *primary*. You guessed that he was asking you if this was your first time in Italy and you are amazed at how this *comunicazione* seemed so *naturale*. Your excitement overshadows your jet lag, and all you want to do is unpack your *bagagli*, find a little *bar* where you can *ordinare* an *espresso*, and begin exploring the *città*.

What's What
Cognates are words in a different language that derive from the same root and are similar in both spelling and meaning, such as with the words, familiar and *familiare*, possible and *possibile*, etc.

False Cognates can be misleading; in Italian, the word *parenti* means "relatives," *not* parents, as one might think.

Your driver turns, and out of nowhere there looms the *Colosseo*; another turn and there's the *Foro Romano*. The driver turns up Aventino hill, winding past a small grove of *arancie*, ready for the picking. "*Siamo arrivati*," he says and smiles as he pulls in front of a small *palazzo* neatly landscaped with trees of *palma*, its *terrazzo* lined with red, pink, and purple *fiori* growing in siena-red clay pots. As you tip the driver, it suddenly dawns on you that you are in *la bella Italia*. There's an oddly *familiare* feeling about this place, as though the *passato* has converged with the *presente*. It's a strange *sensazione*, but you feel as though you've been here before; intuitively, you realize that you know more than you would have ever thought.

Cognates show that languages are all connected. What is *importante* to remember is that the context of a given subject reveals a great deal of itself to the attentive listener. An isolated word may or may not evoke understanding, but when you see that word in relationship (or *in relazione*) to the *situazione*, you might understand a great deal. This chapter presents tricks of the trade, other cognates, and helpful hints, all of which should give you a little more *confidenza* in your endeavor to learn *la bella lingua* of Italian.

If It Looks Like a Duck...

The Italian language has only a few perfect cognates—such as the words *banana, opera, panorama, pizza, via,* and *zebra*—where the English and the Italian are exactly the same, but it does possess many near cognates. Although not exactly the same, the meanings of near cognates are unmistakable. The endings and pronunciation may be slightly different, but the words are essentially the same. Look at Table 4.1 to get an idea of how many *parole simili* exist between Italian and English.

As a Rule

The following endings generally translate from English to Italian. (Note that there are always exceptions to every rule.)

The ending **-ty** in English corresponds to *-tà* in Italian.

The ending **-tion** in English corresponds to *-zione* in Italian.

The ending **-ble** in English corresponds to *-ibile* in Italian.

The ending **-ent** in English corresponds to *-ente* in Italian.

The ending **-ence** in English corresponds to *-enza* in Italian.

The ending **-ism** in English corresponds to *-ismo* in Italian.

The ending **-ous** in English corresponds to *-oso* in Italian.

English has only one definite article: the. Italian has several definite articles, all of which indicate gender (masculine or feminine) and number (singular or plural). When you look at the following list of cognates, you notice that all Italian nouns are marked by a definite article. Although the gender of nouns is easily identifiable in Italian, it is best to learn the noun with its appropriate definite article. It might seem confusing at first. Chapter 6 provides more details on this subject. For now, keep in mind the following:

➤ *il* is for masculine singular nouns.

➤ *lo* is for masculine singular nouns beginning with s + consonant or z.

➤ *l'* is for any singular noun that begins with a vowel.

➤ *la* is for feminine singular nouns.

Table 4.1 Cognates

Adjectives	Masculine Nouns	Feminine Nouns
alto	l'aeroplano	l'agenzia
americano	l'aeroporto	l'arte
basso	l'anniversario	la banca
blu	l'appartamento	la bicicletta
canadese	l'arco	la carota

continues

Table 4.1 Continued

Adjectives	Masculine Nouns	Feminine Nouns
cattolico	l'attore	la cattedrale
cinese	l'autobus	la chitarra
curioso	il balcon	la città
delizioso	il caffè	la classe
desideroso	il centro	la condizione
differente	il cinema	la conversazione
difficile	il colore	la cultura
eccellente	il comunismo	la curiosità
elegante	il continente	la depression
energico	il cotone	la dieta
famoso	il direttore	la differenza
francese	il dizionario	la discussione
frequente	il dottore	l'emozione
geloso	l'elefante	l'esperienza
giapponese	il fatto	l'espressione
grande	il gruppo	la farmacia
greco	l'idiota	la festa
importante	il limone	la fontana
impossibile	il meccanico	la forma
incredibile	il motore	la fortuna
intelligente	il museo	l'idea
interessante	il naso	l'identità
lungo	l'odore	l'inflazione
magnifico	l'ospedale	l'insalata
moderno	il palazzo	la lampada
naturale	il paradiso	la lettera
necessario	il parco	la lista
numeroso	il presidente	la medicina
popolare	il profumo	la musica

Adjectives	Masculine Nouns	Feminine Nouns
possibile	il programma	la nazione
povero	il rispetto	la persona
rapido	il ristorante	la possibilità
ricco	il salario	la probabilità
serio	il servizio	la professione
sicuro	il socialismo	la regione
sincero	lo spirito	la religione
splendido	lo studente	la rosa
stupendo	il supermercato	la stazione
stupido	il tassì	la temperatura
terribile	il tè	la terrazza
tropicale	il teatro	la turista
violento	il telefono	la violenza
virtuoso	il terrazzo	
	il treno	
	il trasporto	

Many English words have been incorporated into the Italian language, including

➤ Autobus   ➤ Film

➤ Bar   ➤ Sport

➤ Computer   ➤ Zoo

As a Rule

In Italian, adjectives must agree in number and gender with the nouns they modify, or describe. Generally speaking, masculine nouns use adjectives ending in *-o* and feminine nouns use adjectives ending in *-a*. Everyone has to get along, as in *la lingua italiana* or *il dizionario italiano*. Tune in to Chapter 9 for more details.

How Much Do You Understand Already?

What's What

An **infinitive** is the unconjugated form of a verb. In Italian, the infinitive forms of verbs end in either *-are*, *-ere*, or *-ire*. There are a few rare exceptions to this rule. Verbs are always listed in the dictionary in this form.

You've unpacked your bags and are ready to hit the town. Read the following sentences and determine their meaning. Check your pronunciation guide (especially with those *c's* and *g's*) to make sure you sound like a native:

1. La città è bella.

2. Il ristorante è terribile.

3. La giacca è grande

4. Il museo è interessante.

5. Il servizio è buono.

6. La montagna è alta.

As a Rule

The letter *e* is actually a word, meaning "and".
The accented letter *è* is also a word, meaning "is."

Your Turn

Now write and say the following sentences in Italian. Look back at your cognate list to make sure you are using the appropriate article:

1. The doctor is elegant.

2. The president is famous.

3. The bank is rich.

4. The violence is terrible.

5. The discussion is important.

6. The idiot is intelligent.

Verb Cognates

Many Italian verbs are so similar to their English counterparts that you will recognize their meaning almost immediately. We do not have this convenient manner of identifying verbs in English because English has borrowed from so many different languages. Fortunately for you, it is easy to identify an infinitive verb in Italian because of the endings. The *infinitive* of a verb is simply a verb in its unconjugated form, as in *to eat, to study, to travel*. There are three kinds of verb endings, *-are*, *-ere*, and *-ire*, or verb families. Every family has its own set of rules that are considered *regular*, which are explained in Chapter 8. Then, of course, there are a few misbehaving verbs, which are considered *irregular*. The only way to remember how an irregular verb works is to memorize it. The largest verb family in Italian is the *-are* family. Take a look at Tables 4.2 through 4.4 and see if you can determine the meanings of the verb cognates listed.

Attenzione!
When you look up a verb in a dictionary, it is important to look it up under its infinitive form. Verbs are perhaps the trickiest aspect of learning any language because they have so many forms, or *tenses*, such as the present, simple past, future, conditional, and so on. Many Italian verbs change significantly after they are conjugated. As in English, if you do not know that the infinitive form of the word "ate" is to eat, you cannot find it in the dictionary.

Table 4.2 -are Verb Cognates

-are Verbs	Pronunciation	English
accompagnare	*ah-kom-pah-nyah-Reh*	to accompany
adorare	*ah-doh-Rah-Reh*	to adore
anticipare	*ahn-tee-chee-pah-Reh*	to anticipate
arrivare	*ah-Ree-vah-Reh*	to arrive
celebrare	*cheh-leh-bRah-Reh*	to celebrate
contare	*kohn-tah-Reh*	to count
controllare	*kohn-tRo-lah-Reh*	to control
conversare	*kohn-veR-sah-Reh*	to converse
cooperare	*koo-oh-peh-Rah-Reh*	to cooperate
costare	*koh-stah-Reh*	to cost
creare	*kray-ah-Reh*	to create
danzare	*dan-zah-Reh*	to dance
desiderare	*deh-zee-deh-Rah-Reh*	to desire
designare	*deh-zee-nyah-Reh*	to design/draw
donare	*doh-nah-Reh*	to donate/give

continues

Table 4.2   Continued

-are Verbs	Pronunciation	English
elevare	*eh-leh-vah-Reh*	to elevate
eliminare	*eh-lee-mee-nah-Reh*	to eliminate
entrare	*ehn-tRah-Reh*	to enter
ignorare	*ee-nyoh-Rah-Reh*	to ignore
immaginare	*ee-mah-jee-nah-Reh*	to imagine
invitare	*een-vee-tah-Reh*	to invite
modificare	*moh-dee-fee-kah-Reh*	to modify
negare	*neh-gah-Reh*	to negate
osservare	*oh-seR-vah-Reh*	to observe
passare	*pah-sah-Reh*	to pass
perdonare	*peR-doh-nah-Reh*	to forgive/pardon
praticare	*pRah-tee-kah-Reh*	to practice
preparare	*pReh-pah-Rah-Reh*	to prepare
presentare	*pReh-zen-tah-Reh*	to present
riparare	*Ree-pah-Rah-Reh*	to repair/fix
riservare	*Ree-zehR-vah-Reh*	to reserve
rispettare	*Ree-speh-tah-Reh*	to respect
studiare	*stoo-dee-ah-Reh*	to study
telefonare	*tel-eh-foh-nah-Reh*	to telephone
usare	*oo-zah-Reh*	to use
verificare	*veh-Ree-fee-kah-Reh*	to verify
visitare	*vee-zee-tah-Reh*	to visit

There are fewer *-ere* verb cognates, as there are also fewer *-ere* verbs. Try not to look at the English until you have studied the Italian to determine the meanings.

Table 4.3   -ere Verb Cognates

-ere Verbs	Pronunciation	English
assistere	*ah-see-steh-Reh*	to assist
decidere	*deh-chee-deh-Reh*	to decide

-*ere* Verbs	Pronunciation	English
descrivere	*deh-skRee-veh-Reh*	to describe
dividere	*dee-vee-deh-Reh*	to divide
scrivere	*skree-veh-Reh*	to write
vendere	*ven-deh-Reh*	to sell (as in vendor)

Table 4.4   -ire Verb Cognates

-*ire* Verbs	Pronunciation	English
diminuire	*dee-mee-noo-ee-Reh*	to diminish
finire	*fee-nee-Reh*	to finish
istruire	*ee-stRoo-ee-Reh*	to instruct
obbedire	*oh-beh-dee-Reh*	to obey
preferire	*pReh-feh-Ree-Reh*	to prefer
prevenire	*pReh-veh-nee-Reh*	to prevent

A Piece of Cake

Try to determine the meaning of the following verb cognates. If you can't figure out a particular verb's significance, refer to the verb chart in Chapter 8.

alludere	disgustare	occupare
attribuire	dissolvere	offendere
cascare	esaminare	offrire
consistere	formare	operare
convertire	funzionare	pronunziare
correspondere	glorificare	raccomandare
deliberare	implicare	rappresentare
detestare	indicare	resistere
difendere	intendere	ricevere
discendere	navigare	rispondere
discutere	notificare	

With all these cognates, you're practically fluent. There shouldn't be too much of a problem deciphering the meaning of these sentences:

1. L'Italia fa parte del continente Europeo.

2. Lo studente studia la matematica e la storia.

3. L'attore è molto famoso nel cinema.

4. Il meccanico ripara l'automobile.

5. Il cuoco prepara un'insalata e un antipasto.

6. Il dottore conversa con il paziente.

7. La famiglia desidera un appartamento moderno e grande.

8. La turista giapponese visita il museo e la cattedrale.

9. Il presidente presenta il programma.

10. Roberto preferisce la musica classica.

What's Your Take?

Imagine you have just arrived in Italy and you want to express your opinions to a fellow traveler. Use what you have learned in this chapter to say the following:

1. The chocolate is delicious.

2. The restaurant is excellent.

3. The city is splendid and magnificent.

4. The perfume is elegant.

5. The conversation is interesting.

6. The doctor is sincere.

7. The student is intelligent.

8. The museum is important.

9. The balcony is high.

10. The train is fast.

Trojan Horses—False Friends

A *false cognate* is a word in Italian that sounds like an English word but means something different. Fortunately, in Italian there aren't many false cognates, or *falsi amici*. Table 4.5 shows you a few false cognates of which you should be aware. Remember the dictionary terms you learned in Chapter 2 to identify what parts of speech the words are.

Table 4.5   False Friends

Italian Word	Pronunciation	Meaning
assumere, *v.*	*ah-soo-meh-Reh*	to hire
attendere, *v.*	*ah-ten-deh-Reh*	to wait
camera, *s.f.*	*kah-meh-Rah*	room
caro, *agg.*	*kah-Roh*	expensive
coincidenza, *s.f.*	*koh-een-chee-den-zah*	connection
come, *av.*	*koh-meh*	how
con, *prep.*	*kohn*	with
corto, *agg.*	*koR-toh*	short
dice, *v.*	*dee-cheh*	he/she says
fabbrica, *s.f.*	*fah-bRee-kah*	factory
fattoria, *s.f.*	*fah-toh-Ree-yah*	farm
firma, *s.f.*	*feeR-mah*	signature
guardare, *v.*	*gwaR-dah-Reh*	to look at
ingenuo, *agg.*	*een-jeh-noo-oh*	naive
libreria, *s.f.*	*lee-bReh-Ree-ah*	bookstore
marrone, *agg.*	*mah-Roh-neh*	brown
parente, *s.m. & f.*	*pah-Rehn-teh*	relative
pesante, *agg.*	*peh-zahn-teh*	heavy
pretendere, *v.*	*preh-ten-deh-Reh*	to demand
testa, *s.f.*	*teh-stah*	head

Are You Well Read?

The following literary titles here all contain cognates. Give their English equivalents:

Dante—*La Divina Commedia*

Di Lampedusa—*Il Gattopardo*

Eco—*Il Nome della Rosa*

Machiavelli—*Il Principe*

Pirandello—*6 Personaggi in Cerca d'Autore*

The Least You Need to Know

➤ Italian and much of English are derived from the same language: Latin. Many words that look similar *are* similar.

➤ Come up with other words that can express your meaning and you may find a cognate more often than you think. For example, *guardare* is to look at. Think of a "guard" standing at his post looking over the landscape.

➤ Beware of false friends. You may think you are saying one thing, when in truth, you are saying another.

Chapter 5

Idiomatic Expressions for Idiots

In This Chapter

➤ An explanation of idioms

➤ Idioms expressing time, location, direction, and weather

➤ Expressions denoting opinion

➤ Idiomatic expressions in Italian

Idioms are important to a complete and correct understanding of a language. They are the spice that makes language interesting. Imagine you are wandering the myriad of Rome's streets in search of a small *caffè* someone recommended to you. You stop to ask an older gentleman for directions. He begins to explain while you stand there dazed, trying to make sense of the jumble of syllables he has just uttered, some of which sound familiar. As you turn to find your way, the kind stranger says, "In bocca a lupo!" You know that *bocca* means mouth, and you look up the word *lupo* (wolf). In the mouth of the wolf? Has that nice old man just sent you to the wolves? Actually, he was wishing you luck. The expression is used much in the same manner as when we say in English, "Break a leg."

What the Heck Is an Idiom, Anyway?

Idiomatic expressions are speech forms that cannot be understood through literal translation; they must be learned and memorized along with their meaning. Often, but not necessarily, there is an allusion to something else, such as the expression, "Happy as a lark." If you didn't know it was an idiom, you might ask yourself, "How happy is that? Are larks happy?" This is not a discussion on the relative condition of larks, but you get the picture.

What's What
An **idiomatic expression** is a speech form or expression that cannot be understood through literal translation.

It's the same with Italian. Most idioms cannot be translated without losing their meaning, although occasionally, the same idiom can exist in two or more languages. In English, we may ask someone, "Can I give a hand?" when offering assistance. In Italian, we say, "Posso dare una mano?" It is the exact translation.

Our speech is peppered with idiomatic expressions or *colloquialisms*, such as:

He was caught red-handed.	It's raining cats and dogs.
No strings attached.	Naked as a jay bird.
Don't hold your breath.	Once in a blue moon.
It runs in the family.	Practice makes perfect.
I'm in seventh heaven.	It's up in the air.

What Is Slang?

Slang refers to unconventional, popular words or phrases that are used in everyday speech. Slang is often regional and not part of the standard vocabulary of a language. Often there is a thin line between what is considered idiomatic versus slang. Idiomatic expressions can be used in almost any context, whereas slang is used primarily within a smaller framework. Vulgarities are considered slang. Check out the following examples:

What's up?	Awesome!
Give it up.	You're playing with my head.
What a scene.	Hang out.

Incidentally, it is no accident that this chapter is riddled with idioms. Can you identify the idiomatic expressions and slang used so far?

Idiomatic Expressions in Italian

The Italian language is packed with idioms. There are so many idiomatic expressions, it is impossible for even an Italian to know all of them. An innocent word in one region might have a completely different idiomatic usage in another part of the country, causing a great deal of snickering and laughing. This has to do with the fact that the standard Italian spoken on television and taught in schools derives from Tuscan Italian, where many of Italy's most prolific writers—most notably Dante and Boccaccio—came from. Meanwhile, all the different nation states that once made up the peninsula have their own speech patterns—all derivative of Latin, but nevertheless, unique and quite colorful.

Many idioms are not as metaphorical or lyrical in nature as others. They can be as simple as *taking a shower, a picture, a walk,* or *a break*. If you were to *take* a shower in Italian, people would ask you where you are taking it. You'll learn more about these idioms later.

You're Off

You can start using Italian idioms immediately. If someone asks you "Are you going on a plane or by boat?" and you say, "Vado sull'aereo," you are saying you are going to ride on top of the plane, meaning its exterior. What you really want to say is "Vado in aereo." A simple preposition can completely change the significance of an expression. These tiny details are what defines a speaker's command of a language. After a while, they will sound so familiar that you'll be questioning your English idioms.

Did You Know?
Once upon a time, a romance was a story told in the vernacular language "of Rome," that boasted of chivalric adventures and heroic deeds. In modern Italian, *un romanzo* describes a novel or short story. The word *romantico* is used to describe someone or something that evokes the spirit of love, as it is used in English.

Look at the following idiomatic expressions that describe various modes of transportation and travel. Whereas English speakers use the preposition *by* to describe how they are going somewhere, in Italian, the preposition changes.

Table 5.1 Idioms for Travel and Transportation

Idiom	Pronunciation	Meaning
a cavallo	*ah kah-vah-loh*	on horseback
a piedi	*ah pee-eh-dee*	by foot
in autobus	*een ow-toh-boos*	by bus
in bicicletta	*een bee-chee-kleh-tah*	by bicycle
in barca	*een bahR-cah*	by boat
in macchina	*een mah-kee-nah*	by car
in moto	*een moh-toh*	by scooter
in metro	*een met-Roh*	by subway
in tassì	*een tah-see*	by taxi
in treno	*een tReh-noh*	by train
in aereo	*een ay-eh-Reh-oh*	by plane

Practice Makes Perfetto

A little repetition and practice can go a long way. Try mastering these idioms by telling how you get to the following places. When followed by a preposition, some of the articles have been turned into *contractions*.

Example: How do you go to the museum (al museo)?

Answer: a piedi

Attenzione!
A simple preposition can greatly alter the meaning of a sentence. From the get go, it's a good idea to memorize certain words along with the prepositions that precede (or follow) them. For example, you may drive *in macchina*, but you must fly *in aereo*.

1. a scuola (to school)

2. al cinema (to the movies)

3. dal dottore (to your doctor)

4. in ospedale (to the hospital)

5. in Europa (to Europe)

6. al parco (to the park)

7. in un'isola tropicale (to a tropical island)

8. a pescare (to go fishing)

9. in farmacia (to the pharmacy)

10. in biblioteca (to the library)

The Time Is Now

The following idioms express time in one manner or another. You may see a literal expression of time or an expression used in particular instances. Some are more practical than others, and a few are quite fun. You can learn a lot about a given culture by the idioms used.

Table 5.2 Timely Expressions

Expression	Pronunciation	Meaning
a domani	*ah doh-mah-nee*	until tomorrow
a più tardi	*ah pyoo tahR-dee*	see you later
a presto	*ah pReh-stoh*	see you soon
a stasera	*ah stah-seh-Rah*	until this evening
a tutte le ore	*ah too-teh leh oh-Reh*	at any time
addio	*ah-dee-yoh*	goodbye (literally, "to God" or like the expression "God speed")

Expression	Pronunciation	Meaning
alla fine	*ah-lah fee-neh*	at the end of
allora	*ah-loh-Rah*	now then
ancora	*ahn-koh-Rah*	again
arrivederci	*ah-Ree-veh-dehR-chee*	see you again soon
buon giorno	*bwohn joR-noh*	good morning/good day
buon weekend	*bwohn weekend*	have a good weekend
buona notte	*bwoh-nah noh-teh*	good night
buona sera	*bwoh-nah seh-Rah*	good afternoon/good evening
Che ore sono?	*kay oh-Reh soh-noh*	What time is it? (literally, "What hours are there?")
dalla mattina alla sera	*dah-lah mah-tee-nah ah-lah seh-Rah*	from morning 'til evening
di buon ora	*dee bwohn oh-Rah*	early
di mattina	*dee mah-tee-nah*	in the morning
di sera	*dee seh-Rah*	in the evening
essere in orario	*eh-seh-Reh een oh-Rah-Ree-yoh*	to be on time
fare presto	*fah-Reh pRe-stoh*	to be early/hurry
fare tardi	*fah-Reh tahR-dee*	to be late
fra un po'	*frah oon poh*	in a while
giorno per giorno	*joR-noh peR joR-noh*	day by day
in anticipo	*een ahn-tee-chee-poh*	early
in ritardo	*een Ree-taR-doh*	late
nel frattempo	*nel fRah-tem-poh*	in the meantime
nelle prime ore del pomeriggio	*neh-leh pRee-meh oh-Reh del poh-meh-ree-joh*	in the early afternoon
nello stesso momento	*neh-loh steh-soh moh-men-toh*	at the same time
ora	*oh-Rah*	now/hour
ora di punta	*oh-Rah dee poon-tah*	rush hour
ora legale	*oh-Rah leh-gah-leh*	daylight saving time

continues

Table 5.2 Continued

Expression	Pronunciation	Meaning
orario	*oh-Rah-Ree-oh*	schedule
ormai	*oR-my*	by now
piano piano	*pee-ah-noh pee-ah-noh*	slowly
presto	*pReh-stoh*	early
qualche volta	*kwahl-kay vohl-tah*	sometimes
un'oretta	*oon oh-Reh-tah*	about an hour
un'ora buona	*oon oh-Rah bwoh-nah*	a full hour

An Idiomatic Workout

Determine what idiomatic expression you would use in the following situations using what you just learned:

1. When someone is speaking Italian too quickly.

2. When you probably will not see someone again.

3. If you're going to meet friends later today, you will see them…

4. If you are an early bird, you are a person who is active…

5. If you hope to soon see someone again, you say…

6. If you are leaving someone but will see them again tomorrow, you say…

7. When you are meeting someone at 1:00 p.m., you are meeting them when?

8. If you think it's going to take you at least 60 minutes to get somewhere, it will take you…

Two Left Feet

Directions are often given using idioms. When you tell someone to "hang a left," you are using an idiom. If you tell them to "take" Main Street until they "get to" Center Street, you are using idioms. Again, it's often a simple preposition that changes, as when you tell someone you are staying "in Via Garibaldi" (on Garibaldi Street). In Italian, you use the preposition *in,* while in English, you normally use the word "on," as in "I live on Tenth Street."

Table 5.3 gives you some practical idioms, as well as some of the more commonly used idiomatic expressions that indicate direction, although they might not necessarily take you somewhere you want to go (like crazy).

As a Rule

In Italian, you use the verb *fare* (to do/make) most often when you would use the English verb "to take." You take a shower in English, but you do a shower *(fare la doccia)* in Italian. This also applies to taking a photo, a nap and so on. The reverse is true for the expression, "make a decision." In Italian, you would use the verb *prendere* (to take) *una decisione*.

Table 5.3 More Idioms

Idiom	Pronunciation	Meaning
a casa	*ah kah-zah*	at home
a destra (di)	*ah deh-stRah (dee)*	to the right (of)
a sinistra (di)	*ah see-nee-stRah (dee)*	to the left (of)
accanto (a)	*ah-kahn-toh (ah)*	next to/beside
al centro	*ahl chen-tRoh*	downtown
all'estero	*ah-leh-steh-Roh*	abroad
andare bene/male	*ahn-dah-Reh beh-neh/mah-leh*	to go well/to go poorly
andare di bene in meglio	*ahn-dah-Reh dee beh-neh een meh-lyoh*	to go from good to better
andare di male in peggio	*ahn-dah-Reh dee mah-leh een peh-joh*	to go from bad to worse
andare in giro	*ahn-dah-Reh een jee-Roh*	to go around
andare in pezzi	*ahn-dah-Reh een peh-tsee*	to go to pieces
andare pazzo	*ahn-dah-Reh pah-tsoh*	to go crazy
avanti	*ah-vahn-tee*	ahead
davanti	*dah-vahn-tee*	in front
Devo andarmene.	*deh-voh ahn-dah-Reh-meh-neh*	I must be going.

continues

Table 5.3 Continued

Idiom	Pronunciation	Meaning
fare un giro	*fah-Reh oon jee-Roh*	to take a spin
in città	*een chee-tah*	in the city
indietro	*een dee-eh-tRoh*	behind
lasciare andare	*lah-shah-Reh ahn-dah-Reh*	to leave something alone/ forget about something
opposto	*oh-poh-stoh*	opposite
sopra	*soh-pRah*	above
sotto	*soh-toh*	below
va bene	*vah beh-neh*	it's going well

What's Your Opinion?

Everyone has an opinion, whether they admit it or not. Some people are more expressive than others when sharing their thoughts. It may be some time before you feel confident enough to use the idioms in Table 5.4 when speaking, but if you listen carefully, you'll hear these used a lot. Later, as your Italian skills increase, you might want to flip back to these idioms and try using them to express what you think.

Table 5.4 If You Ask Me

Italian	Pronunciation	English
al contrario	*ahl kohn-tRah-Ree-oh*	to the contrary
allora	*ah-loh-Rah*	now then, well
capito	*kah-pee-toh*	understood
comunque	*koh-moon-kweh*	anyhow
Credo di sì/no.	*kReh-doh dee see/no*	I believe so/not.
d'accordo	*dah-koR-doh*	agreed
dunque	*doon-kweh*	now then/so
Hai ragione.	*ay Rah-joh-neh*	You are right.
Hai torto.	*ay toR-toh*	You are wrong.
invece di	*een-veh-cheh dee*	instead of
naturalmente	*nah-too-Rahl-mehn-teh*	naturally
non importa	*nohn eem-poR-tah*	it doesn't matter

Italian	Pronunciation	English
peccato	*peh-kah-toh*	too bad/(It's a) shame
Penso di sì/no.	*pen-soh dee see/no*	I think so/not.
per dire la verità	*peR dee-Reh lah veh-Ree-tah*	to tell the truth
secondo me	*seh-kohn-doh meh*	in my opinion
senza dubbio	*sen-zah doob-bee-oh*	without a doubt

What's Happening

Maybe you're feeling a chill or are a bit overheated. You're hungry and thirsty and need a drink. You're tired and in the mood for a nap. All of these things are easily expressed in Italian, using the verb *avere* (to have). If you say to someone, "I am hot," and use the verb *essere* (to be), you might think you're telling someone you feel hot. An innocent assumption—except in Italian, you must say, "I have hot." If you tell someone you *are* hot, you imply, well, that you're *hot*, as in sexy hot. Maybe you are, but it might not be the kind of thing you want to brag about at that moment.

As a Rule

Note that the verb *avere* (to have) is used to describe physical conditions, whereas in English, we use **"to be."** Feelings that are expressed with the verb *avere* (to have) are followed by a noun. Feelings that are expressed with the verb *essere* (to be) are followed by an adjective.

You'll learn how to conjugate the verb *essere* in Chapter 9 and the verb *avere* in Chapter 10. For now, look at how the expressions in Table 5.5 require the use of these two verbs to describe needs and feelings.

Table 5.5   Needs and Feelings

Idiom	Pronunciation	Meaning
avere bisogno di	*ah-veh-Reh bee-zohn-yoh dee*	to need
avere caldo	*ah-veh-Reh kahl-doh*	to be hot (literally, to feel hot)
avere freddo	*ah-veh-Reh fReh-doh*	to be cold (literally, to feel cold)
avere fame	*ah-veh-Reh fah-meh*	to be hungry

continues

Table 5.5 Continued

Idiom	Pronunciation	Meaning
avere sete	*ah-veh-Reh seh-teh*	to be thirsty
avere voglia di	*ah-veh-Reh vohl-yah dee*	to be in the mood
avere male di	*ah-veh-Reh mah-leh dee*	to have pain/to be sick
avere paura	*ah-veh-Reh pow-oo-Rah*	to be afraid
avere ragione	*ah-veh-Reh Rah-joh-neh*	to be right
avere torto	*ah-veh-Reh toR-toh*	to be wrong
avere sonno	*ah-veh-Reh sohn-noh*	to be sleepy
avere ____ anni	*ah-veh-Reh ___ahn-nee*	to be ____ years old
avere vergogna	*ah-veh-Reh veR-gohn-yah*	to be ashamed
essere stanco/a	*eh-seh-Reh stahn-koh/ah*	to be tired
essere contento/a	*eh-seh-Reh kohn-ten-toh/ah*	to be content
essere triste	*eh-seh-Reh tRee-steh*	to be sad
essere arrabbiato/a	*eh-seh-Reh ah-Rah-bee-ah-toh/ah*	to be angry
essere geloso/a	*eh-seh-Reh jeh-loh-soh/ah*	to be jealous

Attenzione!
When you express your needs using the first person (or "I" form) of the verb *avere* (to have), you must not pronounce the *h* in the word *ho* (I have). Instead, simply say it as you do "oh." When using the verb *essere* (to be) in the first person, simply say it like it looks, "sono."

Express Yourself

Express your needs. Start by using either *ho* (I have) or *sono* (I am) and add the appropriate Italian word to say the following:

Example:

Answer:

When you are afraid, you say   Ho paura.

When you are happy, you say   Sono contento.
(Or sono contenta.)

When you want to eat, you say

_____

When the temperature drops below freezing and you don't have a coat, you say

_____

When your legs feel like lead weights and you can't keep your eyes open, you say

_____

When you are happy, you say

_____

When you are angry, you say

_____

And the Forecast Is...

When someone asks, "*Che tempo fa?*" (What's the weather like?) and it's sunny, you say, "*Fa bello.*" (It's nice out.) Even in English, you use idioms when you say it's "nice," or, if there were a storm brewing, you might say, "It's pretty mean out there." In Italian, you must use the verb *fare* (to do or make) to talk about the weather. Essentially you're saying "It makes cold," and must use the third person singular form of the verb, *fare*, as in "*Fa freddo.*" (It's cold out.)

The expressions in Table 5.6 describe the weather. Most of them use the verb *fare*, which has already been conjugated. If you would like a more thorough understanding of the verb, consult Chapter 14. Separate verbs are used for precipitation, such as snow and rain, and as in English, are always used in the third person (unless you are particularly theatrical, "I rain; I snow; therefore, I am").

Attenzione!
When using adjectives, you must always modify the adjective to agree with the subject. If the subject is masculine, you don't have to change the original adjective. If the subject is feminine and the adjective ends in -*o*, you must always change the ending to -*a*. If the adjective ends in -*e*, you don't need to change it.

Table 5.6 Idiomatic Weather Expressions

Idiom	Pronunciation	Meaning
Che tempo fa?	*kay tem-poh fah*	What's the weather?
Fa bello.	*fah beh-loh*	It's beautiful out.
Fa brutto.	*fah bRoo-toh*	It's nasty out.
Fa caldo.	*fah kahl-doh*	It's hot.
Fa freddo.	*fah fReh-doh*	It's cold.
Fa fresco.	*fah fRes-koh*	It's cool.
Nevica.	*neh-vee-kah*	It's snowing.
Piove.	*pee-yoh-veh*	It's raining.
C'è il sole.	*cheh soh-leh*	It's sunny.
C'è nebbia.	*cheh neh-bee-yah*	It's foggy.

As a Rule

In Italian, as in English, many weather conditions are expressed impersonally, as in *Piove,* (It is raining), or *Nevica,* (It is snowing). These verbs are only used in the third person singular since you would never say, "I am snowing" or, "we are raining."

What's Doing?

You've mastered the art of small talk and being the witty, charming individual that you are, you want to warm up a conversation with a few comments on the weather. Using the following descriptions, what would you say to describe the weather? There may be more than one correct answer.

Che tempo fa? (What's the weather like?)

1. You're in the Alps and have your ski boots on. Small, white crystals fall from the sky.

2. You're in Sicily, and the blood oranges are ripe.

3. You can't see more than three feet in front of your car and you feel as though you are driving through a cloud.

4. You're in Chicago, and it's sleeting and the streets are icy.

5. It's high noon and the heat is rising up from the street in squiggly lines.

Some Fun

The idioms you just used are not only practical, but are also frequently used. However, there's a whole other dimension yet to be experienced in the land of colloquial Italian. Try using one of these babies, and you'll really be on the road to fluency.

A few expressions are quite close to English, and many others have similar messages. Did you know that the word proverb derives from Latin (*proverbium*) and literally means "set of words put forth" or "commonly uttered"? Not all idiomatic expressions are proverbs, but often they contain bits of wisdom that can be applied to a variety of situations.

Use an expression only when you are truly sure of its usage. Incidentally, in today's politically correct environment, some of these expressions may be considered trite, slightly rude, or out of fashion. Try out a couple on your Italian friends or simply listen for them in films or around town.

Table 5.7 Idiomatic Expressions and Colloquialisms

Italian Equivalent	Literal Translation	Equivalent English Expression
Chi dorme non piglia pesci.	Those that sleep won't catch fish.	The early bird gets the worm.
Fare alla Romana.	To go Roman.	To go Dutch.
Fare le ore piccole.	To do the wee hours.	To be a night owl.
Dare una mano.	To give a hand.	To give a hand.
Prendere in giro.	To take around.	To tease/joke with.
Andare in giro.	To go around.	To take a spin.
Toccare ferro.	To touch iron.	To knock on wood.
Basta./Basta così.	It's enough.	Enough already!/ That's enough.
Mangiare come una bestia.	To eat like a beast.	To eat like a pig.
Avere una fame da lupo.	To be hungry as a wolf.	To be hungry as a bear.
Fumare come un turco.	To smoke like a Turk.	To smoke like a chimney.
Che cretino/cretina!	What a cretin.	What a jerk!
Fare una vita da cani.	To live like a dog.	It's a dog's life.
Al settimo cielo.	In seventh heaven.	On cloud nine.
Fuori moda.	Out of fashion.	Out of style.
Fa un freddo cane.	It's dog cold.	It's freezing out.
Essere solo come un cane.	To be alone as a dog.	To be without a soul in the world.
Non è tutto oro quello che luccica.	Not everything that shines is gold.	All that glitters is not gold.
Dimmi con chi vai e ti dirò chi sei.	Tell me whom you frequent and I'll tell you who you are.	You are the friends you keep.
Che cavolata.	What cabbage.	What bull!
Perdere il pelo ma non il vizio.	You can lose the skin but not the vice.	A leopard can't change its spots.
Andare all'altro mondo.	To go to another world.	To kick the bucket.
Stanco da morire.	So tired as to die.	Dead tired.

continues

Table 5.7 Continued

Italian Equivalent	Literal Translation	Equivalent English Expression
Di mamma c'è n'è una sola.	Of mothers, there is only one.	You only have one mom.
Come mamma l'ha fatto.	As mom made him.	Stark naked; naked as a jay bird; wearing the emperor's new clothes.
Fare il furbo.	To be sly/clever.	To be sneaky.
Fare lo spiritoso.	To be spirited.	To be a wisenheimer.
Fare finta.	To pretend.	To fake it.
Fare del proprio meglio.	To do one's best.	(Ditto)
Essere nei guai.	To be in trouble.	To be in hot water.
Stringere la cinghia.	To tighten the belt.	(Ditto)
Due gocce d'acqua.	Two drops of water.	Two peas in a pod.
Volere la botte piena e la moglie ubriaca.	To want the bottle full and the wife drunk.	To have your cake and eat it too.
Fare un buco nell' acqua.	To take a dive into the water.	To come up empty handed.
Girare la testa.	To spin one's head.	To be swamped, in over one's head.
Le bugie hanno le gambe corte.	Lies have short legs.	Lies always catch up to you.
Una patata bollente.	A boiling potato.	A hot potato.
Trattare a pesci in faccia.	To act like a fish in the face.	To treat someone like a piece of dirt.
Essere un pesce fuor d'acqua.	To be a fish out of water.	(Ditto)
Avere lo spirito di patata.	To have the spirit of a potato.	To be a deadbeat.
Liscio come l'olio.	Smooth as oil.	To be slick.
Nudo e crudo.	Nude and crude.	The plain truth.
Essere nelle nuvole.	To be in the clouds.	To daydream.
Non sapere nulla di nulla.	To know nothing about anything.	To not know beans about.

Italian Equivalent	Literal Translation	Equivalent English Expression
Sfumare nel nulla.	To fade into nothing.	To go up in smoke.
Andare a nozze.	Like going to a wedding.	To be happy.
Mancino.	Little hand.	Lefty; southpaw.

Did you happen to notice how many idiomatic expressions have to do with food and animals? Dogs, wolves, fish, potatoes—these are but a handful of the thousands of idiomatic expressions that exist in Italian. Many are quite funny. Others impart a certain wisdom. Some can be quite poetic, such as *due gocce d'acqua,* meaning two drops of water and equal to when we say, "two peas in a pod," or *Sogni d'oro,* which translates into dreams of gold (or "Sweet dreams" as we say it).

When someone wishes you good luck (*buona fortuna*), the mere fact of their wishing implies there's a possibility of bad luck. This might explain why actors and others use the expression, "Break a leg." In Italian, we talk about wolves (*In bocca al lupo*) and the appropriate response is, "*Crepi!*" coming from Latin and meaning, "That he dies!" (Animal lovers may be thinking, "Oh, that poor wolf!")

You might want to browse through a few idiom books you can pick up at your local bookstore to see what else is out there. A few books just concentrate on the dirty words, but you probably already know a handful of those words, aptly called *vulgarities*—as they seem to be the first thing anyone learns in a foreign language. By the way, you're going to look awfully silly swearing in Italian if all you know are the bad words and nothing else. Please, spare the world your cynicism for the time being.

The Least You Need to Know

➤ All languages have idiomatic expressions that are particular to them.

➤ There are certain terms, phrases, and expressions in Italian that will be useful to you in practical, everyday situations such as when you want to express location, direction, or opinion.

➤ Be wary of translating an expression directly from one language to another. Often there is an equivalent saying that uses different terminology.

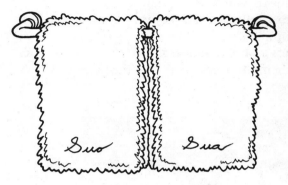

Almost Everything You Wanted to Know About Sex

Once upon a time, the masculine energy of *il sole* (the sun) ruled the earth during the day, and the feminine energy of the *la luna* (moon) ruled the night. When politically correct English speakers came across the land, they called this sexism and made everything neuter. Not so in Italian. In this chapter, you might not learn everything you wanted to know about sex, but you *will* learn about gender.

Determining Gender: He Versus She

Unlike English, where women are women and men are men, and everything else is a non-gender, in Italian, every single noun (person, place, thing, or idea) is designated as masculine or feminine. The sun, the stars, and the moon all have a specific gender. How is this determination made? Sometimes it's obvious, sometimes there are clues, and sometimes it's just downright tricky. A dictionary comes in handy during these times of confusion, and if you imagine yourself as a mystic unveiling the mysteries of the world, determining gender can be an adventure you never imagined.

Masculine or Feminine

Every noun in Italian is either masculine or feminine. Whether you're talking about a *gatto* (cat), a *cane* (dog), or a *macchina* (car), all nouns are one gender or the other.

The reason *why* a particular noun is masculine or feminine is not always obvious. Determining a noun's gender, however, is quite easy in Italian. The key is to look at the endings. Whether a noun is masculine or feminine, the endings are almost always consistent. Occasionally, you will come across a word that does not conform to this rule, making memorization necessary, but even then, the article preceding the noun will indicate its gender.

As a Rule

If a word ends in *-a*, it is generally feminine. If a word ends in *-o*, it is masculine. Some words end in *-e* and require memorization. The article always reflects gender.

The gender of a noun affects its relationship with other words in a sentence, including adjectives (a word that describes a noun), and if you learn the definite articles along with the nouns, it is easier for you to form sentences correctly later. The magic word here is *agreement*. Everyone has to get along. Nouns and adjectives must always agree. For example, if we want to say the small cat (*il gatto piccolo*), the adjective small (*piccolo*) must agree in gender with the word cat (*gatto*). We'll get to adjectives later, but keep in mind that they follow the same rules.

An Article Is Not What You Read in a Newspaper

Before you get into Italian nouns, there's one little challenge you must face: the noun marker that precedes the noun. The term *noun marker* refers to an article or adjective that tells us whether a noun is *masculine* (m.) or *feminine* (f.), *singular* (s.) or *plural* (p.). The noun markers shown in Table 6.1 are singular, definite articles expressing "the" and indefinite articles expressing "a," "an," or "one."

Table 6.1 Singular Noun Markers

Article	Masculine	Feminine
the	il, lo, l'	la, l'
a, an, one	un, uno	una, un'

The Definite Article (The)

What?! Five different singular definite articles? You're probably thinking this is a little too much grammar for you. Rest assured, it's not as confusing as you think. Here's how these definite articles work in the singular:

➤ *Lo* is used in front of all singular, masculine nouns that begin with a *z* or an *s* followed by a consonant, such as *lo zio* (the uncle), *lo studio* (the study), and *lo sci* (the ski/skiing).

➤ *Il* is used in front of all singular, masculine nouns, such as *il ragazzo* (the boy), *il sole* (the sun), and *il vino* (the wine).

➤ *L'* is used in front of all singular nouns, both masculine and feminine, that begin with a vowel, such as *l'uomo* (the man), *l'opera* (the opera), and *l'atleta* (the female athlete).

➤ *La* is used in front of all other singular, feminine nouns, such as *la ragazza* (the girl), *la musica* (the music), and *la luna* (the moon).

> **What's What**
> **Definite articles** are the singular masculine (*il, lo, l'*) and feminine (*la, l'*) articles that precede Italian nouns and correspond with "the" in English. Unlike the English "the," these articles show the gender of a noun. The plural masculine (*i, gli*) and plural feminine (*le*) articles reflect gender and plurality.
>
> A **noun marker** can be any of a variety of articles, such as *il, lo, l', la, i, gli, le* (the equivalent of "the" in English) and *uno, una, un'* (the equivalent of "a" in English).

An Indefinite Article (A, An)

It's much easier with the indefinite articles. Remember that the indefinite article is only used before *singular* nouns.

Masculine:

➤ *Un* is used before all singular masculine nouns beginning with either a consonant or a vowel, such as *un palazzo* (a building), *un signore* (a gentleman), and *un animale* (animal), except those nouns beginning with a *z* or an *s* followed by a consonant.

➤ *Uno* is used just like the definite article *lo*, before singular masculine nouns beginning with a *z* or an *s* followed by a consonant, such as *uno zio* (an uncle) and *uno stadio* (a stadium).

Feminine:

> ➤ *Una* is used before any feminine noun beginning with a consonant, such as *una farfalla* (a butterfly), *una storia* (a story), and *una strada* (a street).

> ➤ *Un'* is the equivalent of "an" in English and is used before all feminine nouns beginning with a vowel, such as *un'italiana* (an Italian woman), *un'amica* (a friend), and *un'opera* (an opera).

Singular Nouns

Some nouns in Italian, such as those shown in Table 6.2, are easy to mark because they obviously refer to masculine or feminine people. Pay special attention to their endings.

Table 6.2   Gender-Obvious Nouns

Masculine Noun	Feminine Noun	Pronunciation	English
il padre		*eel pah-dReh*	the father
	la madre	*lah mah-dReh*	the mother
il marito		*eel mah-Ree-toh*	the husband
	la moglie	*lah mohl-yeh*	the wife
il nonno		*eel noh-noh*	the grandfather
	la nonna	*lah noh-nah*	the grandmother
il fratello		*eel fRah-teh-loh*	the brother
	la sorella	*lah soh-Reh-lah*	the sister
il cugino		*eel koo-jee-noh*	the cousin (m.)
	la cugina	*lah koo-jee-nah*	the cousin (f.)
il ragazzo		*eel Rah-gah-tsoh*	the boy
	la ragazza	*lah Rah-gah-tsah*	the girl
lo zio		*loh zee-oh*	the uncle
	la zia	*lah zee-ah*	the aunt
l'uomo		*lwoh-moh*	the man
	la donna	*lah doh-nah*	the woman
l'amico		*lah-mee-koh*	the friend (m.)
	l'amica	*lah-mee-kah*	the friend (f.)

Pretty soon you're going to be watching Fellini films and you won't have to read the *sottotitoli* (subtitles) anymore. Let's add a few more words to your *vocabolario* (vocabulary).

A few nouns can be either masculine or feminine. All you have to do is simply change their identifier, without changing their spelling, to refer to either gender. Several of those nouns, including many nationalities, end in -*e* but can still be either masculine or feminine.

Attenzione!
All nouns, with the exception of one's immediate family members, require an article.

Let's look at a few:

> *Il dentista* (male) *mangia* (is eating) *la cioccolata.*

> *La dentista* (female) *mangia la frutta.*

Table 6.3 shows several examples of either gender nouns.

Table 6.3   Either Gender Nouns

Noun	Pronunciation	Meaning
artista	*ahR-tees-tah*	artist
atleta	*at-leh-tah*	athlete
cantante	*cahn-tahn-teh*	singer
dentista	*den-tees-tah*	dentist
giovane	*joh-vah-neh*	youth
nomade	*noh-mah-deh*	nomad
parente	*pah-Ren-teh*	relative
turista	*too-Rees-tah*	tourist
inglese	*een-gleh-zeh*	English
francese	*fRahn-cheh-zeh*	French
irlandese	*eeR-lahn-deh-zeh*	Irish
giapponese	*jah-poh-neh-zeh*	Japanese
svedese	*sveh-deh-zeh*	Swedish

Some nouns ending in -*e* may be masculine or feminine. You must memorize the gender of these nouns. You might want to create ways to help you remember the gender of a noun; for example, *la notte* (the night) belongs to the feminine, as does *la luna* (the moon). Be creative—maybe you'll remember the metaphor given at the beginning of this chapter, where the day is ruled by the masculine energy of *il sole* (the sun). When we say *la macchina* or *l'automobile* (a car) runs well, we say *she* runs smoothly. Again, any association you can make to help you remember a word is acceptable, no matter how strange. It's your brain. Work it. If you make a gender mistake, it's really not that serious—as long as you've chosen the correct noun, you'll be understood. See Table 6.4 for common nouns ending in *-e* and their genders.

Table 6.4   Nouns Ending in -e

Masculine	Pronunciation	English	Feminine	Pronunciation	English
cane	*kah-neh*	dog	automobile	*ow-toh-moh-bee-leh*	car
sole	*soh-leh*	sun	stazione	*stah-zee-oh-neh*	station
nome	*noh-meh*	name/noun	notte	*noh-teh*	night
mare	*mah-Reh*	ocean	nave	*nah-veh*	ship

As a Rule

Italian words ending in *-azione* are often the equivalent of English words ending in **-tion**, such as *occupazione* (occupation). These words are always feminine.

Most words of foreign origin ending in a consonant are masculine, such as *autobus*, *bar*, *computer*, *film*, and *sport*.

Did You Know?
Although Ms. is a common feminine form of address in the U.S., an Italian woman can only be addressed as either *signorina* (Miss) or *signora* (Mrs.). However, the Italian women, politically minded as they are, decided to use *signora* in lieu of Ms. In any case, it is still a compliment for a woman to be referred to as *signorina*.

Rules Are Made to Be Broken

Just to drive you crazy, there are a few exceptions to these rules. Remember that rules are man-made, designed by linguists to make sense of an otherwise chaotic universe. All languages, including Italian, are dynamic, changing creatures that evolve, expand, and contract with time, influenced by factors such as trends, other cultures, and values.

Disconcerting Genders

Sometimes the ending of a word completely changes that word's significance. The only way to remember these oddities is to memorize them. If you get the gender wrong, 99% of the time, the person to whom you are speaking will know what you're talking about in any case. Table 6.5 provides a list of words whose meanings change according to the ending.

Table 6.5   Disconcerting Genders

Masculine	Feminine
il ballo (dance)	*la balla* (bundle, bale)
il collo (neck)	*la colla* (glue)
il colpo (blow)	*la colpa* (fault, guilt)
il costo (cost)	*la costa* (coast)
il filo (thread)	*la fila* (line)
il foglio (sheet of paper)	*la foglia* (leaf)
il manico (handle)	*la manica* (sleeve)
il mento (chin)	*la menta* (mint)
il porto (port)	*la porta* (door)
il punto (detail, dot)	*la punta* (tip)
il velo (veil)	*la vela* (sail, sailing)

Words are like the colors on a painter's palette, allowing us to express our thoughts to others. The more colors you have to paint with, the more you can say. Just as there are many more colors than there are words, there are many nouns that just won't conform to the rules, but they exist anyway. Look at Table 6.6 for a few of these misbehaving masculine nouns.

Table 6.6   Masculine Nouns That End in -a

Noun	Pronunciation	English
il clima	*eel klee-mah*	the climate
il cruciverba	*eel kRoo-chee-veR-bah*	the crossword (puzzle)
il drama	*eel dRah-mah*	the drama
il problema	*eel pRoh-bleh-mah*	the problem
il programma	*eel pRoh-gRah-mah*	the program

Feminine nouns can be troublemakers, too. Table 6.7 mentions some of the them.

Table 6.7 Feminine Nouns That End in -o:

Noun	Pronunciation	English
la foto (short for fotografia)	*lah foh-toh*	the photo
la moto (short for motocicletta)	*lah moh-toh*	the motorcycle
la mano	*lah mah-noh*	the hand
la radio	*lah Rah-dee-yoh*	the radio

Sex Changers

Certain words can be made feminine by changing the ending to either *-essa* or *-ice*, as listed in Table 6.8.

Table 6.8 Noun Endings

Masculine	Feminine	English
il professore	la professor*essa*	professor
l'avvocato	l'avvocat*essa*	lawyer
il dottore	la dottor*essa*	doctor
lo studente	la student*essa*	student
l'attore	l'att*rice*	actor/actress
il direttore	la dirett*rice*	director
il pittore	la pitt*rice*	painter

In modern usage, the feminine endings of professionals such as actors, doctors, professors, and lawyers are used with less frequency than they used to be. It is also appropriate to refer to a male or female lawyer as *l'avvocato*.

Fruit is almost always referred to in the feminine, but when the word is made masculine, it becomes the fruit tree. *La mela* (the apple) becomes *il melo* (the apple tree), *la pera* (pear) becomes *il pero* (the pear tree), *la cilegia* (the cherry) becomes *il cilegio* (the cherry tree), *l'arancia* (the orange) becomes *l'arancio* (the orange tree), and so on.

Practice Makes Perfetto

Determine the gender by placing the appropriate definite article in front of the following nouns. You might have to consult a dictionary for a couple of them. Don't forget to look at the endings!

1. ___casa (house)
2. ___cane (dog)
3. ___albero (tree)
4. ___piatto (plate)
5. ___lezione (lesson)

6. ___estate (summer)
7. ___chiesa (church)
8. ___straniero (foreigner)
9. ___cattedrale (cathedral)
10. ___pianeta (planet)

More Is Better: Making Plurals

In English, it's relatively easy to talk about more than one thing; usually, you just add an -s to the word, although there are many plurals that confuse learners of our language. How many *childs* do you have, or rather *children*? Fortunately, forming plural nouns in Italian is as easy as floating in a gondola. Yes, you do have to memorize the endings, and again, the ending must always reflect gender. But you don't have to memorize a hundred different words just to say more than one. Table 6.9 illustrates how the ending should change in the plural.

Table 6.9 Plural Endings

Singular		Plural	Singular		Plural
o	→	i	ragazzo	→	ragazzi
a	→	e	donna	→	donne
ca	→	che	amica	→	amiche
e	→	i	cane	→	cani

What Does It Mean?

Without knowing the significance of a word, it is still easy to determine whether it is singular or plural. Look at the following words and determine their gender and plurality. Remember that some nouns end in -e in the singular. Guess at their meanings:

aeroplani	tavole	vacanza	viaggi
bambini	notte	scuole	invenzione
libro	dollari	supermercati	ragazze
nome	birra	odore	stranieri

Attenzione!

In certain cases, the plural of certain nouns and adjectives follows different rules:

1. Singular feminine nouns and adjectives ending in *-ca* or *-ga* form the plural by changing the endings to *-che* or *-ghe*.

   amica → amiche   bianca → bianche

2. Singular feminine nouns ending in *-cia* and *-gia* form the plural with:

   cie/gie   (if a vowel precedes the singular ending)

   ce/ge   (if a consonant precedes the singular ending)

   camicia → camicie   valigia → valigie

   arancia → arance   pioggia → piogge

3. Singular masculine nouns and adjectives ending in *-co* and *-go* generally form the plural by replacing the singular endings with *-chi* and *-ghi*.

   pacco → pacchi   bianco → bianchi

   lago → laghi   largo → larghi

Do We Agree? Plural Noun Markers

When an Italian noun refers to more than one thing, you must change the noun marker.

As a Rule

Family names do not change endings in the plural. For example, if you were talking about the Leonardo family, you would say *i Leonardo* (the Leonardos).

Nouns accented on the last vowel do not change form in the plural. Only the article changes. For example: *la città* (the city) becomes *le città* (the cities) in the plural.

Table 6.10 shows how singular noun markers change in the plural. Remember that funny rule about the definite article *lo*, which is only used in front of words beginning with s + a consonant or z. The same applies to *gli*.

Table 6.10   Plural Noun Markers—the Definite Article (The)

	Masculine		Feminine	
	Singular	Plural	Singular	Plural
(The)	lo →	**gli***	la →	**le**
	l' →	**gli**	l' →	**le**
	il →	**i**		

*Note that the definite article gli *is pronounced like* ylee.

> ➤ *Gli* is used in front of all plural, masculine nouns beginning with *z* or an *s* followed by a consonant and plural, masculine nouns beginning with a vowel, such as *gli studenti* (the students), *gli zii* (the uncles), *gli animali* (the animals), *gli amici* (the friends).

> ➤ *I* is used in front of all plural, masculine nouns beginning with all other consonants, such as *i ragazzi* (the boys), *i vini* (the wines).

> ➤ *Le* is used in front of all plural, feminine nouns, such as *le ragazze* (the girls), *le donne* (the women), *le automobili* (the cars).

Plural Spelling

Look at what happens to the following nouns in Table 6.11 when made plural.

Table 6.11   Singular and Plural Nouns

Singular Noun	Pronunciation	English	Plural Noun	Pronunciation	English
la monaca	*lah moh-nah-kah*	the nun	le monache	*leh moh-neh-keh*	the nuns
l'amica	*lah-mee-kah*	the friend (f.)	le amiche	*leh ah-mee-keh*	the friends (f.)
l'amico	*lah-mee-koh*	the friend (m.)	gli amici	*ylee-ah-mee-chee*	the friends (m.)
il nemico	*eel neh-mee-koh*	the enemy (m.)	i nemici	*ylee-ah-mee-chee*	the enemies (m.)
l'ago	*lah-goh*	the needle	gli aghi	*ylee-ah-ghee*	the needles
il luogo	*eel lwoh-goh*	the place	i luoghi	*ee-lwoh-ghee*	the places

You already know one plural—spaghetti! Because you could never eat one spaghetto—which isn't a real word—you must always use it in the plural. Let's try a sentence. *In Italia, i turisti mangiano gli spaghetti al pomodoro.*

Irregular Plural Nouns

Some masculine nouns become plural in the feminine. As you can see from Table 6.12, many parts of the body are included.

Table 6.12 Irregular Plural Nouns

Singular	Plural
l'uovo (the egg)	*le uova* (the eggs)
il braccio (the arm)	*le braccia* (the arms)
il dito (the finger)	*le dita* (the fingers)
il labbro (the lip)	*le labbra* (the lips)
il miglio (the mile)	*le miglia* (the miles)
il paio (the pair)	*le paia* (the pairs)
il ginocchio (the knee)	*le ginocchia* (the knees)
la mano (the hand)	*le mani* (the hands)

As a Rule

The word for grapes (*uva*) is always singular and never plural. Whether you are eating one *uva* or 100 *uva*, the word remains the same.

Practice Those Plurals

You've just arrived in Rome, and you need to pick up a few odds and ends. You're in a *negozio* (store), and want to buy more than one of the items listed below. Start by saying, "*Cerco…*" (I am looking for…) and the name of the item. Don't forget to use the appropriate article.

Example: il regalo (gift)

Cerco i regali. (I am looking for the gifts.)

1. la cartolina (postcard)
2. la rivista (magazine)
3. la collana (necklace)

4. il profumo (perfume)
5. la cravatta (tie)
6. la penna (pen)

What Have You Learned About Gender?

You've always wanted to be in a movie. You remember watching all those spaghetti westerns where tall men wore big hats and the women always looked pretty, even with a smudge of dirt across their cheeks. You're in Rome visiting the famous movie studio Cinecittà where those films were made, and you see a listing for auditions. Determine whether the part requires a male or female role.

Attrice matura (40–50 anni), cercasi con la capacità di parlare l'inglese e il francese per interpretare il ruolo di una contessa. Aspetto distinto. Inviare curriculum con foto a Via Garibaldi 36, Roma.

Attore forte, atletico, giovane, cercasi con i capelli chiari per interpretare il ruolo di Cesare. Presentarsi il 25 giugno ore 9:00 alla palestra Superforte, secondo piano.

Uomini e donne veramente sexy, cercasi per apparire nudi in una scena sulla spiaggia: Varie età. Esperienza non necessaria. Telefonare al 06/040357.

Casalinga stanca, che s'innamora del suo vicino mentre il marito viaggia. Pregasi notare che si tratta di un ruolo molto drammatico. Cerchiamo una vera stella. Audizione: 5 luglio allo studio di Cinecittà.

The Least You Need to Know

➤ Certain endings are almost always masculine (*o*, *i*, consonants) or feminine (*a*, *e*).

➤ Some nouns can be changed from masculine to feminine by adding an appropriate ending.

➤ Always look at the article to determine the gender and plurality of a noun.

➤ All plural nouns end in either *-i* or *-e*.

Chapter 7

The Object and Subject of Your Desire

In This Chapter

➤ Subject and object pronouns: the keys to smooth communication in *la bella lingua*

➤ Friendly or polite? Formal and informal pronouns in Italian

➤ You or all of you? Learn how Italians directly address one person or lots of people.

In the previous chapter, you learned about nouns—how to determine their gender and make them plural. You can take *mela* (apple) and make it *mele* (apples); enjoy not just one *libro* (book), but many *libri* (books). And you thought there could be no greater thrill. To add to your plate of joy, this chapter discusses the titillating world of pronouns. This chapter and Chapter 8 are power chapters—meat and potatoes chapters (or if you're a vegetarian, rice and beans chapters). Here you will be freed from the simple-speak of nouns and adjectives and elevated to the level of real communication. Excited yet?

What's the Subject

As you learned in Chapter 4, an infinitive verb is a verb in its unconjugated form, as in *cucinare* (to cook), *mangiare* (to eat), *dormire* (to sleep), and *viaggiare* (to travel).

Determining the subject of a verb is essential to conjugation. To determine the subject, you need to ask the simple question, "What or who is doing the action?" The subject may be a person, a thing (such as the car), or a pronoun replacing the noun (such as he or it).

Look at the sentences in Table 7.1 to better understand what is the subject of the verb.

Table 7.1 Determining the Subject

Sentence	Subject
I want to visit Venice.	I
You want to learn Italian.	You
The bus is leaving at 4:30.	The bus *or* it
Eat, drink, and be merry!	You
Robert and I are brother and sister.	Robert and I *or* we
You are all very intelligent.	You (plural)
The Italians love life.	The Italians *or* they

What's What
There are two kinds of objects: direct and indirect. The **direct object** of a sentence is the recipient of a verb's action. The **indirect object** of a sentence tells *to whom* or *for whom* the action was done.

Subject Pronouns

Way back when linguists began making sense of the universe of words, they realized that there were only three spheres of existence. "I" can exist, "you" can exist, and "he or she" can exist. (In the plural, it's we, you, and they.) There are no other options. The linguists decided to call these *persons*. Look at the subject pronouns in Table 7.2.

Table 7.2 Subject Pronouns

Person	Singular	Plural
First	*io* (I)	*noi* (we)
Second	*tu* (you, informal)	*voi* (you, plural)
Third	*lui/lei/Lei* (he/she/You, polite)*	*loro* (they)

*The pronoun Lei (with a capital "L") signifies "you" (polite, or formal); the pronoun lei signifies "she." Both, however, are third person.

In Italian, subject pronouns are used much less frequently than in English and other languages because the verb endings usually indicate the subject quite clearly. It is not necessary to use a subject pronoun to say the sentence *Mangio la pasta* (I eat the pasta) because the ending *-o* already tells us it's the first person.

What's What
An **object pronoun** replaces the object in a sentence. In English, this is equivalent of "it." Because there isn't a neutral equivalent in Italian, all object pronouns must reflect *gender* and *plurality*.

You're probably wondering, "Why have these idiotic pronouns then?" Why not just eliminate them, make things easier? Well, there are a few reasons. You use subject pronouns for

➤ *Clarity*: To differentiate who is doing the action in cases where verb forms are the same and when there is more than one subject:

Lui parla l'italiano ma lei parla il francese. (He speaks Italian but she speaks French.)

➤ *Emphasis*: To clearly underline the fact that the subject will be performing the action:

Tu viaggi in Italia. Io rimango qui. (You travel to Italy. I'm remaining (I remain) here.)

What's What
The **subject** of a sentence is a noun or pronoun that is generally the doer of the verb's action or the thing being described. The subject usually appears before the verb.

➤ *Politeness*: To show respect and maintain a formality with another person.

Lei è molto gentile. (You are very kind.)

Just to make sure you're on track, determine the subject of the verb in the following sentences; then determine the appropriate subject pronoun for each sentence:

1. The stars twinkled brightly.
2. Jessica knows how to have fun.
3. Leslie travels a lot.
4. My mother was a painter.
5. Louis was an engineer.
6. The food is delicious.
7. Italian is easy to learn.
8. Herby flies a plane.

Now that you're cooking with gas, let's take this one step further: Determine the subject in the following Italian sentences. If you're brave, try translating them:

1. Davide prende l'autobus.
2. Io mangio la cena.
3. Patrizia e Raffaella studiano arte.
4. L'insalata è fresca.
5. La farmacia è aperta.
6. Lo studente conversa con il professore.
7. Io e Gianni andiamo in Italia.
8. La ragazza va a casa.

You and You and You

Have you ever addressed a group of people and not known quite how to acknowledge all of them? In the southern United States, you might say, "Y'all." In the North, you might say, "All of you."

Attenzione!

In English, the subject pronoun "I" is always capitalized, regardless of its position in the sentence. In Italian, *io* is only capitalized at the beginning of a sentence.

The polite "you" subject pronoun *Lei* is always capitalized to distinguish it from the subject pronoun *lei*, meaning "she." At the beginning of a sentence, there is no distinction between the two pronouns, requiring the reader to determine the significance through the context of the sentence.

Italian solves this problem by having a separate, plural form of "you" (the second person plural). It also has an informal "you" (second person singular) used specifically with friends and family members and a separate form of "you" used in formal situations, which we call the *polite* form (third person singular). You've already seen these pronouns in Table 7.1. Take a look at them again in Table 7.3, just to make sure you understand:

Table 7.3 Forms of You

English	Italian	When to Use	Person
you (informal)	*tu*	informal, used with family, friends, children	second singular
you (polite)	*Lei*	polite, used to show respect to strangers, authority figures, elders; always capitalized	third singular
you (plural)	*voi*	plural, used when addressing more than one person	second plural
you (plural polite)	*Loro**	plural, polite; used in extreme cases (as when addressing the Pope)	third plural

*This form, although plural, is used to address the pope as the polite form of voi. *It probably stems from the notion that when speaking to the pope, one is also addressing God. Although Pope John Paul II often uses the first person singular form when giving his own personal opinion, he may also use the plural* noi *(we) form of the verb, as in* pensiamo *(we think), which is the traditional form used by popes.*

What's What

There are actually four forms of "you" in Italian:

Tu is used in informal settings with friends and relatives or when adults address children.

Lei is polite, used with strangers and persons in authority and to show respect or maintain a more formal relationship with someone.

Voi is primarily used to address a group of people, although it can still be used as a formal way of addressing an individual, especially in the south.

Loro is used in rare cases when an extreme form of politeness is required, either when addressing a group of people or someone in a high position, such as a president or the pope. It was once used more commonly and can still be heard in old films.

What pronouns would you use when speaking to the following people:

Anna Maria? Stefano? Mr. and Mrs. Carini? Giorgio e Filippo? Susanna? Pope John Paul II? Your baby brother? Your boss?

Did You Know?

Each region has its own particularities. In Rome, it is not uncommon to use the *tu* form of a verb when addressing a stranger in an informal setting, such as a small shop or while waiting for a bus.

The Florentines tend to be more formal in their interactions and use *Lei* unless it has been established that it is okay to use the *tu*. In English, this is equal to our using a last name to address someone, as in *Mr. Rossi*.

In parts of the south, the *voi* form of a verb may be commonly used in lieu of *Lei*.

The Least You Need to Know

➤ Determining the subject of a verb is essential to conjugation—and therefore speaking.

➤ Subject pronouns are used much less frequently in Italian than in English and other languages because the verb endings usually indicate the subject.

➤ Subject pronouns are used for clarity, emphasis, or courtesy—so don't skip them!

➤ There are four forms of "you" in Italian: the second person plural, the second person singular, the third person singular, and the third person plural.

Chapter 8

An Action-Packed Adventure

In This Chapter

➤ Verb families and conjugation

➤ Common regular Italian verbs

➤ Taking conjugation a step further: asking questions

➤ Forming negative statements

Verbs are the skeleton of a language. Without verbs, nothing would get done; nothing would happen. Verbs are what move us, shape us, and allow us to convey messages, make changes, cook, eat, sleep, dream, travel, study, worship, and live.

You've already studied some verbs in Chapter 4. It is *importante* to know infinitives of verbs in order to look them up in your *dizionario*. The infinitive form is simply the unconjugated verb, as in *to love*, *to dance*, and *to be*. An infinitive, however, doesn't tell us who is doing the action. That's why it's important to know how to conjugate. You do it all the time in English without even realizing it. Most of the time, verbs follow certain rules. We call these regular verbs. However, some verbs conjugate to their own beat; these are called irregular verbs.

All in the Family

All verbs in Italian belong to one of three large families: *-are*, *-ere*, or *-ire*. The rules are the same for each family, so after you've learned the pattern for one family, you know them all. The *-are* family is the largest and most regular. The *-ere* family also has its own set of rules, although there are many misbehaving verbs in this group that dance to their own beat, meaning they follow separate rules of conjugation that must be memorized. (There's one in every family.) The *-ire* family has two methods of conjugation.

The irregular verbs will be covered later. For now, look at the *-are* family and how these verbs are conjugated.

The -are Family

To conjugate *-are* verbs, drop the *-are* from the stem and then add the endings in Table 8.1.

Table 8.1   -are Endings

Pronoun	Singular Endings	Pronoun	Plural Endings
io	*-o*	noi	*-iamo*
tu	*-i*	voi	*-ate*
lui/lei/Lei	*-a*	loro	*-ano*

Now you can conjugate any regular verb that belongs to the *-are* family. Take a look at the verb *celebrare* and see how it conjugates. Break it down to its infinitive stem by detaching the *-are* ending and then attaching the endings you just saw. Check it out:

CELEBR/ARE

(stem)/(infinitive ending)

io	celeb**ro**	noi	celebr**iamo**
tu	celeb**ri**	voi	celeb**rate**
lui/lei/Lei	celeb**ra**	loro	celeb**rano**

Table 8.2 is a fairly comprehensive list of the *-are* verbs, which translates to the following: This is the only book you need when you go on *vacanza* (vacation), except for your

dizionario. Don't be intimidated by the magnitude of words to learn; think of them as colors for your palette. The more you have, the better you will express yourself. For now, study the verbs listed in Table 8.2 carefully. Later, cover the translations with a piece of paper and see if you can ascertain their significance by associating them with English words you already know. Remember that when pronouncing these verbs, double consonants should be emphasized but not separated, and all syllables should slide together.

What's What
Stem + ending = conjugation.

Table 8.2 Regular -are Verbs

Verb	Pronunciation	Meaning
abbracciare	*ah-bRah-chah-Reh*	to hug
abbronzare	*ah-bRohn-zah-Reh*	to tan
abitare	*ah-bee-tah-Reh*	to live
abusare	*ah-boo-zah-Reh*	to abuse
accompagnare	*ah-kohm-pah-nyah-Reh*	to accompany
adorare	*ah-doh-Rah-Reh*	to adore
affermare	*ah-feR-mah-Reh*	to affirm
affittare	*ah-fee-tah-Reh*	to rent
aiutare	*ah-yoo-tah-Reh*	to help
alzare	*ahl-zah-Reh*	to raise/lift up
amare	*ah-mah-Reh*	to love
ammirare	*ah-mee-Rah-Reh*	to admire
anticipare	*ahn-tee-chee-pah-Reh*	to anticipate/wait
arrestare	*ah-Reh-stah-Reh*	to stop/arrest
arrivare	*ah-Ree-vah-Reh*	to arrive
aspettare	*ah-speh-tah-Reh*	to wait/expect
assaggiare	*ah-sah-jyah-Reh*	to taste
avvisare	*ah-vee-sah-Reh*	to inform/advise
baciare	*bah-chah-Reh*	to kiss
ballare	*bah-lah-Reh*	to dance
bloccare	*bloh-kah-Reh*	to block

continues

Table 8.2 Continued

Verb	Pronunciation	Meaning
bruciare	*bRoo-chah-Reh*	to burn
bussare	*boo-sah-Reh*	to knock
calcolare	*kal-koh-lah-Reh*	to calculate
cambiare	*kahm-bee-yah-Reh*	to change
camminare	*kah-mee-nah-Reh*	to walk
cancellare	*kahn-cheh-lah-Reh*	to cancel
cantare	*kahn-tah-Reh*	to sing
cadere	*kah-deh-Reh*	to fall down
causare	*kow-zah-Reh*	to cause
celebrare	*cheh-leb-Rah-Reh*	to celebrate
cenare	*cheh-nah-Reh*	to dine
cercare	*cheR-kah-Reh*	to look for something/to search
chiamare	*kee-ah-mah-Reh*	to call
cominciare	*koh-meen-chah-Reh*	to begin
comprare	*kohm-pRah-Reh*	to buy
comunicare	*koh-moo-nee-kah-Reh*	to communicate
consumare	*kohn-soo-mah-Reh*	to consume
contare	*kohn-tah-Reh*	to count
controllare	*kohn-tRoh-lah-Reh*	to control/to check
conversare	*kohn-veR-sah-Reh*	to converse
costare	*koh-stah-Reh*	to cost
creare	*kray-ah-Reh*	to create
cucinare	*koo-chee-nah-Reh*	to cook
dare	*dah-Reh*	to give
deliberare	*deh-lee-beh-Rah-Reh*	to deliberate/resolve
depositare	*deh-poh-zee-tah-Reh*	to deposit
desiderare	*deh-zee-deh-Rah-Reh*	to desire
determinare	*deh-teR-mee-nah-Reh*	to determine
detestare	*deh-teh-stah-Reh*	to detest
dimostrare	*dee-moh-stRah-Reh*	to demonstrate

Verb	Pronunciation	Meaning
disegnare	*dee-zen-yah-Reh*	to draw/design
disgustare	*dee-sgoo-stah-Reh*	to disgust
disperare	*dee-speh-Rah-Reh*	to despair
diventare	*dee-ven-tah-Reh*	to become
domandare	*doh-mahn-dah-Reh*	to question
donare	*doh-nah-Reh*	to donate/give
elevare	*eh-leh-vah-Reh*	to elevate
eliminare	*eh-lee-mee-nah-Reh*	to eliminate
entrare	*ehn-tRah-Reh*	to enter
esaminare	*eh-zah-mee-nah-Reh*	to examine
evitare	*eh-vee-tah-Reh*	to avoid
festeggiare	*feh-steh-jah-Reh*	to celebrate
firmare	*feeR-mah-Reh*	to sign
formare	*foR-mah-Reh*	to form/create
fumare	*foo-mah-Reh*	to smoke
funzionare	*foon-zee-oh-nah-Reh*	to function
gettare	*jeh-tah-Reh*	to throw
giocare	*joh-kah-Reh*	to play a game
giustificare	*joo-stee-fee-kah-Reh*	to justify
glorificare	*gloh-Ree-fee-kah-Reh*	to glorify
guardare	*gwahR-dah-Reh*	to look at something
guidare	*gwee-dah-Reh*	to drive
ignorare	*ee-gynoh-Rah-Reh*	to ignore
immaginare	*ee-mah-jee-nah-Reh*	to imagine
imparare	*eem-pah-Rah-Reh*	to learn
implicare	*eem-plee-kah-Reh*	to imply
indicare	*een-dee-kah-Reh*	to indicate
informare	*een-foR-mah-Reh*	to inform
invitare	*een-vee-tah-Reh*	to invite
lasciare	*lah-shah-Reh*	to leave something

continues

Table 8.2   Continued

Verb	Pronunciation	Meaning
lavare	*lah-vah-Reh*	to wash
lavorare	*lah-voh-Rah-Reh*	to work
liberare	*lee-beh-Rah-Reh*	to liberate/set free
limitare	*lee-mee-tah-Reh*	to limit
lottare	*loh-tah-Reh*	to struggle/fight
mandare	*mahn-dah-Reh*	to send
mangiare	*mahn-jah-Reh*	to eat
meritare	*meh-Ree-tah-Reh*	to deserve
misurare	*mee-soo-Rah-Reh*	to measure
modificare	*moh-dee-fee-kah-Reh*	to modify
navigare	*nah-vee-gah-Reh*	to navigate
negare	*neh-gah-Reh*	to negate
notificare	*noh-tee-fee-kah-Reh*	to notify
nuotare	*nwoh-tah-Reh*	to swim
obbligare	*oh-blee-gah-Reh*	to obligate
occupare	*oh-koo-pah-Reh*	to occupy
odiare	*oh-dee-ah-Reh*	to hate
operare	*oh-peh-Rah-Reh*	to operate
ordinare	*oR-dee-nah-Reh*	to order
organizzare	*oR-gah-nee-zah-Reh*	to organize
osservare	*oh-seR-vah-Reh*	to observe
pagare	*pah-gah-Reh*	to pay
parlare	*paR-lah-Reh*	to speak
partecipare	*paR-teh-chee-pah-Reh*	to participate
passare	*pah-sah-Reh*	to pass
pensare	*pen-sah-Reh*	to think
perdonare	*peR-doh-nah-Reh*	to forgive/pardon
pesare	*peh-zah-Reh*	to weigh
pettinare	*peh-tee-nah-Reh*	to comb
portare	*poR-tah-Reh*	to bring/carry/wear

Verb	Pronunciation	Meaning
pranzare	*pRahn-zah-Reh*	to eat lunch/to dine
pregare	*pReh-gah-Reh*	to pray/request
prenotare	*pReh-noh-tah-Reh*	to reserve
preparare	*pReh-pah-Rah-Reh*	to prepare
presentare	*pReh-zen-tah-Reh*	to present
prestare	*pReh-stah-Reh*	to lend
pronunziare	*pRoh-noon-zee-ah-Reh*	to pronounce
provare	*pRoh-vah-Reh*	to try
raccomandare	*Rah-koh-mahn-dah-Reh*	to recommend/register
raccontare	*Rah-kohn-tah-Reh*	to tell/recount
rappresentare	*Rah-pReh-zehn-tah-Reh*	to represent
respirare	*Reh-spee-Rah-Reh*	to breath
rifiutare	*Ree-fyoo-tah-Reh*	to refuse/reject
rilassare	*Ree-lah-sah-Reh*	to relax
riparare	*Ree-pah-Rah-Reh*	to repair/fix
riservare	*Ree-seR-vah-Reh*	to reserve/put aside
rispettare	*Ree-speh-tah-Reh*	to respect
ritornare	*Ree-toR-nah-Reh*	to return
saltare	*sahl-tah-Reh*	to jump
salvare	*sahl-vah-Reh*	to save
scambiare	*skahm-bee-ah-Reh*	to exchange
scusare	*skoo-zah-Reh*	to excuse
soddisfare	*soh-dee-sfah-Reh*	to satisfy
sognare	*sohn-yah-Reh*	to dream
spiegare	*spee-yeh-gah-Reh*	to explain
sposare	*spoh-zah-Reh*	to marry
stare	*stah-Reh*	to be/stay
studiare	*stoo-dee-ah-Reh*	to study
suonare	*swoh-nah-Reh*	to play an instrument/to sound
tagliare	*tah-lyah-Reh*	to cut

continues

Table 8.2 Continued

Verb	Pronunciation	Meaning
telefonare	*teh-leh-foh-nah-Reh*	to telephone
terminare	*teR-mee-nah-Reh*	to terminate
toccare	*toh-kah-Reh*	to touch
trovare	*tRoh-vah-Reh*	to find
usare	*oo-zah-Reh*	to use
verificare	*veh-Ree-fee-kah-Reh*	to verify
viaggiare	*vee-ah-jah-Reh*	to travel
vietare	*vee-eh-tah-Reh*	to forbid/prohibit
visitare	*vee-zee-tah-Reh*	to visit
volare	*voh-lah-Reh*	to fly
votare	*voh-tah-Reh*	to vote

Practice Makes Perfetto

Use the correct form of the verb in the following sentences. Don't forget to determine what your subject is and whether the verb should be conjugated in its singular or plural form:

1. Paolo _____ (lavorare) in ufficio.

2. Noi _____ (aspettare) il treno.

3. Tu _____ (abitare) in una casa splendida.

4. Io _____ (studiare) la lingua italiana.

5. Voi _____ (passare) la notte in una bella pensione.

6. Antonella e Dina _____ (preparare) la cena.

As a Rule

For verbs ending in *-iare*, such as *baciare, mangiare, studiare, tagliare,* and *viaggiare,* drop an *-i* in the second person singular (as in *tu baci*) and first person plural (as in *noi baciamo*) to avoid a double vowel.

The -ere Verbs

In most cases, *-ere* verbs are conjugated similarly to the *-are* verbs. Drop the infinitive ending from your stem and add the endings in Table 8.3.

Table 8.3   -ere Endings

Pronoun	Singular Endings	Pronoun	Plural Endings
io	*-o*	noi	*-iamo*
tu	*-i*	voi	*-ete*
lui/lei/Lei	*-e*	loro	*-ono*

Look at how this works with the verb *scrivere* (to write).

> SCRIV/ERE
>
> (stem)/(infinitive ending)
>
> | io | scriv**o** | noi | scriv**iamo** |
> |----|----------|-----|-------------|
> | tu | scriv**i** | voi | scriv**ete** |
> | lui/lei/Lei | scriv**e** | loro | scriv**ono** |

As you can see from the list in Table 8.4, there are fewer regular verbs in the *-ere* family. Study the verbs in the table.

Table 8.4   Regular -ere Verbs

Verb	Pronunciation	Meaning
accendere	*ah-chen-deh-Reh*	to light/turn on
affliggere	*ah-flee-jeh-Reh*	to afflict
aggiungere	*ah-joon-jeh-Reh*	to add
alludere	*ah-loo-deh-Reh*	to allude/refer
ammettere	*ah-meh-teh-Reh*	to admit
apprendere	*ah-pren-deh-Reh*	to learn
assistere	*ah-see-steh-Reh*	to assist
assumere	*ah-soo-meh-Reh*	to hire
attendere	*ah-ten-deh-Reh*	to attend/to wait for

continues

Table 8.4 Continued

Verb	Pronunciation	Meaning
cadere	kah-deh-Reh	to fall
chiedere	kee-eh-deh-Reh	to ask
chiudere	kee-oo-deh-Reh	to close
commettere	koh-meh-teh-Reh	to commit/join
commuovere	koh-mwoh-veh-Reh	to move/touch/affect
comprendere	kohm-pRen-deh-Reh	to understand
concedere	kohn-cheh-deh-Reh	to concede/grant/award
concludere	kohn-kloo-deh-Reh	to conclude
confondere	kohn-fohn-deh-Reh	to confuse
conoscere	koh-noh-sheh-Reh	to know something
consistere	kohn-see-steh-Reh	to consist
convincere	kohn-veen-cheh-Reh	to convince
correggere	koh-Reh-jeh-Reh	to correct
correre	koh-Reh-Reh	to run
corrispondere	koh-Ree-spohn-deh-Reh	to correspond
credere	kReh-deh-Reh	to believe
crescere	kreh-sheh-Reh	to grow
cuocere	kwoh-cheh-Reh	to cook
decidere	deh-chee-deh-Reh	to decide
descrivere	deh-skRee-veh-Reh	to describe
difendere	dee-fen-deh-Reh	to defend
dipendere	dee-pen-deh-Reh	to depend
dipingere	dee-peen-jeh-Reh	to paint
discutere	dee-skoo-teh-Reh	to discuss
dissolvere	dee-sohl-veh-Reh	to dissolve
distinguere	dee-steen-gweh-Reh	to distinguish
distruggere	dee-stRoo-jeh-Reh	to destroy
dividere	dee-vee-deh-Reh	to divide
emergere	eh-meR-jeh-Reh	to emerge
esistere	eh-zee-steh-Reh	to exist

Verb	Pronunciation	Meaning
esprimere	*eh-spree-meh-Reh*	to express
fingere	*feen-geh-Reh*	to pretend
godere	*goh-deh-Reh*	to enjoy
includere	*een-kloo-deh-Reh*	to include
insistere	*een-see-steh-Reh*	to insist
intendere	*een-ten-deh-Reh*	to intend
interrompere	*een-teh-Rohm-peh-Reh*	to interrupt
invadere	*een-vah-deh-Reh*	to invade
leggere	*leh-jeh-Reh*	to read
mettere	*meh-teh-Reh*	to put/place/set
muovere	*mwoh-veh-Reh*	to move
nascondere	*nah-skohn-deh-Reh*	to hide
offendere	*oh-fen-deh-Reh*	to offend
perdere	*peR-deh-Reh*	to lose
permettere	*peR-meh-teh-Reh*	to permit
piangere	*pee-yahn-jeh-Reh*	to cry
prendere	*pRen-deh-Reh*	to take
proteggere	*pRoh-teh-jeh-Reh*	to protect
rendere	*Ren-deh-Reh*	to render/give back
resistere	*Reh-zee-steh-Reh*	to resist
ricevere	*Ree-cheh-veh-Reh*	to receive
ridere	*Ree-deh-Reh*	to laugh
riflettere	*Ree-fleh-teh-Reh*	to reflect
ripetere	*Ree-peh-teh-Reh*	to repeat
risolvere	*Ree-sohl-veh-Reh*	to resolve
rispondere	*Ree-spohn-deh-Reh*	to respond
rompere	*Rohm-peh-Reh*	to break
scendere	*shen-deh-Reh*	to descend
scrivere	*skRee-veh-Reh*	to write
sorridere	*soh-Ree-deh-Reh*	to smile

continues

Table 8.4   Continued

Verb	Pronunciation	Meaning
sospendere	*soh-spen-deh-Reh*	to suspend
spendere	*spen-deh-Reh*	to spend
succedere	*soo-cheh-deh-Reh*	to happen/occur
temere	*teh-meh-Reh*	to fear
uccidere	*oo-chee-deh-Reh*	to kill
vedere	*veh-deh-Reh*	to see
vendere	*ven-deh-Reh*	to sell
vincere	*veen-cheh-Reh*	to win
vivere	*vee-veh-Reh*	to live

Practice Makes Perfetto II

Your plate is full and your eyes are bloodshot from the feast of verbs. Refer to the table and provide the correct verb form that best completes the sentences.

prendere   vedere   accendere   spendere   risolvere   scrivere

1. Loro _____ molti soldi.

2. Io _____ una lettera.

3. Tu _____ la luce.

4. Noi _____ il film, *Cinema Paradiso*.

5. Lei _____ il problema.

6. Voi _____ il treno.

As a Rule

When two verbs appear together in series, the first is conjugated and the second remains in its infinitive form.

Giovanni preferisce studiare.   Giovanni prefers to study.

The -ire Family

There are two groups of *-ire* verbs. The first group follows conjugation rules that are similar to those for the *-ere* verbs. As a matter of fact, they are the same except for the second person plural, as shown in Table 8.5.

Table 8.5 Group I: -ire Endings

Pronoun	Singular Endings	Pronoun	Plural Endings
io	*-o*	noi	*-iamo*
tu	*-i*	voi	*-ite*
lui/lei/Lei	*-e*	loro	*-ono*

See how this works with the verb *dormire* (to sleep).

DORM/IRE

(stem)/(infinitive ending)

io	dorm**o**	noi	dorm**iamo**
tu	dorm**i**	voi	dorm**ite**
lui/lei/Lei	dorm**e**	loro	dorm**ono**

Attenzione

Don't forget that when a double *i* might occur after you add your ending, one *i* must be dropped, as with the verb *cucire* (to sew):

cucio	cuciamo
cuci	cucite
cuce	cuciono

Table 8.6 Group I: Regular -ire Verbs

Verb	Pronunciation	Meaning
aprire	*ah-pRee-Reh*	to open
bollire	*boh-lee-Reh*	to boil

continues

Table 8.6 Continued

Verb	Pronunciation	Meaning
convertire	*kohn-veR-tee-Reh*	to convert
coprire	*koh-pRee-Reh*	to cover
cucire	*koo-chee-Reh*	to sew
dormire	*doR-mee-Reh*	to sleep
fuggire	*foo-jee-Reh*	to escape
mentire	*men-tee-Reh*	to lie
offrire	*oh-fRee-Reh*	to offer
partire	*paR-tee-Reh*	to depart
seguire	*seh-gwee-Reh*	to follow
servire	*seR-vee-Reh*	to serve

More -ire Verbs

The second group of *-ire* verbs is sill considered regular but must be conjugated differently from other *-ire* verbs. Once you learn the endings, you'll have no problem conjugating them.

Table 8.7 Group II: -ire Endings

Pronoun	Singular Endings	Pronoun	Plural Endings
io	*-isco*	noi	*-iamo*
tu	*-isci*	voi	*-ite*
lui/lei/Lei	*-isce*	loro	*-iscono*

A commonly used verb from this family is the verb *capire* (to understand). Look at how this verb conjugates. If you can remember this verb, the others follow quite easily:

CAP/IRE

(stem)/(infinitive ending)

io	cap**isco**	noi	cap**iamo**
tu	cap**isci**	voi	cap**ite**
lui/lei/Lei	cap**isce**	loro	cap**iscono**

Table 8.8   Group II: -ire Verbs

Verb	Pronunciation	Meaning
aderire	*ah-deh-Ree-Reh*	to adhere
attribuire	*aht-Ree-boo-ee-Reh*	to attribute
capire	*kah-pee-Reh*	to understand
colpire	*kohl-pee-Reh*	to hit/strike
costruire	*koh-stroo-ee-Reh*	to construct
definire	*deh-fee-nee-Reh*	to define
digerire	*dee-jeR-ee-Reh*	to digest
diminuire	*dee-mee-noo-ee-Reh*	to diminish
esaurire	*eh-zow-Ree-Reh*	to exhaust
fallire	*fah-lee-Reh*	to fail/go bankrupt
finire	*fee-nee-Reh*	to finish
garantire	*gah-Rahn-tee-Reh*	to guarantee
gestire	*jeh-stee-Reh*	to manage/administrate
guarire	*gwah-Ree-Reh*	to heal/recover
impazzire	*eem-pah-tsee-Reh*	to go crazy
istruire	*ee-stRoo-ee-Reh*	to instruct/teach
obbedire	*oh-beh-dee-Reh*	to obey
preferire	*pReh-feh-Ree-Reh*	to prefer
proibire	*pRoh-ee-bee-Reh*	to prohibit/forbid
pulire	*poo-lee-Reh*	to clean
punire	*poo-nee-Reh*	to punish
riunire	*Ree-yoo-nee-Reh*	to reunite
spedire	*speh-dee-Reh*	to send
stabilire	*stah-bee-lee-Reh*	to establish
suggerire	*soo-jeh-Ree-Reh*	to suggest
tradire	*tRah-dee-Reh*	to betray/deceive
trasferire	*tRah-sfeh-Ree-Reh*	to transfer
unire	*oo-nee-Reh*	to unite

As a Rule

To make a negative statement, add the word *non* in front of the verb.

Non capisco la lezione.   *I don't understand the lesson.*

Antonio non mangia la carne.   *Antonio doesn't eat meat.*

(Noi) non partiamo per l'America.   *We're not leaving for America.*

Double negatives are acceptable in Italian, as in *"No, (noi) non desideriamo niente."* (No, we don't want anything.)

Use the verb charts in Appendix B to conjugate useful verbs.

Attenzione!
Be careful of sounding like a robot when you read aloud. Say it like you mean it! When asking questions, your voice should start out lower and gradually rise until the end of a sentence.

Ask Away

No one knows everything. The curious mind wants to understand and so it needs to ask questions. In Italian, it is very easy (thank God!) to ask a question. This section shows you how to ask anything you could ever want to know.

Intonation

The easiest way to indicate that you're asking a question is by changing your intonation. All you need to do is raise your voice at the end of a sentence, just like in English.

(Tu) parli l'italiano?   Do you speak Italian?

The Tags Vero?, No?, and Giusto?

Another way to ask a simple yes/no question is to add the tags *vero?* ("true?" or "right?"), *no?*, and *giusto?* ("is that so?" or "is that correct?") to the end of a sentence, such as:

(Noi) partiamo alle otto, no?   We're leaving at 8:00, no?

(Tu) desideri mangiare un gelato, giusto?   You want to eat an ice cream, right?

Inversion

Another way of asking a question (options are good, no?) is by inversion, a technique whereby the word order of the subject (noun or pronoun) and the conjugated verb form is reversed. You still have to raise your voice at the end of the sentence to make it sound like a question.

(Tu) Sei di Roma?	Are you from Rome?
(Voi) Preferite il pesce o la carne?	Do you (plural) prefer fish or meat?
(Lei) Parla l'italiano?	Do you (polite) speak Italian?

And the Answer Is...

To answer a question affirmatively (yes), use *sì* and give your response.

To answer a question negatively (no), use *no* attached to ***non*** before the conjugated verb form. This is equivalent to our "don't" as in, "No, I don't smoke."

(Lei) Fuma le sigarette?	Sì, fumo le sigarette.	No, non fumo le sigarette.
(Tu) Capisci la lezione?	Sì, capisco la lezione.	No, non capisco la lezione.

If you are answering a question and starting your sentence with "No," these negative expressions come directly after "No," but before the conjugated verb. Try to determine the meaning of the examples. If you have difficulty determining the significance of the verbs, find the stem of the verb and use the charts to find the infinitive form:

mai	never	As in, "No, non fumo mai."
niente	nothing	As in, "No, non desidero niente."
nulla	nothing	As in, "No, non compra nulla."
nessuno	no one	As in, "No, nessuno arriva."

Take a deep breath and let it out. Crack your spine, stretch your arms, and roll your head around a couple of times.

If you're finding the lessons increasingly challenging, it's because you're in the thick of the woods right now. Even if you went no further than this chapter, you would have enough Italian to get by. However, you might want to browse your bookstore for a good verb book, such as Barron's *501 Italian Verbs*, to deepen your understanding of them.

The Least You Need to Know

➤ Any verb that follows a subject noun or pronoun must be properly conjugated.

➤ There are three verb families: *-are*, *-ere*, and *-ire*. Each has its own set of rules of conjugation.

➤ Ask a question like you mean it. Raise the intonation of your voice at the end of the sentence.

➤ Use the verb charts in Appendix B to practice conjugating the verbs you've just learned.

Part 2
You're Off and Running

Language learning is a process that occurs intuitively on many levels. Yes, the memorization part is hard work. A great deal can be said, however, for what happens underneath the surface of your conscious efforts. Language is about people and espressione; *it's about* communicazione. *When you consider the magnificence of words, you realize that you are undertaking a noble endeavor. Think about this: Until we deem to share our thoughts with another, most of those thoughts occur without language. We're just swimming around with all this knowledge locked inside our heads. Words, therefore, are symbols, or reflections, of our thoughts. Still, until written language developed, there was no way to convey that information except through story telling.*

We tend to take our ability to read for granted, but if you think about it, the fact that you're sitting here reading this book brings communication to a completely new level. Every house needs a foundation, and Part 1 focused on giving you the basics. You've learned about parts of speech, developed an idea about how the Italian language works, and studied the verbs. Now you're ready to begin applying what you've learned to everyday situations. Part 2 focuses on common introductory phrases used by Italian speakers in a variety of manners. Although you may not yet be able to engage in deep, philosophical conversations about the nature of life, as you expand your vocabulary, you'll be able to have conversations with all sorts of people on myriad topics. Most important, you'll have enough traveler's Italian to get yourself off the plane and into a taxi that will bring you to a hotel where a scrumptious meal of your choice awaits you—welcome to the streets of the living fairy tale that is l'Italia.

Chapter 9

Working the Crowd

In This Chapter

➤ Common greetings

➤ The verbs *essere* and *stare*

➤ Professions

➤ Getting the information you need

In the previous chapters, you learned many things: how to create simple Italian *frasi*, more vocabulary, how to *rispondere* to a question with a simple *sì* or *no*, and the value of making associations with familiar words. However, you probably haven't done that much speaking yet, not because you're so shy, but because you want to wait until you know what you're doing before putting your neck on the line.

Get over it! If you don't talk, you'll never speak Italian. It's that simple. Here's the scenario: You're sitting in a plane bound for Italy waiting for takeoff when an attractive Italian (man or woman—it's your fantasy) sits down next to you. You've got a few hours ahead of you and a couple of books (including this one) to read and your blow-up neck pillow tucked securely behind your head. The gorgeous Italian turns to you and says, "*Buona sera.*" What are you going to do about it, just sit there?

What's What
To ask someone what something means, you say:

Cosa vuole dire? or *Che cosa significa?*

To ask someone how to say something in Italian, say:

Come si dice [what you want to say] *in italiano?*

You Say Hello and I Say Goodbye

As a starter, it might help if you could introduce yourself. Then, ask a couple of questions, such as where the hot spots are in Tuscany, what sites you should see in Rome, and where the best wine in the country is.

You almost always want to begin a conversation with a stranger in the formal, or polite, form of address. It gives you a chance to warm up to someone and then switch into the *tu* once a relationship has been established.

Table 9.1 offers you some helpful greetings and salutations you can use with anyone.

Table 9.1 Formal and Generic Salutations and Expressions

Italian	Pronunciation	English
Buon giorno.	*bwon joR-noh*	Good morning/Good day/Good afternoon/Hello; use until early afternoon.
Buona sera.	*bwoh-nah seh-Rah*	Good evening; begin using after 3:00 p.m.
Buona notte.	*bwoh-nah not-teh*	Good night/Goodbye.
signore	*see-nyoh-Reh*	Mr./Sir
signora	*see-nyoh-Rah*	Mrs./Ms.
signorina	*see-nyoh-Ree-nah*	Miss
Mi chiamo...	*mee kee-ah-moh*	My name is (I call myself)...
Come si chiama?	*koh-meh see kee-ah-mah*	What is your name?
Come sta?	*koh-meh stah*	How are you?
Molto bene.	*mohl-toh beh-neh*	Very well.
Non c'è male.	*nohn cheh mah-leh*	Not bad.
Abbastanza bene.	*ah-bah-stahn-zah beh-neh*	Pretty well.
A presto.	*ah pRes-toh*	See you soon.
Mi scusi.	*mee skoo-zee*	Excuse me.
Per favore.	*peR fah-voh-Reh*	Please.
Per piacere.	*peR pee-ah-cheh-Reh*	Please.

Italian	Pronunciation	English
Grazie.	*grah-tsee-yeh*	Thank you.
Prego	*pray-goh*	You're welcome.

Informal Greetings and Salutations

What's What

Ciao is informal for hello and more often for goodbye almost everywhere. The term *salve* is also used in informal greetings. *Arrivederci* literally means "to re-see one another" and is commonly used to say goodbye to friends or colleagues. *ArrivederLa* is used under more formal circumstances.

Using a combination of your new Italian skills and a lot of hand gestures, you and your Italian companion are hitting it off. You're not sure of whether you should use the informal when the issue is decided for you. Your companion, noticing your discomfort, says, "*Usiamo il tu; dai, siamo amici.*" (Let's use the *tu*; come on, we're friends.) By the way, the term *dai* comes from the verb *dare* (to give) and is idiomatic. Table 9.2 contains some useful informal greetings and phrases you can use in more intimate, friendly situations.

Table 9.2 Informal Salutations

Italian	Pronunciation	English
Ciao!	*chow*	Hi/Bye-bye!
Saluti!	*sah-loo-tee*	Greetings!
Come stai?	*koh-meh sty*	How are you?
Salve!	*sahl-veh*	Hello!
Non c'è male.	*nohn cheh mah-leh*	Not bad.
Come va?	*koh-meh vah*	How's it going?
Va bene.	*vah beh-neh*	Things are good.
Va male.	*vah mah-leh*	Not so good.
Va benissimo.	*vah beh-nee-see-moh*	Things are great.
OK.	*oh-kay*	Okay.

continues

Table 9.2 Continued

Italian	Pronunciation	English
Così così.	*koh-zee koh-zee*	So-so.
Arrivederci.	*ah-Ree-veh-deR-chee*	See you later.
A più tardi.	*ah pyoo taR-dee*	Later.
A domani.	*ah doh-mah-nee*	See you tomorrow.

What's What

A **helping verb** is used to form other tenses, including the *present perfect* tense. In English, we usually use the auxiliary verb *to have,* as in "I have eaten." In Italian, there are three helping verbs: *essere* (to be), *avere* (to have), and *stare* (to be), which is used principally to create the *present progressive* tense (as in "I am leaving").

To Be or Not to Be

In the last chapter, you learned all about regular verbs and the power they can add to your life. The most important verb, *to be,* wasn't covered because in Italian, there are two *to be* verbs: *stare* and *essere.* When you ask someone *Come stai?* (How are you?), you're using the verb *stare.* When you say, *Lui è molto simpatico* (He is very nice), you're using the verb *essere.* Because the two verbs mean the same thing, the difference between the two concerns usage. Both verbs are used on their own, but they can also be used as *helping* or *auxiliary* verbs. You'll get to helping verbs later.

The verbs *essere* and *stare* are *importantissimi* and you should go no further until you have memorized them. If the only thing you get from this book is a list of familiar words (*cognates*) and how to conjugate the verbs *essere* and *stare*, you'll have gained a lot. You should already know the subject pronouns by now, which, as you remember, should only be used to emphasize the subject or when asking a question. Therefore, the verb conjugations in Table 9.3 are without subject pronouns.

As a Rule

The verb *essere* uses the same conjugation for the first person singular as the third person plural—*sono.* To ascertain the subject (*I* or *they*), you must look for either a subject pronoun (*io* or *loro*) or infer the subject through the context of the statement by looking at either the noun or adjective endings (which always reflect gender and plurality).

(Io) Sono una persona simpatica.   I am a nice person.

(Loro) Sono persone simpatiche.   They are nice people (persons).

Table 9.3 The Verb Essere

Person	Singular	Plural
First	*sono* (I am)	*siamo* (we are)
Second	*sei* (you are)	*siete* (you are)
Third	*è* (he/she is; You are)	*sono* (they are)

Although the verbs *essere* and *stare* both mean "to be," they are not interchangeable. The verb *essere* is used in several different ways:

➤ To describe nationalities, origins, and inherent unchanging qualities:

Maurizio è di Verona.	Maurizio is from Verona.
Siamo italiani.	We are Italians.
La banana è gialla.	The banana is yellow.

➤ To identify the subject or describe the subject's character traits:

Voi siete simpatici.	You all are nice.
Michele è un musicista.	Michael is a musician.
Sono io.	It's me.

➤ To talk about the time and dates:

Che ore sono?	What time is it?
È il 25 di giugno.	It's June 25.

➤ To indicate possession:

Questa è la zia di Anna.	This is Anna's aunt.
Quella è la mia casa.	That is my house.

➤ For certain impersonal expressions:

È una bella giornata.	It is a beautiful day.
È molto importante studiare.	It is very important to study.

The verb *stare* is easy to learn. Study Table 9.4 to see how it is conjugated.

Table 9.4 The Verb Stare

Person	Singular	Plural
First	*sto* (I am)	*stiamo* (we are)
Second	*stai* (you are)	*state* (you are)
Third	*sta* (he/she is; You are)	*stanno* (they are)

Attenzione!
You should always address a man as *Signore* (Mr./Sir) and a woman as *Signora* (Mrs./Ms.); young girls can be addressed as *Signorina* (Miss). Always use the third person singular of a verb when addressing strangers, unless they begin to use the *tu* form of the verb or indicate to you that it's okay.

The verb *stare* is used in the following ways:

➤ To describe a temporary state or condition of the subject:

Come sta?	How are you?
Sto bene, grazie.	I am well, thanks.

➤ To express location:

Stiamo in città.	We are staying in the city.
Patrizia sta a casa.	Patricia is at home.

➤ In many idiomatic expressions:

Sta attento!	Pay attention!
Sta zitto!	Be quiet!

➤ To form the progressive tenses:

Stiamo andando al cinema.	We are going to the movies.
Sto studiando il mio libro.	I am studying my book.

Present Progressive Tense (-ing)

You're someone who lives in the moment, and the present progressive is the tense that does just that. It describes an action as it is occurring. Generally, the present tense of Italian verbs serves as both the simple present and the progressive, which explains the difficulty native Italian, French, and Spanish speakers have distinguishing the difference between, "I am going to the store now," and "I go to the store now"; in English, we use the present progressive much more often than the simple present tense.

In Italian, however, if you want to indicate an action in progress (hence the term *present progressive*) that is happening in this moment, you can use this tense.

To form the present progressive, you need the verb *stare*. This helping verb does most of the work here because it is the verb that must be conjugated to reflect the subject. It's easy to learn how to make a verb present progressive because all you need to do is slice off the infinitive ending of the verb and add the progressive endings.

Once more, you must think in terms of verb families. Notice how the *-ere* and the *-ire* progressive tense endings are the same.

Table 9.5   Present Progressives

Infinitive	Present Progressive	English
studi*are*	studi*ando*	studying
scriv*ere*	scriv*endo*	writing
fin*ire*	fin*endo*	finishing

Table 9.6 takes the verb *studiare* and shows what happens when we attach the auxiliary verb *stare* to the present progressive.

Table 9.6   Forming the Present Progressive

Singular	Plural
sto studiando (I am studying)	*stiamo studiando* (we are studying)
stai studiando (you are studying)	*state studiando* (you are studying)
sta studiando (he/she is studying)	*stanno studiando* (they are studying)

Making Progress

Turn the following sentences into the present progressive. (Hint: You need to determine the infinitive of the verb before you can find the appropriate progressive form. If you can't remember the verb families to which they belong, flip back to Chapter 8.

1. (Noi) Guardiamo il film.
2. (Tu) Scrivi una lettera.
3. Nicola cucina la cena.
4. I bambini dormono.
5. (Loro) Leggono un libro.
6. Pulisco la camera.

As a Rule

The preposition *di* (of, from) is often used to show origin or possession or to describe something's material constitution. It is always preceded by the verb *essere*. If the noun it precedes begins with a vowel, the *i* is dropped and a contraction is formed:

Siamo di Napoli.	We are from Naples.
Questa macchina è di Peppino.	This car is Beppino's.
L'anello è d'argento.	The ring is (made of) silver.

Chit Chat

You're having a conversation with the person sitting next to you on the plane. Should you use the verb *essere* or *stare*? Complete the following sentences with the correct form of the necessary verb:

1. Noi _____ nel hotel Paradiso.

2. Io _____ di New York.

3. Come _____, Lei?

4. Loro _____ turisti.

5. Il ristorante "Caffè Greco" _____ molto famoso.

6. Questa villa _____ della Contessa.

C'è and Ci Sono (There Is; There Are)

You've arrived in Italy and have your flying companion's *numero di telefono* neatly tucked into your wallet where you won't lose it. You've checked into your hotel and used your new salutations whenever there's been an opportunity, and you are now confronted with a new problem: Whenever you ask someone how they are, they immediately launch into a *conversazione*, not realizing that your language abilities are still a work in progress. You stutter, smile, and *sì-sì* everyone, hoping that by saying "yes" enough times, they'll understand you are a nice person, perhaps a little lost, but well-intended just the same.

Out and About

It's time to go exploring. First you need to change money. Then you want to make a long distance *telefonata* (phone call) to let friends and family know you've arrived in Italy safely. It would be nice to find a *cartoleria* (stationery store) so that you can write a couple of *cartoline* (postcards). And finally, you would like to go to a good *ristorante* where you can relax and reflect on all the things you want to do.

Here's where the verb *essere* comes in handy. You want to ask, "Is there an exchange nearby?," "Is there a bank?," or "Are there many tourists at this hour?" When you say the word "there," what you're really asking is if a bank is nearby, if many tourists visit the museum at this hour, or if a money exchange exist somewhere in the vicinity.

C'è (from *ci è*) and *ci sono* correspond to the English *there is* and *there are*. They state the existence or presence of something or someone:

C'è tempo; non c'è fretta.	There's time; there is no hurry.
Ci sono molti turisti a Roma.	There are many tourists in Rome.

When asking a question, again, intonation is everything. The word order stays the same:

C'è una banca?	Is there a bank?
Ci sono ristoranti buoni?	Are there good restaurants?

To make negative statements, simply add the word *non* in front of the sentence:

Non c'è speranza.	There is no hope.
Non ci sono letti.	There are no beds.

Circle Marks the Spot

Look at the following phrases and circle the appropriate answer. Then translate the sentences. Don't forget to look at the endings to determine whether the subject is singular or plural.

Esempio: C'è/ci sono un supermercato?

1. C'è/ci sono un museo?
2. C'è/ci sono molte persone.
3. C'è/ci sono due piazze.
4. C'è/ci sono un cambio (*exchange*).
5. Dove (*where*) c'è/ci un ristorante buono?
6. C'è/ci sono quattro chiese (*churches*).
7. C'è/ci sono molti treni?
8. Non c'è/ci sono benzina (*gasoline*).

Ecco! (Here It Is!)

Ecco is not what you hear when you scream into a canyon. It's very similar to the French *voilà*, meaning, "Here it is! Got it!" Although idiomatic, it is also used frequently to express agreement, as when someone might say, "Now you're talking! Yes, that's right."

Ecco la stazione!	Here's the station!
Eccola!	Here it (the station) is!

As a Rule

In Italian, object pronouns can be tricky because they resemble the articles. Object pronouns can be attached to the end of the word *ecco* to express, "Here *it* is!" Because there is no neuter "it" in Italian, object pronouns must always reflect gender and plurality. The singular object pronouns used for "it" are simple:

Lo is used for masculine singular nouns, as in *"Eccolo!"* (Here it is!)

La is used for feminine singular nouns, as in *"Eccola!"* (Here it is!)

Ecco is often used with object pronouns (words that substitute for a noun), which you'll learn more about in Chapter 17.

Eureka!

Try expressing the fact that you've found the following things. You can use the noun itself, or you can use the appropriate masculine or feminine singular object pronoun:

il museo (the museum)	*la stazione* (the station)
il ristorante (the restaurant)	*l'albergo* (the hotel)
una banca (a bank)	*un bar* (a bar)
il negozio (the store)	*un ospedale* (a hospital)
un autobus (a bus)	*lo stadio* (the stadium)
la strada (the street)	*il supermercato* (the supermarket)

So, What's Your Story?

You can only go so far with the niceties; it's time to get into the nitty-gritty. You want to ask someone about themselves, and the first thing that comes to mind is their profession. This is where the verb *essere* comes in handy. Begin your response with *"sono"* (I am), as in *"Sono dentista."*

Formal use:

Qual è la sua professione?	What is your profession?

Informal use:

Qual è la tua professione?	What is your profession?

What's What

In Italian, one way to show possession is with the use of possessive adjectives (my, your, his, her, its, our, and their). They're called adjectives and not pronouns because they must agree in gender and number with the noun possessed and not with the possessor. The definite article must always precede the possessive adjective. For example:

la mia casa (my house), *la nostra casa* (our house)

il tuo libro (your book, informal), *il suo libro* (your book, polite)

Many professions end in *-a*, such as *dentista* and *artista*. In these cases, you may not be able to tell whether the subject is a man or a woman.

Table 9.7 lists several common professions. If you have a profession that is atypical, such as a dog walker or flower designer, you may want to consult your dictionary.

Table 9.7   Professions

Profession	Pronunciation	Meaning
artista	*ahR-tees-tah*	artist
attore	*ah-toh-Reh*	actor
attrice	*ah-tRee-cheh*	actress
amministratore	*ah-mee-nee-stRah-toh-Reh*	manager
avvocato	*ah-voh-kah-toh*	lawyer
bancario	*bahn-kah-Ree-yoh*	banker
cameriere	*kah-meh-Ree-eh-Reh*	waiter/waitress
casalinga	*kah-zah-leen-gah*	housewife
cassiere	*kah-see-eh-Reh*	cashier
commerciante	*koh-mehR-chahn-teh*	merchant
dentista	*den-tees-tah*	dentist
dottore	*doh-toh-Reh*	doctor (m.)
dottoressa	*doh-toh-Reh-sah*	doctor (f.)
elettricista	*eh-leh-tRee-chee-stah*	electrician
gioielliere	*joh-yeh-lee-yeh-Reh*	jeweler

continues

Table 9.7 Continued

Profession	Pronunciation	Meaning
infermiera	*een-feR-mee-yeh-Rah*	nurse
insegnante	*een-sehn-yahn-teh*	teacher
mecchanico	*meh-kah-nee-koh*	mechanic
musicista	*moo-zee-chee-stah*	musician
operaio	*oh-peh-Rah-yoh*	worker
parrucchiere	*pah-Roo-kee-eh-Reh*	hair dresser
pompiere	*pom-pee-eh-Reh*	firefighter
professore	*pRoh-fes-oh-Reh*	professor (m.)
professoressa	*pRoh-fes-oh-Reh-sah*	professor (f.)
scienziato	*shee-ehn-zee-ah-toh*	scientist
scrittore	*skRee-toh-Reh*	writer (m.)
scrittrice	*skRee-tRee-cheh*	writer (f.)
segretaria	*seh-gReh-tah-Ree-ah*	secretary
studente	*stoo-den-teh*	student (m.)
studentessa	*stoo-den-teh-sah*	student (f.)
vigile	*vee-jee-leh*	police officer

It's Not What You Do, But Whom You Do It With

You want to find out the bus schedule, where the museum is, how much the tickets will cost you, and with whom you should speak to make reservations for the opera. Getting the information you need is an essential communication skill that will take you places. Table 9.8 contains a list of words and expressions that will help you get what you want, find out where you want to go, and meet the people you would like to know.

Table 9.8 Information Questions

Word/Phrase	Pronunciation	Meaning
a che ora	*ah kay oh-Rah*	at what time
a chi	*ah kee*	to whom
a che	*ah kay*	to what

Word/Phrase	Pronunciation	Meaning
che cosa (can be broken up to *che* or *cosa*)	*kay koh-zah*	what
come	*koh-meh*	how
con chi	*kohn kee*	with whom
con che	*kohn kay*	with what
di	*dee*	of/from
dove	*doh-veh*	where
perché	*peR-kay*	why
quando	*kwahn-doh*	when
quanto	*kwahn-toh*	how much

Questions, Questions

The best way to get to know someone is to ask questions; they're the best ice breakers. The easiest way to ask a question is to make your sentence using your new list of verbs and add the question word immediately afterward. In Italian, you can also put the question word before the conjugated verb. Don't forget to sound like you're asking a question by raising the intonation of your voice at the end of the phrase. You don't want to sound like you're reading from a phrase book. You don't need to use a subject pronoun unless it helps clarify the subject.

As a Rule

When asking a question using the word *dove* (where) with the third person of the verb *essere* (*è*), you must form a contraction, as in *dov'è*, to avoid a double vowel and maintain the flow of the pronunciation.

(Lei) viaggia con chi?	With whom are you traveling? (polite)
A che ora apre il museo?	At what hour does the museum open?
Quando c'è il treno per Roma?	When is the train for Rome?
Dov'è la fermata per l'autobus?	Where is the bus stop?
Quanto costa?	How much does this cost?

Di dov'è Lei?	Where are you from? (polite)
Di dove sei?	Where are you from? (informal)
Per quanto tempo state in Italia?	For how long are you in Italy? (you, plural)
C'è un'ospedale qui vicino?	Is there a hospital nearby?
Ci sono molti turisti a quest'ora?	Are there many tourists at this hour?

Ask Away

Each of the following paragraphs is an answer to a question. Figure out what the questions are based on the following information. In the first paragraph, use the *tu* form to ask Cinzia about herself based on her responses. In the second paragraph, ask Signore Pesce about himself, using the *Lei* form of the verb.

Mi chiamo Cinzia e abito negli Stati Uniti. Sono una studentessa. Studio la storia d'arte. Viaggio in macchina con la mia famiglia in Italia. Passiamo un mese in Italia. Desidero visitare tutte le città importanti. Ritorno all'università in settembre.

Mi chiamo Signore Pesce e sono un bancario. Non parlo l'inglese molto bene. Abito a Milano con mia moglie. Abbiamo due figli, Giorgio e Isabella. In settembre viaggio con mia moglie a New York.

The Least You Need to Know

➤ You should always begin a conversation with a stranger in the formal, or polite, form of address.

➤ There are two verbs that express the action "to be": *essere* (used to express various states of existence) and *stare* (used to describe a temporary condition).

➤ *Avere* (to have) is an auxiliary verb but is also used with many idiomatic expressions.

➤ Questions are a great way to start a conversation—but you have to learn your verbs first!

Chapter 10

Tell Me About Your Childhood

In This Chapter

➤ Introducing relatives

➤ Expressing possession

➤ Describing things—adjectives

➤ Nationalities

In Italy, one of the first things people will want to know about is your family. Do you have brothers or sisters? Are you of Italian descent or one of the many who have fallen in love with the *cultura*, the beautiful landscapes, and the *arte*? It's time to take the chit-chat a step further. First, let's take a look at who's who in *la famiglia* in Table 10.1. (Figure out which articles you should use. Are you able to easily tell which nouns take the feminine and which take the masculine?)

Table 10.1 Family Members

Female	Pronunciation	Meaning	Male	Pronunciation	Meaning
madre	*mah-dReh*	mother	padre	*pah-dReh*	father
moglie	*moh-lyeh*	wife	marito	*mah-Ree-toh*	husband
nonna	*noh-nah*	grand-mother	nonno	*noh-noh*	grand-father
figlia	*fee-lyah*	daughter	figlio	*fee-lyoh*	son
bambina	*bahm-bee-nah*	infant	bambino	*bahm-bee-noh*	infant
sorella	*soh-Reh-lah*	sister	fratello	*fRah-teh-loh*	brother
cugina	*koo-jee-nah*	cousin	cugino	*koo-jee-noh*	cousin
zia	*zee-ah*	aunt	zio	*zee-oh*	uncle
nipote	*nee-poh-teh*	grand-daughter	nipote	*nee-poh-teh*	grandson
nipote	*nee-poh-teh*	niece	nipote	*nee-poh-teh*	nephew
suocera	*swoh-cheh-Rah*	mother-in-law	suocero	*swoh-cheh-Roh*	father-in-law
nuora	*nwoh-Rah*	daughter-in-law	genero	*jen-eh-Roh*	son-in-law
cognata	*koh-nyah-tah*	sister-in-law	cognato	*koh-nyah-toh*	brother-in-law
sorellastra	*soh-Reh-lah-stRah*	stepsister	fratell-astro	*fRah-teh-lah-stRoh*	step-brother
madrina	*mah-dRee-nah*	godmother	padrino	*pah-dRee-noh*	godfather
ragazza	*Rah-gah-tsah*	girlfriend	ragazzo	*Rah-gah-tsoh*	boyfriend
fidanzata	*fee-dahn-zah-tah*	fiancée	fidanzato	*fee-dahn-zah-toh*	fiancé
vedova	*veh-doh-vah*	widow	vedovo	*veh-doh-voh*	widower

As a Rule

When discussing one's "children" of both sexes, Italian reverts to the masculine plural: *figli*. The same goes for friends: *amici*. One's *genitori* (parents) can be simply referred to as *i miei*, coming from the possessive adjective "my" as in "my parents." The word used to describe niece/nephew and granddaughter/grandson is the same: *nipote*.

Are You Possessed?

You will always be somebody's somebody: your mother's child, your brother's sister, your dog's owner, your wife's husband. In English, we use *'s* or *s'* to show possession. In Italian, however, you show possession by using *di*, as in

Silvia è la figlia di Pepe. Silvia is Pepe's daughter. (Silvia is the daughter of Pepe.)

As a Rule

The phrases *of mine, of his, of yours*, and so on do not require the definite article.

una mia speranza	a hope of mine
due suoi amici	two friends of his
una sua collega	a colleague of his

If the possessor is referred to by a common noun such as *the father*, you must attach an article to the preposition (that is, if the preposition is "of," you need to say "of the").

Lei è la madre del ragazzo. She is the boy's mother. (She is the mother of the boy.)

As a Rule

The terms *signore, signora*, and *signorina* are often used in place of the man, the woman, the young woman:

Quella è la macchina della signora.	That is the woman's car.
Il libro del signore sta sulla tavola.	The man's book is on the table.

If the possessor is not referred to by name but by a common noun such as *la zia* (the aunt) or *i genitori* (the parents), then *di* contracts with the appropriate definite article to express *of the*. You've already seen some of these contractions before. Note that contractions with *di* change the spelling. Contractions are explained in more detail in Chapter 11.

Singular	Plural
di + il = del	di + i = dei
di + lo = dello	di + gli = degli
di + l' = dell'	di + le = delle
di + la = della	

Examples using contractions with *di* are

Ecco sono le chiave della macchina.	Here are the car's keys.
C'è il figlio del presidente.	There is the president's son.

Possessive Adjectives

"A possessive what?" you ask. Don't panic. In English, we just call them possessive pronouns, such as my, your, his, and our. In Italian, the possessive adjectives must be followed by a noun (my house, your house, and so on). They're not complicated but it will help you to keep a few things in mind.

Attenzione!
When it isn't clear who the possessor is, use *di* to indicate the subject:

il libro di Rosetta. Rosetta's book. (The book of Rosetta.)

la macchina di Walter. Walter's car. (The car of Walter.)

First, you have to ask what is being possessed. Second, you need to choose the possessive adjective that agrees with it. In Italian, what is important is the gender of the noun. For instance, if what is being possessed is masculine singular, then your possessive adjective must also be masculine singular. Compare the English possessives to their Italian counterparts in Table 10.2.

Table 10.2 Comparisons

English	Italian
He loves his mother.	Lui ama **sua** madre.
She loves her mother.	Lei ama **sua** madre.
He loves his father.	Lui ama **suo** padre.
She loves her father.	Lei ama **suo** padre.

Notice that the third person singular possessive adjectives *sua* and *suo* can mean both *his* or *her* because the possessive adjective agrees with the noun it modifies, not with the subject.

As a Rule

When speaking of family members, there is no article required before the possessive adjective. The following examples:

Mia madre è una donna forte.

My mother is a strong woman.

Tuo fratello e io andiamo al cinema.

Your brother and I are going to the movies.

Table 10.3 summarizes the use of possessive adjectives. Remember, the article must precede the possessive adjective, except when you are referring to family members.

Table 10.3 Possessive Adjectives

Person	Possessive Adjective	Singular		Plural	
		Masculine	Feminine	Masculine	Feminine
First singular	my	il mio	la mia	i miei	le mie
Second singular	your	il tuo	la tua	i tuoi	le tue
Third singular	his/her/its	il suo	la sua	i suoi	le sue
	Your (polite)*	il Suo	la Sua	i Suoi	le Sue
First plural	our	il nostro	la nostra	i nostri	le nostre
Second plural	your	il vostro	la vostra	i vostri	le vostre
Third plural	their	il loro	la loro	i loro	le loro

As you remember, Lei, the polite form of you, is capitalized to distinguish it from lei (she). The possessive adjectives are also capitalized to make this distinction.

A Sense of Belonging

Determine the appropriate possessive adjective using the list above for the following:

Example: her house

Answer: la sua casa

1. His house
2. My school
3. Her books

4. His books
5. Your (familiar) friend (m.)

Let Me Introduce You

In the last chapter, you learned a few conversation openers when you befriended the great-looking Italian who was sitting next to you on the plane. Now it's your first day in Italy, and your new friend has agreed to escort you to the Vatican. You're already on familiar terms, which in Italian means you're using *tu*.

It's time to introduce your new friend to your traveling companions and family members (who have been patiently standing in a cluster as you flirt in Italian with this gorgeous person). It might help if you can express the *demonstrative pronouns this* and *these* shown in Table 10.4 because you want to say, "*This* is my sister and *these* are my parents."*

When standing alone, they are considered pronouns, as in, "This is mine, that is yours," and must always agree in gender and number with the nouns they replace. If you were to say, "This car is mine, that car is yours," they would be considered possessive adjectives. Whatever it may be grammatically called, they are the same.

Table 10.4   The Demonstrative Pronouns This and These

Demonstrative	Masculine	Feminine
this	questo	questa
these	questi	queste

Again, agreement, agreement, agreement. If you are introducing your *fratello* (brother), then you have to use a masculine singular demonstrative pronoun, as in *Questo è mio fratello*. (This is my brother.) If it's your mother you are introducing, you have to use a feminine singular demonstrative pronoun, *Questa è mia madre*. (This is my mother.) By now, you know that you don't have to worry about the articles when referring to family members (but remember, in most other cases, you must always include the article before the noun). A friend, on the other hand, would be introduced as **la mia amica**.

Who Is Who

You can alter the expressions in Table 10.5 to suit your needs. You'll have a chance to use all the material you've learned so far.

Table 10.5 Helpful Introductory Expressions

Italian	English
Vorrei presentare (mia madre, mio padre...)	I'd like to present (my mother, my father...)
Conosci (mia zia, mio cugino...)?	Do you know (my aunt, my cousin...)? (informal)
Conosce...	Do you know... (polite)
È un piacere conoscerti.	It's a pleasure to meet you. (informal)
È un piacere conoscerLa.	It's a pleasure to meet you. (formal)
Il piacere è mio.	The pleasure is mine.
Questo è mio fratello.	This is my brother.
Questa è mia sorella.	This is my sister.
Questi sono i miei amici.	These are my friends. (m.p.)
Questi sono le mie amiche.	These are my friends. (f.p.)
Questa è la mia collega.	This is my colleague.

As a Rule

There are two verbs equivalent to the English verb *to know: sapere* (an irregular verb) and *conoscere*.

Sapere: to know something

so	sappiamo
sai	sapete
sa	sanno

Conoscere: to know someone/to be acquainted

conosco	conosciamo
conosci	conoscete
conosce	conoscono

What's What
A common expression is *Non lo so*, meaning "I don't know," and referring to when you don't know *something*.

The Haves and the Have Nots

In Chapter 5, you learned about the verb *avere* (to have) and were given many idioms that express physical conditions (*ho freddo, ho fame, ho sete…*). Like the verb *essere*, the verb *avere*, shown in Table 10.6, is irregular and must be memorized.

Table 10.6 Avere

Singular	Plural
io ho (I have)	*noi abbiamo* (we have)
tu hai (you have)	*voi avete* (you have)
lui/lei/Lei ha (he/she has; You have)	*loro hanno* (they have)

Remember that the "h" is always silent. Its importance, however, should not be underestimated. For example, take the "h" out of "ho" and you have "o," meaning *or*. Take the "h" out of "hai" and you have the contraction "ai," meaning *to the*. Take the "h" out of "ha" and you have the preposition "a," meaning *to*; take the "h" out of "hanno" and you have the word "anno," meaning *year*.

You can use the expressions in Table 10.7 to help you continue your relationships with the wonderful people you have already met and will get to know on your journey.

Table 10.7 Idioms with Avere

Italian	Pronunciation	English
(avere) l'occasione di	*loh-kah-zee-oh-neh dee*	to have the chance to
(avere) l'opportunità di	*loh-poR-too-nee-tah dee*	to have the opportunity to/of
(avere) la possibilità di	*lah poh-see-bee-lee-tah dee*	to have the possibility to
(avere) la fortuna di	*lah foR-too-nah dee*	to have the fortune to/of
(avere) l'intenzione di	*lah een-ten-see-oh-neh dee*	to have the intention of
(avere) l'abitudine di	*lah ah-bee-too-dee-neh dee*	to have the habit of

There's really no mystery to language learning. Just keep at it, step by step, and you'll climb the *montagna*.

Using Avere

From the list you just read above as well as the idioms you learned in Chapter 5, determine the idiom that goes with each of the following sentences. There's more than one correct response. Don't be lazy: Translate the sentences using your gut and your *dizionario*. You have to conjugate *avere* so that the verb agrees with the subject.

Example: Io ho l'opportunità di studiare in italia.

I have the opportunity to study in Italy.

1. Io _____ di giocare a carte ogni settimana (every week).

2. Giuseppe _____ di viaggiare tutta l'Europa.

3. Andiamo a mangiare. Io _____!

4. Cristoforo e Gina _____ di essere inammorati (in love).

5. Tu _____? Ecco una Coca Cola.

6. Voi siete poveri. _____ dei soldi.

Tall, Dark, and Handsome

What a bland world it would be without descriptive adjectives. Everything would be all action but no fluff. If verbs are the skeleton of a language and nouns are the flesh, adjectives are the color. They're pretty, ugly, big, little, black, white, young, old, and all of what's in between.

Guess what: Adjectives have to agree with the nouns and pronouns they modify. (So what's new?) They have to agree in *gender* (masculine or feminine) and *number* (singular or plural):

Tua sorella è una ragazza simpatica.   Your sister is a nice girl.

Tuo fratello è un ragazzo simpatico.   Your brother is a nice boy.

Adjectives are easy to modify because they follow simple rules that correspond to the same rules nouns have. If modifying a masculine noun, then simply leave the adjective as it is (adjectives default to the masculine—it goes way back before women's lib).

When you change an adjective to the feminine, the ending will be *-a* 90% of the time. Occasionally, you will come across adjectives that end in *-e*, such as *intelligente, giovane,*

Attenzione!
Except at the beginning of a sentence, remember that an *s* is pronounced like *z*, as in the word "plaza." A double *ss* is pronounced like the *s* in "gasoline." One *R* is slightly rolled; a double *RR* is trilled. The real key to success is to make sure you are pronouncing your vowels correctly: *a* (ah), *e* (eh), *i* (ee), *o* (oh), and *u* (oo).

grande, *verde*, *triste*, and *cortese*, in which case you don't have to do a thing (at least in the singular) because they can be used to describe both masculine and feminine nouns. The plural endings of these adjectives follow the same rules as nouns ending in -*e*. As a reminder, -*e* turns to -*i*, as in the example *il signore intelligente*, which in turn becomes *i signori intelligenti*.

You've already seen how many Italian adjectives are cognates to English in Chapter 4. Look at the following endings and compare them to the noun endings you learned in Chapter 6.

Table 10.8 Adjective Endings

Singular		Plural	Adjective		
o	→	i	famos*o*	→	famos*i*
a	→	e	curios*a*	→	curios*e*
ca	→	che	magnifi*ca*	→	magnifi*che*
e	→	i	intelligent*e*	→	intelligent*i*

Just to refresh your memory, look again at the list of adjective cognates:

alto	eccellente	incredibile
americano	elegante	intelligente
basso	energico	interessante
blu	famoso	lungo
canadese	francese	magnifico
cattolico	frequente	moderno
cinese	geloso	naturale
curioso	giapponese	necessario
delizioso	grande	numeroso
desideroso	greco	popolare
differente	importante	possibile
difficile	impossibile	povero

rapido	sincero	terribile
ricco	splendido	tropicale
serio	stupendo	violento
sicuro	stupido	virtuoso

You want to describe your wonderful wife or husband, your children, your new boyfriend or girlfriend, your ex, your best friend, or your cat. Are they kind or cruel, good or bad, generous or stingy? The list of adjectives in Table 10.9 will add to your palette.

> **What's What**
> To indicate that you're in a good or bad mood, use the expressions *Sono di buon umore* (I am in a good mood) and *Sono di cattivo umore* (I am in a bad mood).

Table 10.9 Emotions and Characteristics

English	Italian	Pronunciation	English	Italian	Pronunciation
ambitious	ambizioso	*ahm-bee-zee-oh-zoh*	lazy	pigro	*pee-gRoh*
beautiful	bello	*beh-loh*	ugly	brutto	*bRoo-toh*
blond	biondo	*bee-ohn-doh*	brunette	bruno	*bRoo-noh*
calm	calmo	*kahl-moh*	nervous	nervoso	*neR-voh-zoh*
clever/sly	furbo	*fooR-boh*	slow/dull	lento	*len-toh*
courageous	coraggioso	*koh-Rah-joh-zoh*	cowardly	codardo	*koh-dahR-doh*
courteous	cortese	*koR-teh-zeh*	discourteous	scortese	*skoR-teh-zeh*
cultured	educato	*eh-doo-kah-toh*	ignorant	ignorante	*ee-nyoh-Rahn-teh*
cute/pretty	carino	*kah-Ree-noh*	unattractive	bruttino	*bRoo-tee-noh*
fat	grasso	*gRah-soh*	skinny	magro	*mah-groh*
funny	buffo	*boo-foh*	boring	noioso	*noy-oh-zoh*
generous	generoso	*jeh-neR-oh-zoh*	stingy	tirchio	*teeR-kee-yoh*
good	bravo	*bRah-voh*	evil	cattivo	*kah-tee-voh*
happy	allegro	*ah-leh-gRoh*	sad	triste	*tRee-steh*
healthy	sano	*sah-noh*	sick	malato	*mah-lah-toh*
honest	onesto	*oh-nes-toh*	dishonest	disonesto	*dee-soh-nes-toh*
intelligent	intelligente	*een-tel-ee-jen-teh*	stupid	stupido	*stoo-pee-doh*
kind/polite	gentile	*jen-tee-leh*	rude	male-ducato	*mah-leh-doo-kah-toh*

continues

Table 10.9   Continued

English	Italian	Pronunciation	English	Italian	Pronunciation
loyal	fedele	*feh-deh-leh*	unfaithful	infedele	*een-fed-eh-leh*
lucky	fortunato	*foR-too-nah-toh*	unlucky	sfortunato	*sfoR-too-nah-toh*
married	sposato	*spoh-zah-toh*	divorced	divorziato	*dee-voR-zee-ah-toh*
nice	simpatico	*seem-pah-tee-koh*	mean	antipatico	*ahn-tee-pah-tee-koh*
organized	organizzato	*oR-gah-nee-zah-toh*	unorganized	disorganizzato	*dee-zoR-gah-nee-zah-toh*
perfect	perfetto	*peR-feh-toh*	imperfect	imperfetto	*eem-peR-feh-toh*
proud	orgoglioso	*oR-goh-lyoh-zoh*	humble	umile	*oo-mee-leh*
romantic	romantico	*Roh-mahn-tee-koh*	practical	pratico	*prah-tee-koh*
sensitive	sensibile	*sen-see-bee-leh*	insensitive	insensibile	*een-sen-see-bee-leh*
sincere	sincero	*seen-cheh-Roh*	insincere	bugiardo	*boo-jaR-doh*
strong	forte	*foR-teh*	weak	debole	*deh-boh-leh*
tall	alto	*ahl-toh*	short	basso	*bah-soh*
young	giovane	*joh-vah-neh*	old	vecchio	*veh-kee-yoh*
wise	saggio	*sah-joh*			

What's What
Some adjectives have different words for men and woman, such as *celibe* (a single man) and *nubile* (a single woman).

What's He Like?

If you were to describe someone, what adjectives would you use to talk about

Your boyfriend   Your teacher

Your sister   Your father

Your best friend

For example:

Lui è generoso, intelligente, sincero e ricco. He is generous, intelligent, sincere, and rich.

If you want to describe things, including the lamp you just bought, the food you just ate, and the cost of something, the list of adjectives and their opposites in Table 10.10 will help you.

Table 10.10 Adjectives and Their Antonyms

English	Italian	Pronunciation	English	Italian	Pronunciation
big	grande	*grahn-deh*	small	piccolo	*pee-koh-loh*
clean	pulito	*poo-lee-toh*	dirty	sporco	*spoR-koh*
complete	completo	*kohm-pleh-toh*	incomplete	incompleto	*een-kohm-pleh-toh*
dear/ expensive	caro	*kah-Roh*	inexpensive	economico	*eh-koh-noh-mee-koh*
first	primo	*pRee-moh*	last	ultimo	*ool-tee-moh*
full	pieno	*pee-eh-noh*	empty	vuoto	*vwoh-toh*
good	buono	*bwoh-noh*	bad	male	*mah-leh*
hard	duro	*doo-Roh*	soft	morbido	*moR-bee-doh*
heavy	pesante	*peh-zahn-teh*	light	leggero	*leh-jeh-Roh*
hot	caldo	*kahl-doh*	cold	freddo	*fReh-doh*
light	leggero	*leh-jeh-Roh*	heavy	pesante	*peh-zahn-teh*
long	lungo	*loon-goh*	short	basso	*bah-soh*
new	nuovo	*nwoh-voh*	used	usato	*oo-zah-toh*
next	prossimo	*pRoh-see-moh*	last	ultimo	*ool-tee-moh*
normal	normale	*noR-mah-leh*	strange	strano	*stRah-noh*
open	aperto	*ah-peR-toh*	closed	chiuso	*kee-yoo-soh*
perfect	perfetto	*peR-feh-toh*	imperfect	imperfetto	*eem-peR-feh-toh*
pleasing	piacevole	*pee-ah-cheh-voh-leh*	displeasing	spiacevole	*spee-ah-cheh-voh-leh*
real	vero	*veh-Roh*	fake	finto	*feen-toh*
safe/sure	sicuro	*see-koo-Roh*	dangerous	pericoloso	*peR-ee-koh-loh-zoh*
strong	forte	*foR-teh*	weak	debole	*deh-boh-leh*
true	vero	*veh-Roh*	false	falso	*fahl-zoh*

One Yellow Banana, Please

Fill in the blank with the adjective modified by the subject and then translate the sentences:

What's What
You might also want to use colors when being descriptive:

rosso (red)   *bianco* (white)
azzurro (sky blue)   *verde* (green)
nero (black)   *rosa* (pink)
blu (blue)   *marrone* (brown)
viola (purple)   *giallo* (yellow)
beige (beige)   *arancione* (orange)
grigio (gray)

P.S. The word for rainbow is *arcobaleno*.

Example: La banana è _____. (yellow)

Answer: La banana è <u>gialla</u>.

1. La casa _____ (white) è _____ (clean).
2. Il Colosseo è molto _____ (old).
3. Le montagne in Svizzera sono _____ (high).
4. Il negozio è _____ (closed) la domenica.
5. Quest'albergo è _____ (inexpensive).
6. Lo Scrooge è un'uomo molto _____ (cheap).

Nationalities

It's *impossibile* not to meet people from different nationalities and backgrounds when you are traveling. Aside from the guidebook you carry in your right hand and the camera hanging from your neck, it's obvious that you are a *straniero* (foreigner), and the Italians are going to be curious about why you have come to Italy. Don't be surprised if you are asked your origins when you visit Italy. It's a natural question to the Italians and is not regarded as too personal.

Lei è d'origine italiana?   Sì, sono d'origine italiana.

Sei d'origine italiana?   No, sono d'origine russa.

Table 10.11 provides a general listing of nationalities. With only a few exceptions, most of these should be easy to remember because they're similar to their English counterparts (good news for you *americano*!).

Table 10.11   Nationalities

English	Italian	Pronunciation
African	africano	*ahf-Ree-kah-noh*
American	americano	*ah-meh-Ree-kah-noh*
Belgian	belga	*bel-gah*
Canadian	canadese	*kah-nah-deh-zeh*

English	Italian	Pronunciation
Chinese	cinese	*chee-neh-zeh*
English	inglese	*een-gleh-zeh*
French	francese	*fRahn-cheh-zeh*
German	tedesco	*teh-des-koh*
Greek	greco	*gReh-koh*
Indian	indiano	*een-dee-ah-noh*
Irish	irlandese	*eeR-lahn-deh-zeh*
Japanese	giapponese	*jah-poh-neh-zeh*
Korean	coreano	*koh-Ree-ah-noh*
Mexican	messicano	*meh-see-kah-noh*
Polish	polacco	*poh-lah-koh*
Russian	russo	*Roo-soh*
Scandinavian	scandinavo	*skahn-dee-nah-voh*
Spanish	spagnolo	*spahn-yoh-loh*
Swiss	svizzero	*svee-tseh-roh*

As a Rule

In Italian, nationalities are *not* capitalized. Countries are always capitalized. Countries should always be preceded with the definite article.

italiano	Italian
l'Italia	Italy

You also might be asked about your religion; some answers are provided in Table 10.12. Again, this isn't considered a personal question to Italians, so don't be surprised if someone is curious about if, how, or what you worship.

Table 10.12   Religions

English	Italian	Pronunciation
agnostic	agnostico	*ah-nyoh-stee-koh*
atheist	ateo	*ah-teh-oh*
Buddhist	buddista	*boo-dees-tah*
Catholic	cattolico	*kah-toh-lee-koh*
Christian	cristiano	*kRee-stee-ah-noh*
Jewish	ebreo	*eh-bReh-oh*
Hindu	indù	*een-doo*
Muslim	mussulmano	*moo-sool-mah-noh*

Back to Your Roots

Translate the following sentences into Italian. Determine what the subject is and modify your adjective accordingly. Don't forget to use the correct preposition.

Example: Wen Wen Lin is Chinese.

Answer: Wen Wen Lin è cinese.

1. Olivier is French and lives (abitare) in Paris (Parigi).
2. Patrizia is Catholic and has five sisters.
3. My grandmother is Jewish.
4. Massimo is of Italian origin.
5. There are many Japanese tourists in Italy.

What's What
Bello is used to describe anything wonderful: a good meal, a sunset, a beautiful person. If you want to sound like an Italian, use this expression the next time you are moved: *Che bello/a!* (literally meaning "How Beautiful!")

Bello and Quello

The adjectives *bello* (beautiful, handsome, nice, good, fine) and *quello* (that/those) follow the same rules, as you can see in Table 10.13. Both have forms similar to those of the definite article.

Table 10.13　Bello and Quello

Gender	Singular	Plural	When It Is Used
Masculine	bello/quello	begli/quegli	Before s + consonant or z
	bel/quel	bei/quei	Before consonants
	bell'/quell'	begli/quegli	Before vowels
Feminine	bella/quella	belle/quelle	Before all consonants
	bell'/quell'	belle/quelle	Before vowels

Generally speaking, *bello* and *quello* come before the noun, just like in English. However, when the adjective is used after the verb *essere*, it retains its full form:

Quella ragazza è molto bella.	That girl is very beautiful.
Che bei bambini!	What beautiful children!
Quell'albergo è bello.	That hotel is beautiful.
Quelle donne sono simpatiche.	Those women are nice.

Buono

The adjective *buono* (good) must change its form in the singular when preceding a noun. The plural form of this adjective is regular. Consult Table 10.14 for the different forms.

Table 10.14　Buono

Gender	Singular	Plural	When It Is Used
Masculine	buono	buoni	Before s + consonant or z
	buon	buoni	Before consonants
	buon	buoni	Before vowels
Feminine	buona	buone	Before all consonants
	buon'	buone	Before vowels

The following are a few examples of how to use this adjective:

Trovare un buon amico è difficile.	A good friend is hard to find.
Tu sei una buon´ amica.	You are a good friend.

What's What
Quello (that) is used as an adjective to describe a noun, as in *quel ragazzo* (that boy), *quelle ragazze* (those girls), and so on. The following example illustrates *quello* when used as an adjective:

Quella casa è bella. That house is beautiful.

Quello is also used as a pronoun when standing alone and, like *questo* (this), must reflect the gender and number of the noun it replaces, as in the following example:

La casa di Marco è grande; quella di Federico è piccola. (Marco's house is big; Federico's house is small.)

The Least You Need to Know

➤ To show possession in Italian, use the possessive adjectives or the preposition *di*.

➤ *Avere* is an important verb that can also be used to express expressions of luck, intention, and opportunity.

➤ Italian adjectives must agree in gender and number with the nouns they modify.

Chapter 11

Finally, You're at the Airport

In This Chapter

➤ All about planes and airports

➤ The verb *andare* (to go)

➤ How to give and receive directions

➤ Expressing confusion

➤ Getting help

Whenever you are in a fix and want to communicate something, it's amazing how quickly all the hard work you invested in your new language goes out the window. That's why it's important to remember that the best way to communicate is often in the simplest manner. No need to start quoting Dante here; just get your point across. Sometimes this means simply pointing to something and saying, "questo" (this). Other times it may mean that you use a combination of vocabulary, mime, and facial expressions to make yourself understood.

On the Plane

Most international flights going to and from Italy communicate with passengers in both English and Italian. This is a wonderful opportunity to develop your listening skills. Instead of relying on your native tongue, pay close attention to the voice coming over the loud speaker when Italian is used. Are you able to grasp the general meaning? The vocabulary in Table 11.1 contains many of the words you might hear.

Table 11.1 Inside the Plane

English	Italian	Pronunciation
airline	la linea aerea	*lah lee-neh-yah ay-eh-Reh-ah*
airline terminal	il "terminal"	*eel teR-mee-nahl*
airplane	l'aeroplano	*lah ay-eh-Roh-plah-noh*
airport	l'aeroporto	*lah-ay-Roh-poR-toh*
aisle	il corridoio	*eel koh-Ree-doy-oh*
aisle seat	un posto vicino al corridoio	*oon pos-toh vee-chee-noh ahl koh-Ree-doy-oh*
to board/embark	imbarcare	*eem-baR-kah-Reh*
emergency exit	l'uscita d'emergenza	*loo-shee-tah deh-meR-jen-zah*
to exit/get off the plane	salire	*sah-lee-Reh*
flight (domestic/international)	il volo (nazionale/internazionale)	*eel vo-loh nah-zee-oh-nah-leh/een-teR-nah-zee-oh-nah-leh*
flight number	il numero del volo	*eel nooh-meh-Roh dehl voh-loh*
gate	il cancello	*eel kahn-cheh-loh*
headphones	le cuffie	*leh koo-fee-ay*
landing	l'atterraggio	*lah-teR-ah-joh*
life vest	il giubotto di salvataggio	*eel joo-boh-toh dee sahl-vah-tah-joh*
luggage	i bagagli	*ee bah-gahl-yee*
magazine	la rivista	*lah Ree-vee-stah*
newspaper	il quotidiano	*eel kwoh-tee-dee-ah-noh*

English	Italian	Pronunciation
non-smoking seat	un posto per non fumatori	*oon pos-toh peR nohn foo-mah-toh-Ree*
on board	a bordo	*ah boR-doh*
row	la fila	*lah fee-lah*
seat	il posto	*eel poh-stoh*
seat belt	la cintura di sicurezza	*lah cheen-too-Rah dee see-koR-eh-zah*
to smoke	fumare	*foo-mah-Reh*
steward/stewardess	l'assistente di volo	*lah-sees-ten-teh dee voh-loh*
take-off	il decollo	*eel deh-koh-loh*
trip	il viaggio	*eel vee-ah-joh*
window seat	un posto vicino al finestrino	*oon poh-stoh vee-chee-noh ahl fee-nes-tReh-noh*

In the Comfort Zone

Look at the following paragraph taken from an Italian in-flight magazine describing the various services offered passengers and see how much you can understand:

> A bordo dell'aereo sono a disposizione dei passeggeri: riviste italiane e straniere, coperte e cuscini, medicine, carta da lettera, giochi per bambini, penne, cartoline, sigarette, spumanti italiani, vino, birra, e bibite varie.

On the Inside

You've landed safely and are ushered off the plane toward customs. After your *passaporto* is stamped, many thoughts fill your mind as you grab your bags off the luggage carousel: You need to find a bathroom, change money, and find out when your connecting flight to Sicily (or Milan, or Pisa) is leaving. Did you lose something *importante* and now need to find the *Ufficio oggetti smarriti* (lost and found)? How are you going to communicate all of these things? Look no further; Table 11.2 gives you all the vocabulary you need.

Table 11.2   Inside the Airport

English	Italian	Pronunciation
arrival	l'arrivo	*lah-Ree-voh*
arrival time	l'ora d'arrivo	*loh-Rah dah-Ree-voh*
baggage claim	la riconsegna bagagli	*lah Ree-kohn-sehn-yah bah-gahl-yee*
bathroom	la toilette	*lah toy-leht*
	il bagno	*eel-bah-nyoh*
to be late/delayed	essere in ritardo	*eh-seh-Reh een Ree-taR-doh*
bus stop	la fermata (dell'autobus)	*lah feR-mah-tah*
car rental	l'autonoleggio	*low-toh-noh-leh-joh*
cart	il carrello	*eel kah-Reh-loh*
connection	la coincidenza	*lah koh-een-cheh-den-zah*
customs	la dogana	*lah doh-gah-nah*
departure	la partenza	*lah paR-ten-zah*
departure time	l'ora di partenza	*loh-Rah dee pahR-ten-zah*
destination	la destinazione	*lah des-tee-nah-zee-oh-neh*
elevator	l'ascensore	*lah-shen-soh-Reh*
entrance	l'entrata	*len-tRah-tah*
exit	l'uscita	*loo-shee-tah*
information	l'informazione	*leen-foR-mah-zee-oh-neh*
to miss a flight	perdere un volo	*peR-deh-Reh oon voh-loh*
money exchange	lo scambio	*loh skahm-bee-oh*
porter	il portiere	*eel poR-tee-eh-Reh*
reservation	la prenotazione	*lah pReh-noh-tah-zee-oh-neh*
to reserve	prenotare	*pReh-noh-tah-Reh*
stairs	le scale	*leh skah-leh*
taxi	il tassì	*eel tah-see*
telephone	il telefono	*eel tel-eh-foh-noh*
ticket	il biglietto	*eel bee-lyeh-toh*

In addition, the following helpful expressions will at the very least get you to Italy comfortably:

Dov'è la dogana?	Where is customs?
Vorrei un posto vicino al finestrino/corridoio.	I'd like a seat near the window/aisle.
Vorrei viaggiare in prima/seconda classe.	I'd like to travel in first/second class.
Vorrei fare il biglietto di andata e ritorno.	I'd like to order a round-trip ticket.
Vorrei prendere l'aereo.	I'd like to take a plane.
Vorrei consegnare i bagagli al deposito bagagli.	I'd like to consign bags in the baggage claim.
Vorrei prenotare un posto.	I'd like to reserve a place.
Dove si trova la biglietteria?	Where does one find the ticket office?

Going Crazy: The Verb Andare

The verb *andare* (to go) can come in handy as you make your way out of the airport. This is an irregular verb, so you need to memorize the parts outlined in Table 11.3. (You can cram on the seven-hour plane ride.) Keep in mind that the Italian present tense often corresponds to the English present progressive (**-ing** words).

Table 11.3   The Verb Andare

Person	Singular	Plural
First	*vado* (I go)	*andiamo* (we go)
Second	*vai* (you go)	*andate* (you go)
Third	*va* (he/she goes; You go)	*vanno* (they go)

As a Rule

You use the preposition *a* when you want to express going to or staying in a city:

Vado a Roma.

The preposition *in* is generally used when you are traveling to a country:

Andiamo in Italia.

Did You Know?
The Italians often say "Andiamo!" much in the same way we say, "Let's go!"

Andare is generally followed by the preposition *a* (to), as it usually is in English (I am going to...) when you want to say you're going somewhere or going to do something. Often, you must create a contraction when using the preposition *a* with a definite article (you'll learn about contractions later in this chapter):

Vado all'università.   I am going to the university.

Andiamo al ristorante. We're going to the restaurant.

Andate a mangiare?   Are you going to eat?

Attenzione!
When using the verb *andare* to say you are going "by foot," you use the preposition *a* (*not* in): *Vado a piedi.* (I am going by foot.)

Andare is also followed by the preposition *in* (to) when describing means of transportation:

andare in macchina	to go by car
andare in bicicletta	to go by bicycle
andare in treno	to go by train
andare in aeroplano	to go by plane

Going, Going, Gone

Fill in the appropriate form of *andare*:

1. Luisa e Marta _____ in macchina all'aeroporto.

2. Io _____ a New York.

3. Tu _____ alla stazione.

4. Roberto ed io _____ a mangiare una pizza.

5. Voi _____ a piedi. Loro _____ in bicicletta.

Attenzione!
Once you've arrived somewhere or found what you are looking for, remember the words *c'è* (there is), *ci sono* (there are), and *ecco*:

C'è una toilette vicino?	Is there a toilet nearby?
Sì, ci sono le toilette vicino all'uscita.	Yes, there are toilets near the exit.
Dov'è ci sono i bagagli?	Where are the bags?
Ecco i bagagli!	Here are the bags!

Prepositions: Sticky Stuff

You've used these words thousands of times and probably didn't know they were all prepositions. You've already seen a lot of prepositions because they are often the glue of a phrase, tying the words together. Table 11.4 provides a comprehensive list of Italian prepositions and their meanings.

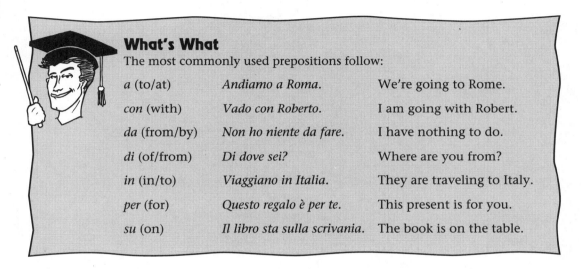

What's What

The most commonly used prepositions follow:

a (to/at)	*Andiamo a Roma.*	We're going to Rome.
con (with)	*Vado con Roberto.*	I am going with Robert.
da (from/by)	*Non ho niente da fare.*	I have nothing to do.
di (of/from)	*Di dove sei?*	Where are you from?
in (in/to)	*Viaggiano in Italia.*	They are traveling to Italy.
per (for)	*Questo regalo è per te.*	This present is for you.
su (on)	*Il libro sta sulla scrivania.*	The book is on the table.

Table 11.4 Prepositions

Preposition	Meaning
a	to/at
accanto a	beside
attorno a	around
avanti	in front of/before/ahead
circa	about/around (when making an estimation)
con	with
contro	against/opposite to
da	from/by
davanti a	before
dentro a	inside

continues

Table 11.4   Continued

Preposition	Meaning
di	of, from, about
dietro a	behind
dopo	after
eccetto	except/save
fino a	until/as far as
fra/tra	between/among
fuori di	outside
lontano da	far from
oltre	besides/beyond
per	for/in order to
senza	without
sopra	above
sotto	under
su	on top of
vicino a	near

Contractions

No one is having a baby here. A *contraction*, in linguistic terms, is a single word made out of two words. The prepositions in Table 11.5 form contractions when followed by a definite article. Notice that the endings remain the same as the definite article. A contraction can be as simple as *alla* (to the) or *sul* (on the).

Table 11.5   Contractions

Preposition	Masculine					Feminine		
	Singular			Plural		Singular		Plural
	il	*lo*	*l'*	*i*	*gli*	*la*	*l'*	*le*
a	al	allo	all'	ai	agli	alla	all'	alle
in	nel	nello	nell'	nei	negli	nella	nell'	nelle

	Masculine					Feminine		
Preposition	Singular			Plural		Singular		Plural
	il	*lo*	*l'*	*i*	*gli*	*la*	*l'*	*le*
di	del	dello	dell'	dei	degli	della	dell'	delle
su	sul	sullo	sull'	sui	sugli	sulla	sull'	sulle
da	dal	dallo	dall'	dai	dagli	dalla	dall'	dalle

As a Rule

Pronunciation in Italian is relatively easy. Sometimes it can be a little confusing remembering when a *c* should be pronounced like a *ch* or like a *k*. Review the pronunciation rules in Chapter 3 if you're still confused. As an aid, keep in mind the following:

c + a, h, o, u = hard c (like cat)

Examples: *candela, con, contro, Chianti*

c + e, i = ch (like chest)

Examples: *centro, ci, ciao, vicino*

As a reference point, pick a word, any word, that follows these pronunciation rules. For example, can't remember the c + i rule? Remember the word *ciao*. The c + h rule? Remember the word *Chianti*.

There are so many different ways you can use prepositions that it's almost *impossibile* to outline every one of them here. The best way to learn them is to study the basic rules and listen for idiomatic usage. If you want a more comprehensive explanation of speech parts and their different uses, you might want to pick up a copy of a good Italian grammar book such as *Italian Verbs and Essentials of Grammar* by Carlo Graziano (Passport Books).

Switcharoo

Replace the italicized words with the words in parentheses, changing the preposition or contraction as necessary. Accommodate any changes in gender or plurality.

1. Silvia ed io andiamo *al cinema*. (festa)

2. Il tassì va *in centro*. (piazza)

3. Andate *a piedi*? (macchina)

4. La giacca sta *sulla tavola*. (armadio)

5. Mangiamo *del riso*. (spaghetti)

As a Rule

The preposition *da* (from/by/of/since) can mean "since" or can describe an amount of time. For example, use the present tense of the verb *essere* + *da* to create the following:

Da quanto tempo sei in Italia?	Literally, "You are in Italy from how much time?"
Sono in Italia da ottobre.	Literally, "I am in Italy since October."

What's What

You can use the preposition *di* plus an article to express an unspecified quantity or "some" of a greater amount:

Mangio della pasta.	I am eating some pasta.
Bevo del vino.	I am drinking some wine.
Vuole della frutta?	Do you want some fruit?

Take a Left, a Right, Go Straight, and Keep Walking...

Getting lost while traveling can be half the fun, but sometimes you have a particular place in mind and don't want to spend your entire afternoon wandering around the streets. Being able to ask for directions is easy enough. You can point to your map or you can form a simple question using what you've just learned in this book.

To start you on the right foot, the verbs in Table 11.6 will help you find your way around town.

Table 11.6 Verbs Giving Direction

Verb	Pronunciation	Meaning
andare	*ahn-dah-Reh*	to go
attraversare	*ah-tRah-veR-sah-Reh*	to cross
camminare	*kah-mee-nah-Reh*	to walk
continuare	*kohn-teen-oo-ah-Reh*	to continue
fare	*fah-Reh*	to make/do/take (idiomatic)
girare	*jee-Rah-Reh*	to turn
passare	*pah-sah-Reh*	to pass
prendere	*pRen-deh-Reh*	to take
salire	*sah-lee-Reh*	to go up
scendere	*shen-deh-Reh*	to go down
seguire	*seh-gwee-Reh*	to follow
stare	*stah-Reh*	to stay/be

Understanding the response you're given is another story. When someone directs you to a location, that person is giving you a command (also called the imperative form of a verb). To keep it simple, all you really need to learn for a command are the endings for the two forms of *you* (*tu* and *Lei*) and then you conjugate the verb accordingly:

What's What
nord = north
sud = south
ovest = west
est = east
a sinistra = to the left
a destra = to the right
diritto = straight

Familiar imperative:

Va a destra.   Go right.

Polite imperative:

Vada a destra.   Go right.

Plural imperative:

Andate a destra.   Go right.

Look at the following endings to see how you can make any verb imperative. Notice in Table 11.7 that the *-ere* and *-ire* verbs use the same endings. Then, check out the verbs in Table 11.8 for some common commands that might come in handy.

143

Table 11.7   Imperative Endings

	-are Verbs	*-ere* and *-ire* Verbs
Tu	-a	-i
Lei	-i	-a

Table 11.8   Imperative Form

Verb	Tu	Lei	Meaning
attraversare	Attraversa!	Attraversi!	Cross!
camminare	Cammina!	Cammini!	Walk!
continuare	Continua!	Continui!	Continue!
girare	Gira!	Giri!	Turn!
passare	Passa!	Passi!	Pass!
prendere	Prendi!	Prenda!	Take!
salire	Sali!	Salga!	Go up!
scendere	Scendi!	Scenda!	Go down!
seguire	Segui!	Segua!	Follow!
stare	Stai!	Stia!	Stay!

As a Rule

To form a negative command, such as "Don't go!" in the *tu* form, you don't need to worry about endings. Just use the formula of *non* + infinitive:

Non andare!	Don't go!
Non girare!	Don't turn!

Some important verbs that you need for making commands are irregular. Look at Table 11.9 and memorize the ones you think you'll need most.

Table 11.9 Irregular Imperative Forms

Verb	Tu	Lei	Meaning
andare	Va!	Vada!	Go!
avere	Abbi!	Abbia!	Have!
dire	Di'!	Dica!	Say/Tell!
essere	Sii!	Sia!	Be!
fare	Fa'! or Fai!	Faccia!	Do! Make! Take!
venire	Vieni!	Venga!	Come!

You may hear some of the following imperatives used while you're shopping or chatting.

Abbia pazienza!	Have patience! (polite)
Mi dica!	Tell me. (polite)
Dimmi tutto.	Tell me everything. (familiar)
Faccia quello che vuole.	Do what you want. (polite)

Tell Me What to Do

Use the imperative form with the following non-directional verbs:

	Tu	*Lei*
aiutare	_____	_____
mangiare	_____	_____
portare	_____	_____
telefonare	_____	_____

Dazed and Confused

You've figured out how to ask for the help you need and you've been given a beautifully articulated response. What do you do if you don't understand the response? Rather than sit there with a dumb look on your face, just have them repeat themselves, but slower this time. Table 11.10 gives you a few phrases you can use to let people know you just don't get it. Anything in parentheses is the familiar (*tu*).

Table 11.10 Expressing When You Just Don't Get It

Italian	English
Mi scusi. (Scusami.)	Excuse me.
Parli (Parla) piano, per favore, non parlo bene l'italiano.	Speak slowly please, I don't speak Italian well.
Parli (Parla) più lentamente, per favore.	Speak more slowly, please.
Ripeti (Ripeta) un'altra volta, per favore.	Repeat another time, please.
Non ho capito.	I didn't understand.
Ho capito.	I understood.
Come?	How? (a much nicer way of saying "huh?")
Sono perso.	I'm lost.

Impersonally Yours

The *si* construction is used to express the passive voice or when *one* is talking about an unspecified subject. This form is used in Italian to make general statements such as:

Si mangia bene in Italia.   One eats well in Italy.

Very often, this tense is used to ask or give directions:

Con l'autobus si arriva subito.   With the bus, one arrives immediately.

Come si arriva in centro?   How does one get to center?

Per andare in piazza si va diritto.   One goes straight to arrive in piazza.

The Least You Need to Know

➤ The irregular verb *andare* is one verb used to give directions.

➤ The imperative is the command form of a verb; it is used to tell people what to do and where to go.

➤ Prepositions are the glue that ties words together and are frequently used with an article, forming a contraction.

Chapter 12

Moving Around

In This Chapter

➤ Getting around town

➤ Renting a car

➤ Numbers

➤ Telling time

You're in Italy and all of your bags somehow made it intact. You've breezed through customs, changed enough money to get through the next couple of days, and, unless you had friends or family waiting for you, you've had to take a bus or other public means of transportation to get to *centro*. That's where you really feel, for the first time, that you are in a foreign country. No longer are the signs in English; it's all Italian now and you're on your own.

This chapter gives you all the vocabulary you need to be as independent as *possibile* and the means to *navigare* through just about any travel challenge.

Hoofing and Spinning

When traveling within a *città*, you have a few choices about how you're going to get around. It's best to take advantage of the *economico* and quite efficient modes of public *trasporti*. However, walking or cycling is always a terrific way of getting to know the corners of a city that you won't see from inside a bus or taxi—as well as a great way to stay in shape. Or, if you dare, you can rent a car.

Before you decide how you're going to get around, however, you need to know what you're talking about (in Italian, that is). Table 12.1 covers all your bases (and wheels).

Did You Know?

In Italy, public transportation is quite efficient, with buses, trains, and *la metro* (subway) to take you just about anywhere you want to go. It's a good idea to purchase bus tickets at a *cartoleria* or *tabacchi* to keep in your wallet because buses do not accept cash or coins. You can also buy *biglietti* (tickets) at train stations and from automated machines. Once you get on *l'autobus*, you must validate your ticket by punching it into a small box located on the back of the bus. Hold onto your ticket in case of surprise inspection by stern-faced inspectors eager to find transgressions. When using *la metro*, you must also buy a ticket from either one of the automated machines or from a ticket booth. It's possible to buy daily, weekly, and monthly tickets.

Table 12.1 Modes of Transportation

Italian	Pronunciation	English
l'autobus	*low-toh-boos*	bus
l'automobile	*low-toh-moh-bee-leh*	car
la bicicletta	*lah bee-chee-kleh-tah*	bicycle
la macchina	*lah mah-kee-nah*	car
la metro	*lah meh-tRoh*	subway
il tassì	*eel tah-see*	taxi
il treno	*eel tReh-noh*	train

Take a Ride

You've already learned the verb *andare* (to go), which you use when you want to indicate "going by car" (*andare in macchina*). The regular verb *prendere* (to take) is particularly useful when using public transportation. You've already seen the endings in Chapter 8, but take another look at these important verbs in Tables 12.2 and 12.3.

Table 12.2   The Verb Prendere

Person	Singular	Plural
First	*prendo* (I take)	*prendiamo* (we take)
Second	*prendi* (you take)	*prendete* (you take)
Third	*prende* (he/she takes; You take)	*prendono* (they take)

Table 12.3   The Verb Andare

Person	Singular	Plural
First	*vado* (I go)	*andiamo* (we go)
Second	*vai* (you go)	*andate* (you go)
Third	*va* (he/she goes; You go)	*vanno* (they go)

All Verbed Up and Everywhere to Go

Use the two verbs *prendere* and *andare* in the following sentences. Remember that the gerund form in English is equivalent to the simple present in Italian.

1. (Io) _____ l'autobus per andare in centro. (*prendere*)

   I am taking the bus to get downtown.

2. (Noi) _____ in macchina in spiaggia. (*andare*)

   We are going by car to the beach.

3. (Loro) _____ il treno da Roma per arrivare a Milano. (*prendere*)

   They are taking the train from Rome to get to Milan.

4. (Tu) _____ a piedi al negozio. (*andare*)

   You are going by foot to the store.

5. (Voi) _____ la metro per arrivare alla piramide in Via Ostiense. (*prendere*)

   You (plural) are taking the subway to get to the pyramid on Via Ostiense.

6. (Lui) _____ in bicicletta a vedere la campagna. (*andare*)

   He is going by bicycle to see the country.

Which One?

Quale means "which" or "what." By now, you've become used to the notion of agreement and are looking at endings and constantly making sure that everything gets along. As a reward for your diligence, the literary gods created an interrogative that only requires you to change it when there's more than one. Yes, Virginia, there is a *Babbo Natale*.

Singular	Plural
Quale (which)	Quali (which ones)
Qual (in front of è (is))	Quali (which ones)

Here are few commonly asked questions using the interrogative pronoun *quale*:

Quale *il treno per Venezia?*	Which is the train for Venice?
Quel treno parte fra due minuti.	That train leaves in (within) two minutes.
Quale *binario?*	Which track?
Questo treno parte dal binario tre.	This train leaves from track three.
Quali *sono gli autobus per centro?*	What are the buses (going) downtown?
Il quattrocento e il ventitre vanno a centro.	The number 400 and the number 23 go downtown.

As a Rule

Quale refers to a choice between two or more alternatives. *Che* (what) can be substituted for *quale* in almost any given situation:

Quale (or che) ristorante è il migliore? Which restaurant is the best?

Go back to Chapter 10 to review the demonstrative adjectives *this*, *these*, *that*, and *those*.

On the Road

Italy's *autostrade* are among the best in the world, but *le automobili* move pretty fast (often drivers do not abide by the speed limit), so keep in the right lane unless you're prepared to speed. Getting a handle on international driving laws is always a smart idea, and your local AAA can probably give you a hand in learning more about the dos and don'ts. It also wouldn't hurt to be able to understand directions and signs. Although most signs are fairly obvious, some can be pretty tricky:

You also should get to know the names of the amenities inside a car before you get in one. You can't keep your eyes on the road while searching for the button that means "air conditioner," now can you? Check out Table 12.4 for hints about car features.

Table 12.4 Inside the Car

English	Italian	Pronunciation
accelerator	l'acceleratore	*lah-cheh-leh-Rah-toh-Reh*
air conditioning	l'aria condizionata	*lah-Ree-yah kohn-dee-zee-oh-nah-tah*
brakes	i freni	*ee fReh-nee*
dashboard	il cruscotto	*eel kroo-skoh-toh*
gear stick	il cambio	*eel kahm-bee-yoh*

continues

Table 12.4   Continued

English	Italian	Pronunciation
glove compartment	il ripostiglio	*eel Ree-poh-stee-lyoh*
handbrake	il freno a mano	*eel fReh-noh ah mah-noh*
horn	il clacson	*eel klak-son*
ignition	l'accensione	*lah-chen-see-oh-neh*
keys	le chiavi	*leh kee-ah-vee*
radio	la radio	*lah Rah-dee-oh*
rear-view mirror	lo specchietto	*loh speh-kee-yeh-toh*
speedometer	il tachimetro	*eel tah-kee-met-Roh*
steering wheel	il volante	*eel voh-lahn-teh*
turn signals	le frecce	*leh fReh-cheh*

Behind the Wheel

Renting a car is easiest from the airport because most of the competitors have booths with English-speaking staff. If you find yourself in a small, out-of-the-way town, however, the following phrases will help you get some wheels:

> *Vorrei noleggiare una macchina.*
> I would like to rent a car.

> *Preferisco una macchina con il cambio automatico.*
> I prefer a car with automatic transmission.

> *Quanto costa al giorno (alla settimana) (al chilometro)?*
> How much does it cost per day (per week) (per kilometer)?

> *Quanto costa l'assicurazione per l'auto?*
> How much does automobile insurance cost?

> *Quale tipo di pagamento preferite?*
> What form of payment do you prefer?

> *Accettate carte di credito?*
> Do you accept credit cards?

If you've decided to rent *una macchina*, carefully inspect it inside and out. Make sure there is *un cricco* (a jack) and *una ruota di scorta* (a spare tire) in the trunk, in case you get a *gomma a terra* (flat tire) and it doesn't hurt to check for any pre-existing damages you could later be charged for.

Table 12.5 gives you the Italian words for car parts and predicaments. You never know—that cherry-red Ferrari you rented could turn out to be a lemon.

Table 12.5 Automobile Parts and Predicaments

English	Italian	Pronunciation
antenna	l'antenna	*lahn-teh-nah*
battery	la batteria	*lah bah-teR-ee-yah*
breakdown	un guasto	*oon gwah-stoh*
bumper	il paraurti	*eel pah-Rah-ooR-tee*
carburetor	il carburatore	*eel kaR-booR-ah-toh-Reh*
door	la portiera	*lah poR-tee-eh-Rah*
door handle	la maniglia	*lah mah-nee-lyah*
fan belt	la cinghia del ventilatore	*lah cheen-ghee-yah del ven-tee-lah-toh-Reh*
fender	il parafango	*eel pah-Rah-fahn-goh*
flat tire	una gomma a terra una ruota bucata	*oo-nah goh-mah ah teR-Rah,* *oo-noh Roo-woh-tah boo-kah-tah*
gas tank	il serbatoio	*eel seR-bah-toy-oh*
headlights	i fari	*ee fah-Ree*
hood	il cofano	*eel koh-fah-noh*
license plate	la targa	*lah taR-gah*
motor	il motore	*eel moh-toh-Reh*
muffler	la marmitta	*lah maR-mee-tah*
radiator	la radiatore	*lah Rah-dee-yah-toh-Reh*
spark plug	la candela d'accensione	*lah kahn-deh-lah dah-chen-see-oh-neh*
tail light	la luce di posizione	*lah loo-cheh dee poh-zee-zee-oh-neh*
tire	la ruota	*lah rwoh-tah*
trunk	il bagagliaio	*eel bah-gah-lyah-yoh*
window	il finestrino	*eel fee-neh-stRee-noh*
windshield	il parabrezza	*eel pah-Rah-bReh-zah*
windshield wiper	il tergicristallo	*eel teR-jee-kRee-stah-loh*

Just in case that wasn't enough, Table 12.6 contains some more useful terms related to the road that might come in handy.

Table 12.6 More Words for the Road Warrior

English	Italian
license	la patente
sign	il segnale
speed limit	il limite di velocità
to be prohibited	essere vietato
to break down	guastare
to change a tire	cambiare la ruota
to check	controllare
…the water	…l'acqua
…the oil	…l'olio
…the tires	…le ruote
to drive	guidare
to get a ticket	prendere una multa
to give a ride	dare un passaggio
to obey traffic signs	rispettare i segnali
to park	parcheggiare
to run out of gas	rimanere senza benzina
to run/function	funzionare
traffic officer	il vigile

Tell Me Your Worries

You're driving along, minding your own business, when Pop! You blow a tire. A kind stranger pulls over and asks you what happened and whether you need help. Fill in the blanks in the following paragraph to describe to the good Samaritan what your problem is and how he can help:

Signore: C'è un problema?

Turista: Si, c'è _____. (a flat tire)

Signore: _____ è sua? (the car)

Turista: No, _____ questa macchina per una settimana. Sono in vacanza. (I am renting)

Signore: C'è _____ nel portabagagli? (a jack)

Turista: Credo di sì. Lei è molto _____.
(kind)

Trains and Buses

Public transportation is a great way to get around, but how are you going to get on the right bus if you don't know which number it is or take the right train if you don't know what time it leaves? Numerically speaking, you'd have a pretty hard time. Take *un momento* to learn how to count and tell time (and you won't be late for your date with that good-looking stranger from the plane).

Baby, I Got Your Number

In Italy, you're going to need to be able to count to a million since the Italian currency (*lira*) requires you to be able to understand high numbers. For instance, a cappuccino on average is 2,000 lira (£2.000). (Don't panic; it's only about a buck and a half.) If you want to make a date, tell the time, or find out prices, you need to know numbers.

Fortunately, you don't need to use Roman numerals to do your math. Numbers that express amounts, known as cardinal numbers, are called *numeri cardinali* in Italian. Let the counting begin with Table 12.7.

> **Did You Know?**
> In Italy, schedules are given in military time. If you are leaving at 2:00 p.m., for example, you are told 14:00 hours. This may be tricky at first, so confirm that you have understood correctly by asking if it is a.m. (*di mattino*) or p.m. (*di sera*).

> **Attenzione!**
> Numbers under 100 ending in a vowel, such as *venti* (20), drop the vowel when connected to secondary numbers. Examples are *ventuno* (21), *trentotto* (38), *quarantuno* (41), and so on.
>
> *Mille* (1000) turns to *mila* in the plural, as with the number *due mila* (2000).

Table 12.7 Numeri Cardinali

English	Italian	Pronunciation
0	zero	*zeh-Roh*
1	uno	*oo-noh*
2	due	*doo-weh*
3	tre	*tRay*
4	quattro	*kwah-tRoh*
5	cinque	*cheen-kweh*

continues

Table 12.7   Continued

English	Italian	Pronunciation
6	sei	*sey*
7	sette	*seh-teh*
8	otto	*oh-toh*
9	nove	*noh-veh*
10	dieci	*dee-ay-chee*
11	undici	*oon-dee-chee*
12	dodici	*doh-dee-chee*
13	tredici	*tReh-dee-chee*
14	quattordici	*kwah-toR-dee-chee*
15	quindici	*kween-dee-chee*
16	sedici	*sey-dee-chee*
17	diciassette	*dee-chah-seh-teh*
18	diciotto	*dee-choh-toh*
19	diciannove	*dee-chah-noh-veh*
20	venti	*ven-tee*
21	ventuno	*ven-too-noh*
22	ventidue	*ven-tee-doo-eh*
23	ventitre	*ven-tee-tReh*
24	ventiquattro	*ven-tee-kwaht-Roh*
25	venticinque	*ven-tee-cheen-kweh*
26	ventisei	*ven-tee-sey*
27	ventisette	*ven-tee-seh-teh*
28	ventotto	*ven-toh-toh*
29	ventinove	*ven-tee-noh-veh*
30	trenta	*tRen-tah*
40	quaranta	*kwah-Rahn-tah*
50	cinquanta	*cheen-kwahn-tah*
60	sessanta	*seh-sahn-tah*
70	settanta	*seh-tahn-tah*

English	Italian	Pronunciation
80	ottanta	*oh-tahn-tah*
90	novanta	*noh-vahn-tah*
100	cento	*chen-toh*
101	centouno	*chen-toh-oo-noh*
200	duecento	*doo-ay-chen-toh*
300	trecento	*tReh-chen-toh*
400	quattrocento	*kwah-tRoh-chen-toh*
500	cinquecento	*cheen-kweh-chen-toh*
1,000	mille	*mee-leh*
1,001	milleuno	*mee-leh-oo-noh*
1,200	milleduecento	*mee-leh-doo-eh-chen-toh*
2,000	duemila	*doo-eh-mee-lah*
3,000	tremila	*treh-mee-lah*
10,000	diecimila	*dee-ay-chee-mee-lah*
20,000	ventimila	*ven-tee-mee-lah*
100,000	centomila	*chen-toh-mee-lah*
200,000	duecentomila	*doo-eh-chen-toh-mee-lah*
1,000,000	un milione	*oon mee-lyoh-neh*
1,000,000,000	un miliardo	*oon mee-lyaR-doh*

Time Is of the Essence

Time is easy to learn. You need to remember the verb *essere* for asking what time it *is*. You use the verb *sapere* to ask if someone *knows* the time.

You can ask the time in one of two ways:

Che ore sono?	What time is it?
Che ora è?	What time is it?
Sa l'ora?	Do you know what time it is?

Attenzione!
Be careful of the Italian word *tempo* because this word is primarily used when talking about the weather (as in *temperatura*), not time.

You can respond in only two ways using either *È* _____ or *Sono le*:

È l'una.	It is one o'clock.
È mezzogiorno.	It is noon.
Sono le due.	It is two o'clock.
Sono le nove.	It is nine o'clock.

If someone is already wearing a watch and asks you for the time, beware. Otherwise, the following expressions in Table 12.8 will help talk about the time.

Table 12.8   Time Expressions

Italian	English
Che ore sono? Che ora è?	What time is it?
A che ora?	At what time?
e	and
meno (le)	less than
e mezzo	half past
e un quarto	a quarter past
meno un quarto	a quarter to
di mattino	in the morning
di pomeriggio	in the afternoon
di sera	in the evening
un minuto	a minute
due minuti	two minutes
un secondo	a second
due secondi	two seconds
un'ora	an hour
due ore	two hours
un mezz'ora	a half hour
(fra) un'ora, una mezz'ora, cinque minuti	(in) an hour, a half hour, five minutes
fra un po'	in a while
da quando?	since when?
dalle sei	since 6:00

Italian	English
(un'ora, cinque minuti...) fa	(an hour, five minutes...) ago
dopo le tre	after 3:00
prima delle tre	before 3:00
in tempo	on time
in ritardo	late
in anticipo	early
A che ora andiamo a mangiare?	At what time are we going to eat?
Andiamo a mangiare alle otto e mezzo.	We are going to eat at 8:30.
A che ora c'è il treno per Roma?	At what time is the train to Rome?
C'è un treno che parte alle sei.	There is a train that leaves at 6:00.

Use *è* when it is one o'clock. For all other times, because they are plural, use *sono*.

> *È l'una.*   It is 1:00.
>
> *Sono le tre.*   It is 3:00.

To express time after the hour, use *e* (without the accent, meaning "and") plus the number of minutes past the hour:

> *Sono le quattro e dieci.*   It is 4:10.
>
> *Sono le sei e cinque.*   It is 6:05.
>
> *È l'una e un quarto.*   It is 1:15.

To express time before the next hour (in English, we say "ten to," "quarter to," and so on), use the next hour + *meno* (meaning less) + whatever time is remaining before the next hour:

> *Sono le otto meno un quarto.*   It is a quarter to eight—literally, eight minus a quarter.
>
> *È l'una meno dieci.*   It's ten to one—literally, one minus ten.

It is not unusual to hear the time expressed as follows:

> *Sono le sette quarantacinque.*   It is 7:45.

Table 12.9 spells out exactly how to tell the time minute by minute, hour by hour.

Table 12.9 Telling Time

English	Italian
It is 1:00.	È l'una.
It is 2:00.	Sono le due.
It is 2:05.	Sono le due e cinque.
It is 3:10.	Sono le tre e dieci.
It is 4:15.	Sono le quattro e un quarto.
It is 5:20.	Sono le cinque e venti.
It is 6:25.	Sono le sei e venticinque.
It is 6:30.	Sono le sei e trenta.
It is 7:30.	Sono le sette e mezzo.
It is 8:40. (20 min. to 9)	Sono le nove meno venti.
It is 9:45. (a quarter to 10)	Sono le dieci meno un quarto.
It is 10:50. (10 min. to 11)	Sono le undici meno dieci.
It is 11:55. (5 min. to noon)	È mezzogiorno meno cinque.
It is noon.	È mezzogiorno.
It is midnight.	È mezzanotte.

Time Will Tell

Answer the following questions as best you can using complete sentences. Remember that the answer is usually in the question.

Example: A che ora finisci di lavorare? (What time do you finish working?)

Answer: Finisco di lavorare alle sei e mezzo. (I finish working at 6:30.)

1. A che ora andiamo al cinema? (6:00 p.m.)

2. A che ora parte il volo? (8:25 a.m.)

3. A che ora è la cena? (7:00 p.m.)

4. Quando c'è un'autobus per Verona? (noon)

5. Che ore sono? (4:44 p.m.)

All Aboard

Now that you know when to get on board, you need to know what you're getting onto. In Table 12.10, you'll find the what, where, and how to complement the when.

Table 12.10 Getting Around

English	Italian	Pronunciation
bus	l'autobus	*low-toh-bus*
bus stop	fermata dell'autobus	*feR-mah-tah dow-toh-boos*
taxi	tassì	*tah-see*
train	il treno	*eel treh-noh*
by railway	per ferrovia	*peR feh-Roh-vee-yah*
train station	la stazione ferroviaria	*lah stah-zee-oh-neh*
ticket	il biglietto	*eel bee-lyeh-toh*
round-trip ticket	il biglietto di andata e ritorno	*...dee ahn-dah-tah eh ree-toR-noh*
one-way ticket	il biglietto di andata	*...dee ahn-dah-tah*
ticket counter	la biglietteria	*lah bee-lyeh-teh-Ree-yah*
schedule	l'orario	*loR-ah-Ree-oh*
track	il binario	*eel bee-nah-Ree-oh*
waiting room	la sala d'aspetto	*lah sah-lah dah-speh-toh*
connection	la coincidenza	*lah koh-een-chee-den-zah*
first/second class	prima/seconda classe	*pree-mah/sehk-ohn-dah klah-seh*
seat	il sedile/il posto	*eel sed-ee-leh/eel pohs-toh*
window	il finestrino	*eel fee-neh-stRee-noh*
information	l'ufficio informazioni	*loo-fee-choh een-foR-mah-zee-oh-nee*
to be (running) late	essere in ritardo	*eh-seh-Reh een Ree-taR-doh*
to be (running) early	essere in anticipo	*...een ahn-tee-chee-poh*
to be (running) on time	essere in orario	*...een oR-ah-Ree-yoh*
to change	cambiare	*kahm-bee-ah-Reh*
to commute	fare il pendolare	*fah-Reh eel pen-doh-lah-Reh*
to get on	salire su	*sah-lee-Reh su*

continues

Table 12.10 Continued

English	Italian	Pronunciation
to get off	scendere da	*shen-deh-Reh da*
to stop	fermarsi	*feR-mahR-see*
to leave	partire	*paR-tee-Reh*
to take	prendere	*pRen-deh-Reh*
to lose	perdere	*peR-deh-Reh*
stop	la fermata	*lah feR-mah-tah*
last stop/ end of the line	il capolinea	*eel kah-poh lee-nee-yah*

In addition, some handy phrases include the following:

Vorrei un biglietto di andata e ritorno.	I would like a round-trip ticket.
Dov'è la fermata dell'autobus?	Where is the bus stop?
C'è la coincidenza?	Is there a connection?
A che ora parte il treno?	At what times does the train leave?
I voli sono in orario.	The planes (are running) on time.
Partiamo subito.	We're leaving immediately.
Su quale binario parte il treno?	On what track does the train leave?
Prenda quest'autobus.	Take this bus.
C'è un posto vicino al finestrino?	Is there a seat near the window?
Posso aprire il finestrino?	May I open the window?

Things to Do: The Verb Fare

The verb *fare* means "to do/make." In Italian, the verb *fare* is often used similarly to the English verb "to take" and appears in many idiomatic expressions. For example, in Italian, you don't "take a trip," but rather "make a trip" (*fare un viaggio*).

You also use the verb *fare* to tell the weather or to take a picture, a shower, a walk, or a spin. You can go shopping, pretend, or indicate where something hurts. You'll see this verb a lot—and use it often during your travels. Because it is irregular, you must memorize the different parts in Table 12.11.

Table 12.11 The Verb Fare: to Do/Make

Singular	Plural
io faccio (I do)	*noi facciamo* (we do)
tu fai (you do)	*voi fate* (you do)
lui/lei/Lei fa (he/she does; You do)	*loro fanno* (they do)

Table 12.12 contains some idiomatic expressions using the verb *fare*.

Table 12.12 Expressions Using Fare

Italian	English
fare un viaggio	to take a trip
fare una passeggiata	to take a walk
fare una fotografia	to take a picture
fare una domanda	to ask a question
fare l'amore	to make love
fare la doccia	to take a shower
fare il bagno	to take a bath
fare un giro	to take a spin
fare finta	to pretend
fare vedere	to show
fare le spese	to go shopping
fare le valigie	to pack/prepare one's bags
fare male	to hurt
fare benzina	to get gas
fare un regalo	to give a gift
fare il pieno	to fill it up
fare l'autostop	to hitchhike

Which Way Do I Go

The verb *fare* is also used to indicate direction. Instead of telling someone to "take a left and then take a right," you tell them to "*make* a left," using either the *si* construction you

163

learned in Chapter 11 or the first person singular of the verb you are using. The response you get will probably use the interrogative form of the verb.

Come si arriva a piazza Navona?	How do you get to piazza Navona?
Si va a sinistra e poi a destra.	Take a left and then a right.

Look at the following sentences to get a better idea of what you can express with the verb *fare:*

Perché non facciamo un giro?	Why don't we take a spin?
Devo fare le valigie per la mia vacanza in Italia.	I must prepare my bags for my vacation in Italy.
Noi facciamo un bel viaggio.	We are taking a beautiful trip.
Posso fare una domanda?	May I ask a question?
Ti voglio fare vedere qualcosa.	I want to show you something.
Fammi vedere!	Show me!
Lui sta facendo una passeggiata.	He is taking a walk.
Mi fa male lo stomaco.	My stomach hurts.

What to Do, What to Do

Fill in the appropriate form of *fare* in the following sentences:

1. Perché non (noi) _____ un giro?

2. Io mi _____ una bella doccia quando arrivo in albergo.

3. Mi _____ male la gola (throat).

4. Lui _____ una domanda all'ufficio informazioni.

The Least You Need to Know

➤ The verbs *andare* (to go) and *fare* (to do/make) are two important irregular verbs you need to memorize.

➤ Telling time is easy; remember the key words *meno* (less than) and *e* (and).

➤ You use the verb *prendere* (to take) when traveling.

➤ *Che?* and *Quale?* are used to ask "what?" and "which?"

Chapter 13

Hallelujah, You've Made It to the Hotel

In This Chapter

➤ The comfort zone: getting the most from your hotel

➤ First things first: ordinal numbers

➤ How to get what you want with *volere*, *potere*, and *dovere*

➤ Verbs that need a little help

Whether you're willing to live on a shoestring or you want the best of the best, this chapter will help you get what you need, when you want it.

A Cave Will Do

For most people with limited vacation time, it's a good idea to make reservations in advance, especially during the busy season (called *alta stagione*), which usually lasts from May through August.

For others, the fun of travel is the unexpected, the sense of living in the moment. You don't mind not knowing where you'll be next week because you want to go with the flow. In that case, it's a good idea to shop around before settling on a hotel or *pensione* (inn); prices may vary, and with a smile and bit of wit, you might be able to get yourself a terrific deal.

Whether you decide to pick a place to lay your head early in the game or later on, you're going to need the vocabulary in Table 13.1 to help you find the place that's right for you.

Table 13.1 The Hotel and Nearby

Facilities	Italian	Pronunciation
bar	il bar	*eel baR*
barber	il barbiere	*eel baR-bee-eh-Reh*
cashier	la cassa	*lah kah-sah*
doorman/concierge	il portiere	*eel poR-tee-eh-Reh*
dry cleaner	la tintoria	*lah teen-toh-Ree-ah*
elevator	l'ascensore	*lah-shen-soh-Reh*
gift shop	il negozio di regali	*eel neh-goh-zee-oh dee Reh-gah-lee*
gym	la palestra	*lah pah-leh-stRah*
hairdresser	il parrucchiere	*eel pah-Roo-kee-eh-Reh*
hotel	l'albergo	*lahl-beR-goh*
laundry service	la lavanderia	*lah lah-vahn-deh-Ree-yah*
maid	la cameriera	*lah kah-meR-ee-eh-Rah*
parking lot	il parcheggio	*eel pahR-keh-joh*
pension	la pensione	*lah pen-see-oh-neh*
pharmacy	la farmacia	*lah faR-mah-chee-ah*
room service	il servizio in camera	*eel seR-vee-zee-oh een kah-meh-Rah*
sauna	la sauna	*lah sah-oo-nah*
swimming pool	la piscina	*lah pee-shee-nah*
tailor	la sartoria	*lah saR-toh-Ree-yah*

A Room with a View

You might think you want to stand at your window and look at the wonderful chaos that makes Rome such a lively place. Beware: Windows facing the street can often be murder on your rest, especially if you want to sleep in a little. Early morning traffic can be quite merciless on one's ears. After you unpack, maybe you want to take a nice bath to unwind. Don't assume there will be a tub in your room; you must ask. Table 13.2 will help you ask for the kind of room you want.

Table 13.2 Your Room

Amenity	Italian	Pronunciation
a double room	una doppia	*oo-nah doh-pee-yah*
with a double bed	con matrimoniale	*kohn mah-tRee-moh-nee-ah-leh*
a single room	una singola	*oo-nah seen-goh-lah*
bathroom	il bagno	*eel bah-nyoh*
bathtub	la vasca da bagno	*lah vah-skah dah bah-nyoh*
elevator	l'ascensore	*lah-shen-soh-Reh*
fax	il fax	*eel faks*
heat	il riscaldamento	*eel Ree-skahl-dah-men-toh*
key	la chiave	*lah kee-yah-veh*
on the courtyard	sul cortile	*sool koR-tee-leh*
on the garden	sul giardino	*sool jaR-dee-noh*
on the sea	sul mare	*sool mah-Reh*
refrigerator	il frigorifero	*eel fRee-goh-Ree-feh-Roh*
room	la stanza, la camera	*lah stan-zah, lah kah-meh-Rah*
safe (deposit box)	la cassaforte	*lah kah-sah-foR-teh*
shower	la doccia	*lah doh-chah*
telephone	il telefono	*eel teh-leh-foh-noh*
television	la televisione	*lah teh-leh-vee-zee-oh-neh*
toilet	il gabinetto	*eel gah-bee neh-toh*
with air conditioning	con l'aria condizionata	*kohn lah-Ree-yah kohn-dee-zee-oh-nah-tah*

continues

Table 13.2   Continued

Amenity	Italian	Pronunciation
with bathroom	con bagno	*kohn bah-nyoh*
with terrace	con terrazza	*kohn teh-Rah-tsah*
with every comfort	con ogni confort	*kohn oh-nyee kohn-foRt*

Did You Know?
Italy has few, if any, laundromats. Traditionally, you must give your laundry to the hotel or bring it to a *lavanderia* where it will be cleaned and pressed for you. Usually, you pay per piece and not by weight. If you want something dry-cleaned, you must bring it to *la tintoria*.

Simply Said

It's nice to understand how a language works, but it can take a while for it all to sink in. In the meantime, the following simple phrases will help you ask for what you need without breaking out your list of conjugated verbs:

Frase	Phrase
Vorrei…	I would like…
Ho bisogno di…	I need…
Mi serve, Mi servono…	I need…

Table 13.3 will help you find the word for whatever amenity you may be lacking.

Table 13.3   Inside Your Room

Necessities	Italian	Pronunciation
alarm clock	la sveglia	*lah sveh-lyah*
ashtray	una portacenere	*oo-nah poR-tah-cheh-neh-Reh*
blanket	la coperta	*lah koh-peR-tah*
blow-dryer	l'asciugacapelli	*lah-shoo-gah-kah-peh-lee*
cot	un lettino	*oon leh-tee-noh*
hanger	la stampella	*lah stahm-peh-lah*
ice	il ghiaccio	*eel ghee-ah-choh*
matches	i fiammiferi	*ee fee-ah-mee-feh-Reh*
mineral water	l'acqua minerale	*lah-kwah mee-neR-ah-leh*
pillow	il cuscino	*eel koo-shee-noh*

Necessities	Italian	Pronunciation
shampoo	lo shampoo	*loh sham-poo*
soap	il sapone	*eel sah-poh-neh*
stationery	la carta da lettere	*lah kahR-tah dah leh-teh-Reh*
tissues	i fazzolettini di carta	*ee fah-tsoh-leh-tee-nee dee kahR-tah*
toilet paper	la carta igienica	*lah kahR-tah ee-jen-ee-kah*
towel	l'asciugamano	*lah-shoo-gah-mah-noh*
transformer	il trasformatore	*eel tRah-sfoR-mah-toh-Reh*

As a Rule

When using the reflexive verb *servirsi*, the number of things you need must agree with the verb. You'll learn more about reflexive verbs later.

Mi serve una coperta in più.   I need an extra blanket.

Mi servono due coperte in più.   I need two extra blankets.

Room Service, Please

Ask the hotel for something from the previous list using one of the expressions you just learned. You might have to add the words *in più* after the item if you want an extra towel, blanket, and so on.

If you want to ask for "some" more, don't forget to use the preposition *di* + the article, as in *del*, *della*, *dei*, and so on:

Example: un cuscino

Answer: Vorrei un cuscino in più, per favore.

Example: la carta igienica

Answer: Mi serve della carta igienica.

1. carta da lettere
2. chiave
3. asciugamano
4. sveglia
5. saponetta

169

In a pinch, you can use the phrases in Table 13.4 to express yourself and get the information you need. The last thing you want to do is rifle through your *dizionario* while the concierge taps his foot.

Table 13.4 Useful Expressions

Expression	L'Espressione
At what time is check-out?	Qual è l'ora di partenza?
Can you give me a discount?	Mi potete fare uno sconto?
Did I receive any messages?	Ho ricevuto dei messaggi?
Do you speak English?	Parla l'inglese?
How much does it cost per day?	Quanto costa al giorno?
...per week?	...alla settimana?
I'm remaining for about a week.	Rimango per circa una settimana.
I need...	Ho bisogno di...
extra	in più
I'd like to make a reservation.	Vorrei fare una prenotazione. Vorrei prenotare...
I'll take this room.	Prendo questa stanza.
Is breakfast included?	Colazione compresa?
Is there anything less expensive?	Non c'è qualcosa più economico?
Is there...?	C'è...?
Can I pay with...	Posso pagare con...
...cash?	...contanti?
...check?	...assegno?
...credit card?	...carta di credito?
compliments	complimenti
May I leave a message?	Posso lasciare un messaggio?
Thank you so much.	Grazie tanto.
This room is too...	Questa stanza è troppo...
...small	...piccola
...dark	...buia
...noisy	...rumorosa

Expression	L'Espressione
This is too expensive.	Questo è troppo caro.
to make a reservation	fare una prenotazione
to take a vacation	fare una vacanza

Practice Makes Perfetto

Complete the following sentences with the appropriate Italian word. Don't forget to use the correct article when necessary. Then translate the sentences.

1. Mi servono _____ in più per favore. Fa freddo stasera! (two blankets)

2. Ho bisogno di un altro _____. (pillow)

3. Vorrei un _____ per i miei capelli. (hair dryer)

4. C'è un'altra _____ per la nostra camera? (key)

5. Ci sono dei buoni _____ qui vicino? (restaurants)

6. Vorrei _____ diversa. Questa non va bene. (a room)

7. Mi serve _____. (a bottle of mineral water)

Who's on First?

When you *ordinare* (order) your dinner in a *ristorante*, you start with your *primo piatto* (first course). Maybe you order *pasta primavera* (which means springtime and translates literally as "first green"). You move along to your *secondo piatto* (second course), and afterwards, you might have *per ultimo* (for last)—a nice *tiramisù*, so sweet and light and lovely that you'll feel like you died and went to heaven.

What do all these things have in common (other than the fact that they all taste really good)? They all use *ordinal numbers*.

Ordinal numbers specify the order of something in a series. It's probably obvious (but in case it's not) that the word *primo* is similar to the English word "primary," *secondo* is like "secondary," *terzo* is like "tertiary," *quarto* is like "quarter," *quinto* is like "quintuplets," and so on and so forth. (Remember: You should always be thinking of like-sounding words in English to help you retain your Italian vocabulary.) Table 13.5 gives you a rundown of the ordinal numbers you need and how to write them in abbreviated form.

Table 13.5 Ordinal Numbers

English	Italian	Masc.	Fem.	Pronunciation
first	primo	1°	1ª	*pRee-moh*
second	secondo	2°	2ª	*seh-kohn-doh*
third	terzo	3°	3ª	*teR-zoh*
fourth	quarto	4°	4ª	*kwahR-toh*
fifth	quinto	5°	5ª	*kween-toh*
sixth	sesto	6°	6ª	*sehs-toh*
seventh	settimo	7°	7ª	*seh-tee-moh*
eighth	ottavo	8°	8ª	*oh-tah-voh*
ninth	nono	9°	9ª	*noh-noh*
tenth	decimo	10°	10ª	*deh-chee-moh*
eleventh	undicesimo	11°	11ª	*oon-dee-cheh-zee-moh*
twelfth	dodicesimo	12°	12ª	*doh-dee-cheh-zee-moh*
twentieth	ventesimo	20°	20ª	*ven-teh-zee-moh*
twenty-first	ventunesimo	21°	21ª	*ven-too-neh-zee-moh*
twenty-third*	ventitreesimo	23°	23ª	*ven-tee-tReh-eh-zee-moh*
sixty-sixth*	sessantaseiesimo	66°	66ª	*seh-sahn-tah-seh-eh-zee-moh*
seventy-seventh	settantasettesimo	77°	77ª	*seh-tahn-tah-seh-teh-zee-moh*
hundredth	centesimo	100°	100ª	*chen-teh-zee-moh*
thousandth	millesimo	1000°	1000ª	*mee-leh-zee-moh*

Note: The final vowel of the cardinal number is not dropped with numbers ending in 3 (-tre) and 6 (-sei).

There are some basic rules for using ordinal numbers in Italian:

➤ Like any adjective, ordinal numbers must agree in gender and number with the nouns they modify. As in English, they precede the nouns they modify. Notice how they are abbreviated, as in 1° (1st), 2° (2nd), and 3° (3rd)—much easier than the English. The feminine abbreviation reflects the ending -a, as in 1ª, 2ª, and 3ª.

la prima volta (1ª) the first time

il primo piatto (1°) the first course

➤ The first ten ordinal numbers all have separate forms, but after the tenth ordinal number, they simply drop the final vowel of the cardinal number and add the ending -*esimo*.

tredici	tredicesimo	13th
venticinque	venticinquesimo	25th
ventisei	ventiseiesimo	26th

➤ You need to use ordinal numbers whenever you reference a Roman numeral, as in Enrico V (*quinto*) or Papa Giovanni Paolo II (*secondo*).

➤ Unlike in English, dates in Italian require cardinal numbers, unless you are talking about the first day of a month, as in *il primo ottobre*. June 8th is *l'otto (di) giugno* because the day always comes before the month. The use of the preposition *di* is optional. Therefore, it's important to remember that in Italian, *8/6/98* is actually June 8, 1998 (and not August 6, 1998).

Did You Know?
In Italian, the word for floor is *piano* (just like the instrument). The *primo piano* (first floor) is actually the floor above the *pianterreno* (ground floor) and equal to what is considered the second floor in the U.S. By the way, the number 13 is considered *buona fortuna*—just the opposite from what one might expect.

There's No Stopping You Now

Are you up to the challenge of learning a few more irregular verbs? "I want! I can! I must!" you say. And that's exactly what you're going to learn. The following verbs will help you to be able to (*potere*) do what you have to do (*dovere*) to get what you want (*volere*).

Before you plunge in, take stock of what you've already learned—and be patient with yourself. Learning a language, you'll hear again and again, is a *processo*. It takes time—time to sink in, time to kick in—but when it does, there's nothing like it.

I Want What I Want! (Volere)

An important verb you have already been using in its conditional form is the verb *volere*. When you say, "Vorrei," you are saying, "I would like." You are using the conditional form because you *would like* to express your wants as delicately as possible. Sometimes, however, you just want what you want and there's no doubt about it. Table 13.6 shows you how to express want, pure and simple. (You should definitely know your subject pronouns by now. If not, review Chapter 6.)

Table 13.6 Volere—to Want

Singular	Plural
io voglio (I want)	*noi vogliamo* (we want)
tu vuoi (you want)	*voi volete* (you want)
lui/lei/Lei vuole (he/she wants; You want)	*loro vogliono* (they want)

I bambini vogliono mangiare un gelato.	The children want to eat an ice cream.
(Lei) Vuole una mano?	Do you want a hand?

I Think I Can, I Think I Can! (Potere)

The verb *potere* is what you use to say you are able to do something. It's the same as what the little train said as it puffed up the hill—and it's what you use to express that you *can* speak Italian (it's not just a dream). Using it will help you to remember it. Your "potential" is unlimited, as long as you think you can. One thing to keep in mind, however, as you examine Table 13.7: *Potere* is always used with an infinitive.

Table 13.7 Potere—to Be Able to/Can

Singular	Plural
io posso (I can)	*noi possiamo* (we can)
tu puoi (you can)	*voi potete* (you can)
lui/lei/Lei può (he/she/You can)	*loro possono* (they can)

Posso venire con te?	Can I come with you?
Possiamo imparare questa lingua.	We can learn this language.

I Have to... (Dovere)

The verb *dovere*, outlined in Table 13.8, is what you use to express "to have to," "must," or "to owe." Like the verb *potere*, *dovere* is always used in front of an infinitive, such as when you say, "I have to study," except when it is used to mean "to owe."

Table 13.8 Dovere—to Have to/Must/to Owe

Singular	Plural
io devo (I must)	*noi dobbiamo* (we must)
tu devi (you must)	*voi dovete* (you must)
lui/lei/Lei deve (he/she/You must)	*loro devono* (they must)

Devo trovare una banca.	I must find a bank.
Dobbiamo partire subito.	We have to leave immediately.
Devo molti soldi.	I owe a lot of money.

Infinitive Verbs and Prepositions

The infinitive of a verb, as you know, is a verb before it has been conjugated, or the "to" form of a verb, as in *to study*, *to laugh*, and *to cry*. Sometimes an infinitive takes a different form, as in the sentence "I plan *on studying* a lot this summer."

In Italian, when a verb does not have a subject, it is usually in its infinitive form, even if this form resembles the present progressive.

Some Italian verbs are preceded by a preposition, others are followed by a preposition, and some take none at all. Knowing when to use a preposition is often a question of usage because the meaning of a verb can change when used with one. This applies in English as well; compare these two sentences and see how the meaning changes by changing the preposition:

I want to go **on** the plane.   I want to go **to** the plane.

Watch what happens to the meaning of the following Italian sentences when you change the preposition.

Verbo	*Esempio*	*Example*
pensare di	Penso di andare in italia.	I am thinking (of going) to Italy.
pensare a	Penso a te.	I'm thinking of you.

Memorization might work for the few who have a photographic memory, but for the rest of us, practice and usage are the only way to remember what verb takes what.

Alone at Last

For some verbs, you don't have to worry about the preposition at all. The verbs in Table 13.9 like being alone and thus require no preposition before an infinitive.

Table 13.9   Verbs Without a Preposition

Italian	English
ascoltare	to listen
amare	to love
desiderare	to desire
dovere	to have to
fare	to do/make
guardare	to look at
lasciare	to leave (something behind)
preferire	to prefer
sapere	to know (something)
sentire	to listen
vedere	to see
volere	to want

Anna preferisce bere la birra.	Anna prefers to drink beer.
Vogliamo vedere un menu.	We want to see a menu.
Dobbiamo andare subito.	We must go immediately.

Oddballs

There are always going to be peculiarities that cannot be translated. The prepositions in Table 13.10 are examples.

As a Rule

It is important to avoid literally translating from one language to another—context is key—because you might get caught up in details that cannot be completely "decoded."

Table 13.10 Verbs Taking di Before an Infinitive

Italian	English
accettare di	to accept (from)
ammettere di	to admit (to)
aspettare di	to wait (for)/expect
avere bisogno di	to have need (of)
avere intenzione di	to intend (to)
avere paura di	to be afraid (of)
avere ragione di	to be right (about)
avere voglia di	to be in the mood (for)
cercare di	to try (to)/to look (for)/to search (for)
chiedere di	to ask (for)
credere di	to believe (in)
decidere di	to decide (to)
dimenticare di	to forget (to)
dire di	to say (to)
finire di	to finish (to)
offrire di	to offer (to)
ordinare di	to order (to)
parlare di	to speak (of)
pensare di	to think (of)
permettere di	to permit (to)
pregare di	to pray (to)
ricordare di	to remember (to)
ripetere di	to repeat (to)
rispondere di	to respond (to)
sognare di	to dream (of)
sperare di	to hope (to)

*Ho voglia **di** mangiare un gelato subito.*	I'm in the mood to eat an ice cream.
*Ho paura **di** essere in ritardo.*	I am afraid of being late.

177

*Cristina sogna **di** sposarsi.*	Christina dreams of getting married.
*Natalia ha bisogno **di** studiare.*	Natalia needs to study.

A Is for Apple

Finally, you learn some verbs in Table 13.11 that take the preposition *a* before an infinitive. Pay attention to how the preposition in the English changes from one verb to the next. You may "help *to* protect someone," but you "succeed *at* your job." (This flexibility that prepositions have is what makes them as annoying as fruit flies.)

Table 13.11 Verbs Taking a Before an Infinitive

Italian	English
aiutare a	to help (to)
andare a	to go (to)
cominciare a	to begin (to)
correre a	to run (to)
entrare a	to enter (into)
essere pronto a	to be ready (to)
imparare a	to learn (to)
invitare a	to invite (to)
passare a	to pass (to)
portare a	to bring (to)
riuscire a	to succeed (at)
stare a	to be/stay (at)
stare attento a	to be careful (to)
tornare a	to return (to)
uscire a	to go out/exit (to)
venire a	to come (to)

Watch how some of these verbs work in the following sentences:

Comincio a capire.	I am beginning to understand.
Impariamo a parlare l'italiano.	We are learning to speak Italian.
Vengo a trovarti.	I am coming to see you.

Learning by Example

Complete the sentences using the subjects in parentheses. Translate the sentences.

Example: (Io) _____ essere brava. (cercare di)

Answer: (Io) cerco di essere brava.

Translation: I try to be good.

1. (Voi) _____ studiare. (avere bisogno di)

2. (Tu) _____ parlare l'italiano. (imparare a)

3. (Cristoforo) _____ lavorare mentre studia. (continuare a)

4. (Noi) _____ dormire presto. (andare a)

5. (Io) _____ fumare le sigarette. (smettere di)

6. (Loro) _____ mangiare alle 8:00. (finire di)

A Review of the Irregular Verbs

You've studied verbs until you think you'll go nuts trying to understand the different conjugations, stems, tenses, and persons. Don't try to rush through any of it. You'll learn Italian with perseverance and patience. It might be a good idea to look over the first two parts of this book to pause and reflect on what you have learned. In the meantime, Table 13.12 offers a quick review of some of the more important verbs you learned in this chapter.

Table 13.12 Irregular Verbs

Italian	English	Conjugation—Present Indicative
andare	to go	vado, vai, va, andiamo, andate, vanno
avere	to have	ho, hai, ha, abbiamo, avete, hanno
dovere	to must/have to	devo, devi, deve, dobbiamo, dovete, devono
essere	to be	sono, sei, è, siamo, siete, sono
fare	to do/make	faccio, fai, fa, facciamo, fate, fanno
potere	to be able to/can	posso, puoi, può, possiamo, potete, possono
stare	to be/to stay	sto, stai, sta, stiamo, state, stanno
volere	to want	voglio, vuoi, vuole, vogliamo, volete, vogliono

Practice with a friend and see if you have these verbs memorized. At first, you'll probably fumble a bit, but after a while, they'll begin to come naturally. It's like doing scales on a musical instrument. Once you can play them three times in a row with no mistakes, you've pretty much got them down pat.

Practice Makes Perfetto II

Conjugate and insert the correct verb where appropriate in each of the sentences below. Conjugate as appropriate and note that not all verbs will be used.

avere bisogno di	finire di
amare	fare
chiedere di	volere
aiutare a	credere di

1. Io _____ mangiare la pasta.

2. Enrico _____ fare la valigia.

3. Sandra e Filippo _____ preparare la cena.

4. Voi _____ essere poveri, ma siete ricchi—avete l'amore.

5. Tu _____ pulire la tua camera!

6. Posso _____ una domanda?

The Least You Need to Know

➤ Ordinal numbers specify the order of things, as in first, second, and third.

➤ If you can't remember the Italian word for an ordinal number, think about how you'd say it in English; chances are you'll remember the Italian word because the English is so similar.

➤ Some verbs require a preposition when followed by an infinitive.

Part 3
Fun and Games

The next few chapters are all about fun and give you the vocabulary you need to talk about just about anything—your horoscope, the weather, movies, art, and music.

You've learned how to count, an essential skill when it comes to money. Now it's time to go out and spend some of those hard earned lire, which make you feel like a rich person. After the exchange, you're practically a millionaire!

It may feel like monopoly money, but it's real and how you spend it is all up to you. Want to buy something really special to wear to dinner? How about purchasing some genuine gabardine you can then have made into anything you want? Are you a music buff? Check out the latest sounds and bring home some music as a souvenir. An art lover? Discuss Tintoretto when you're in Venice and Michelangelo while you're in Florence, or go to Rome and see them all.

Let's not forget food. You'll learn how to shop for your dinner, make a simple soup using an Italian recipe from the Tuscan countryside, and order a bottle of wine from a restaurant.

If you're still at home, keep finding ways to practice your Italian. The more you can make language a daily part of your life, the more it will seep into your subconscious. Before you know it, you'll be blurting out "Ciao!" everywhere you go.

Incidentally, you'll be seeing less and less of the pronunciation in these chapters. I can't hold your hand every time you want to say something, now can I?

Chapter 14

Rain or Shine

In This Chapter

➤ The weather and the verb *fare*

➤ Days of the week and months of the year

➤ Vocabulary for all seasons

➤ Keeping a date

➤ What's your sign: the zodiac in Italian

You're ready to go. Forget jet lag; you took your Melatonin on the plane, your body's clock is totally in synch with Italian time, and now you're raring to go out and see the sights. You walk downstairs and the *portiere* gives you a big smile and says, *"Fa bello oggi,"* and you agree: The *temperatura* is a perfect 24° and the sky is blue. So, come on; let's talk about the weather.

It's 20 Degrees Celsius and Getting Hotter

You already learned a lot of weather expressions when you studied idioms in Chapter 5. The verb *fare* (to do/make) is necessary to talk about the weather, but you'll see the *ci + essere* combination here too, as in *C'è il sole.* (It's sunny.) Some of the information in Table 14.1 might be review, and some is new.

Table 14.1   Weather Expressions

Italian	English
Che tempo fa?	What's the weather?
C'è il sole.	It's sunny.
C'è nebbia.	It's foggy.
C'è un temperale.	There is a storm.
C'è vento.	It's windy.
Fa trenta gradi.	It's 30° (Celsius).
È nuvoloso.	It's cloudy.
È umido.	It's humid.
È bello.	It's beautiful.
È brutto.	It's bad.
Fa caldo.	It's hot.
Fa freddo.	It's cold.
Fa fresco.	It's cool.
Grandina.	It's hailing.
Nevica.	It's snowing.
Piove.	It's raining.
Quanto fa oggi?	What is the temperature today?
Fa ___ gradi.	It is ___ degrees.

As a Rule

The verbs *piovere* (to rain), *nevicare* (to snow), and *tuonare* (to thunder) are only used in the third person singular.

Piove.	It's raining.
Nevica.	It's snowing.
Tuona.	It's thundering.

Weather or Not

There's a lot more out there than rain, sun, and snow. How about snowflakes? Rainbows? Sunsets and sunrises? If someone says it's raining cats and dogs, you know they mean it's raining very hard. Some of the words and phrases in Table 14.2 will help take your conversation about the weather to a more poetic level.

Table 14.2 Cats and Dogs

Italian	English
affosa	overcast
l'alba	sunrise
l'arcobaleno	rainbow
l'aria	air
l'atmosfera	the atmosphere
la brina	frost
il clima	climate
Fa un tempo da cani.	It's nasty. ("It's dog's weather.")
Fa un tempo da lupi.	It's nasty. ("It's wolf's weather.")
il fango	mud
fare palle di neve	to make snowballs
lanciare palle di neve	to throw snowballs
il fiocco di neve	snow flake
il fulmine	lightning bolt

continues

Table 14.2 Continued

Italian	English
il lampo	lightning bolt
il ghiaccio	ice
grado centigrado	Celsius
l'inquinamento	pollution
la neve	snow
la nuvola	cloud
nuvoloso	cloudy
l'ozono	ozone
pioggia	rain
piovoso	rainy
secco	dry
sereno	calm
lo smog	smog
il tramonto	sunset
tropicale	tropical
umido	humid
la valanga	avalanche

What's Hot and What's Not

To talk about the temperature, you use the verb *fare* in the third person as you do with the weather.

If someone asks, "Quanto fa oggi?" you may find yourself initially confused. What they're really asking is "How many degrees (*gradi*) are there today?" The word *gradi* is implied.

If it's 20 degrees Celsius, you reply, "Fa venti gradi." (It's twenty degrees.)

If it's ten below, you say, "Fa dieci sotto zero."

As a Rule

In Italy, as in all of Europe, the metric system is used to determine the temperature. To convert Centigrade to Fahrenheit, multiply the Centigrade temperature by 1.8 and add 32.

To convert Fahrenheit to Centigrade, subtract 32 from the Fahrenheit temperature and multiply the remaining number by .5.

Here are some basic temperature reference points:

Freezing: 32°F = 0°C

Room Temperature: 68°F = 20°C

Body Temperature: 98.6°F = 37°C

Boiling: 212°F = 100°C

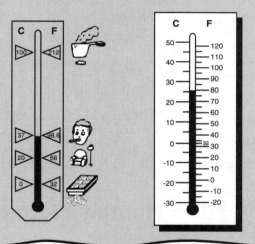

What Day Is It?

You're having so much fun that you've lost track of the days. Monday, Tuesday…it's all the same. Just don't get too carried away; you don't want to miss your plane home.

There are few accents in Italian. The days of the week, however, excepting the weekend, all end with -*ì*. When pronouncing days of the week, which are outlined in Table 14.3, always emphasize the last syllable. One trick for remembering them is to note the corresponding planet each day represents. For example, *lunedì* corresponds with *la luna*, as in "moon day." Italians have adopted the English way of expressing the end of the week by using our word "weekend," but you might also hear *il fine della settimana* expressed as well.

Table 14.3 Days of the Week

Day of the Week		Italian	Pronunciation
Monday	"moon day"	lunedì	*loo-neh-dee*
Tuesday	"Mars day"	martedì	*mahR-teh-dee*
Wednesday	"Mercury day"	mercoledì	*mehR-koh-leh-dee*
Thursday	"Jupiter day"	giovedì	*joh-veh-dee*
Friday	"Venus day"	venerdì	*ven-ehR-dee*
Saturday	"Saturn day"	sabato	*sah-bah-toh*
Sunday	"God's day"	domenica	*doh-meh-nee-kah*
The weekend	"weekend"	il fine settimana	*eel fee-neh seh-tee-mah-nah*

Attenzione!
Days of the week in Italian are not capitalized unless they begin sentences.

There is no equivalent to the preposition *on* before the names of days:

Arriviamo lunedì.	We are arriving (on) Monday.
Giuseppe arriva sabato.	Giuseppe is arriving (on) Saturday.

You use the definite article in front of a day to describe something you always do:

Andiamo in chiesa la domenica.	We go to church on Sundays.
Faccio yoga il mercoledì.	I do yoga on Wednesdays.

Did You Know?
April showers bring May flowers. Italians have a similar saying, "Aprile, ogni goccia un bacile." (April, every drop a kiss.)

Monthly Matters

If you've lost track of the months while you're away, you've been gone for too long. Go home! If, on the other hand, you're planning your next trip, or you want to tell someone when your birthday is, knowing the month is important. Find that special date in Table 14.4.

Table 14.4 I Mesi (The Months)

Month	Mese	Pronunciation
January	gennaio	*geh-nah-yoh*
February	febbraio	*fehb-Rah-yoh*
March	marzo	*mahR-zoh*

Month	Mese	Pronunciation
April	aprile	*ah-pRee-leh*
May	maggio	*mah-joh*
June	giugno	*joo-nyoh*
July	luglio	*loo-lyoh*
August	agosto	*ah-goh-stoh*
September	settembre	*seh-tem-bReh*
October	ottobre	*oh-toh-bReh*
November	novembre	*noh-vem-bReh*
December	dicembre	*dee-chem-bReh*

One of the most beautiful words in any language is the word *vacation*. But what are you going to do when you're on your holiday? Table 14.5 and the sample sentences that follow contain a few expressions and some vocabulary related to trip-taking that will help you express some of the events of your fabulous Italian vacation.

Table 14.5 Expressions of Leisure

Italian	English
al mare	to the seashore
all'estero	abroad
essere in ferie	to be on vacation
essere in vacanza	to be on vacation
fare il campeggio	to go camping
fare una vacanza	to take a vacation
fare un viaggio	to take a trip
fare una crociera	to take a cruise
festeggiare	to party/celebrate
il ferragosto	August 15th
il giro	tour
in campagna	to the country
in montagna	to the mountains
la vacanza	vacation

Andiamo al mare quest'estate.	We are going to the seashore this summer.
Siamo in vacanza il mese d'agosto.	We are on vacation for the month of August.
Facciamo il campeggio in montagna.	We are camping in the mountains.

To express *in* a certain month, the Italians use either the preposition *in* or *a*.

Il mio compleanno è a giugno.	My birthday is in June.
Fa ancora freddo a marzo.	It's still cold in March.

Like the days of the week, the months are not capitalized in Italian. As you learned in the last chapter, dates in Italian require cardinal numbers and not ordinal numbers. The month always comes after the day, when written as well as when abbreviated. This is not difficult to realize when you're talking about 25/12 (December 25), but with some dates it can get tricky. For instance, if you wrote 4/5, in Italy it is read as the fourth of May. If you meant the fifth of April, you were off by a month! It's crucial that you remember to reverse the two numbers when dealing with any kinds of documents, such as a car lease or apartment contract.

In Italian, you must always put the definite article in front of the day after which comes the month.

Il 25 giugno	June 25th
Il tre ottobre	October 3rd

As a Rule

The definite article goes in front of the cardinal number when telling the date, as in *il sette luglio* (July 7th).

The exception here is the first day of the month, which is indicated with the ordinal number *primo* (first), as in *il primo giugno* (June 1st).

See if you can answer the following questions. They are asked using the informal form of the verb, but you will answer using the first person:

1. Quando è il tuo compleanno?	When is your birthday?
2. Quando vai in vacanza?	When are you going on vacation?
3. Quando è l'anniversario dei tuoi?	When is your (parents') anniversary?

How Often?

Some things occur once in a lifetime, whereas others, gratefully, reoccur, such as your birthday or getting your daily newspaper. The terms in Table 14.6 may come in handy.

Table 14.6   When?

English	Italian	Pronunciation
annual	annuale	*ah-noo-ah-leh*
biannual	bienuale	*bee-eh-nwah-leh*
bimonthly	bimestrale	*bee-meh-stRah-leh*
biweekly	bisettimanale	*bee-seh-tee-mah-nah-leh*
centennial	centenario	*chen-teh-nah-Ree-yoh*
daily	quotidiano	*kwoh-tee-dee-ah-noh*
monthly	mensile	*men-see-leh*
quarterly	trimestrale	*tRee-me-stRah-leh*
weekly	settimanale	*seh-tee-mah-nah-leh*

What Century?

The history of Italy spans long before the birth of Christ and the beginning of the Christian calendar, and therefore, determining when something occurred is more complicated than it is in North America.

To express centuries up to the year 1000, as in the third century—which in English is a bit tricky because it really means the century before (200–299)—you use cardinal numbers plus the words *dopo Cristo* (literally meaning, "after Christ"). In Italian, it looks like this: *trecento dopo Cristo* (300 D.C.). Italian uses A.D. (as in English) to indicate a date after the birth of Christ.

30 D.C.—Cristo morì.	30 A.D., Christ died.
79 D.C.—Il Vesuvio distrusse Pompei.	79 A.D., Vesuvius destroys Pompei.

To express centuries after the year 1000, as in the 16th century (1500–1599), you again use cardinal numbers but you omit the first thousand and say, "the five hundred," as in *il cinque cento* (1500). There is no need to say that this occurred after the birth of Christ. The apostrophe before the number indicates that it is after the year 1000.

Did You Know?
Many *monumenti* (monuments) in Italy are written with the dates expressed in Roman numerals. Often, you will see A.D. (*anno domini*) written after a date, meaning "in the year of the Lord." This is used in English as well.

'100—*La Crociata*.   12th century—the Crusades.

'300—*Il Rinascimento*.   14th century—the Renaissance.

To express time before the birth of Christ, as in 400 B.C., you still use cardinal numbers and the words *avanti Cristo* (literally, "before Christ").

753 A.C.—*La fondazione di Roma*.   753 B.C., the foundation of Rome.

63 A.C.—*Cicerone, oratore*.   63 B.C., Cicero, orator.

Dating Dilemmas

Determine how to say the following *feste* (holidays) or important dates in Italian:

1. Natale

2. Capodanno

3. Il tuo compleanno

4. L'anniversario dei tuoi genitori

Did You Know?
If you've ordered *pizza quattro stagioni*, you've actually eaten "four seasons pizza."

The Four Seasons

Ah! What's nicer than springtime in *Toscana* or a beautiful summer day lounging on the beaches of *Sardegna*? Before you start daydreaming about the seasons in which you'd like to travel, first you need to learn how to say them in Italian, as shown in Table 14.7.

Table 14.7 The Seasons

Italian	Pronunciation	English
la primavera	*lah pRee-mah-veh-Rah*	spring
l'estate	*leh-stah-teh*	summer
l'autunno	*low-too-noh*	autumn
l'inverno	*leen-veR-noh*	fall
la stagione	*lah stah-joh-neh*	season

To express the notion of being *in* a certain season, the Italians use either the preposition *in* or *di*:

Andiamo in Italia d'inverno.	We are going to Italy in the winter.
In primavera fa bello.	It's beautiful in the spring.

Quale Festa?

Practice your comprehension skills using all the materials you have learned so far. Read the following paragraph and translate:

Le feste in Italia sono molto importanti. Ferragosto è un'opportunità per rilassarsi. Quando c'è una festa, tutte le famiglie mangiano, bevono e festeggiano insieme.* Alcune famiglie vanno al mare, altre vanno in montagna, mentre altre vanno all'estero. Naturalmente sperano di divertirsi.

*together

Do You Have an Appointment?

In Italian, you make an *appuntamento* to meet people, whether it's social or business related. This year, last year, the day before, the day after—all of these times have significance. Was it good for you, too?

Table 14.8 It's a Date

English	Italian	Pronunciation
afternoon	il pomeriggio	*eel poh-meh-Ree-joh*
ago	fa	*fah*
an appointment	un appuntamento	*oon ah-poon-tah-men-toh*
calendar	il calendario	*eel kah-len-dah-Ree-yoh*
date	la data	*lah dah-tah*
day	il giorno	*eel joR-noh*
evening	la sera	*lah seh-Rah*
holiday	la festa	*lah fes-tah*
in two weeks	fra due settimane	*frah doo-yeh seh-tee-mah-neh*
in five years	fra cinque anni	*frah cheen-kweh ah-nee*

continues

Table 14.8 Continued

English	Italian	Pronunciation
last	scorso	*skoR-soh*
last night	ieri notte	*ee-eh-Ree noh-teh*
month	il mese	*eel meh-zeh*
morning	la mattina	*lah mah-tee-nah*
next	prossimo	*pRoh-see-moh*
the day after tomorrow	dopodomani	*doh-poh doh-mah-nee*
the day before yesterday	l'altro ieri	*lahl-tRoh ee-yeh-Ree*
this evening*	stasera	*stah-seh-Rah*
this morning*	stamattina	*stah-mah-tee-nah*
today	oggi	*oh-jee*
tomorrow	domani	*doh-mah-nee*
vacation	la vacanza	*lah vah-kahn-zah*
year	l'anno	*lah-noh*
yesterday	ieri	*ee-eh-Ree*
yesterday evening	ieri sera	*ee-eh-Ree seh-Rah*

Note: The terms stamattina *and* stasera *are abbreviated from* questa mattina *and* questa sera.

The Dating Game

How do you express the following? Remember that adjectives must agree with the nouns they modify. Nouns must always reflect number.

Example: Last week   *Example:* 3 years ago

Answer: La settimana scorsa   *Answer:* Tre anni fa.

1. Last month   6. Next winter
2. Last year   7. Seven years ago
3. Next year   8. Last night
4. In ten years   9. Yesterday evening
5. Last spring   10. This morning

I Pianeti (The Planets)

It is said by some that if you reach for the stars, you might arrive at the moon. Not a bad place to be. But how would da Vinci or Galileo discuss such ethereal topics?

Table 14.9 Planets and Stars

English	Italian	English	Italian
Mercury	Mercurio	Pluto	Plutone
Venus	Venere	sun	il sole
Earth	Terra	moon	la luna
Mars	Marte	star/s	la stella/le stelle
Jupiter	Giove	universe	l'universo
Saturn	Saturno	galaxy	la galassia
Uranus	Urano	constellation	la costellazione
Neptune	Nettuno	the Milky Way	la Via Lattea

What's Your Sign?

If the weather isn't your thing, you can go to another plane and ask someone about their background—astrologically speaking. Find out if you are compatible by asking someone, *"Che segno sei?"* (What's your sign?)

Table 14.10 Astrological Signs

Simbolo	Segno	Elemento	Caratteristiche	Periodo	English
♈	ariete	fuoco	indipendente, aggressivo, impulsivo	21 marzo–19 aprile	Aries
♉	toro	terra	determinato, testardo, fedele, tollerante	20 aprile–20 maggio	Taurus
♊	gemelli	aria	intelligente, ambizioso, capriccioso	21 maggio–21 giugno	Gemini

continues

195

Table 14.10   Continued

Simbolo	Segno	Elemento	Caratteristiche	Periodo	English
♋	cancro	acqua	sensibile, simpatico, impressionabile	22 giugno–22 luglio	Cancer
♌	leone	fuoco	generoso, nobile, entusiasta	23 luglio–22 agosto	Leo
♍	vergine	terra	intellettuale, passivo, metodico	23 agosto–22 settembre	Virgo
♎	bilancia	aria	giusto, organizato, simpatico	23 settembre–23 ottobre	Libra
♏	scorpione	acqua	filosofo, fedele, dominante	24 ottobre–21 novembre	Scorpio
♐	sagittario	fuoco	pragmatico, maturo, creativo	22 novembre–21 dicembre	Sagittarius
♑	capricorno	terra	ambizioso, fedele, perseverante	22 dicembre–19 gennaio	Capricorn
♒	acquario	aria	generoso, idealistico, originale	20 gennaio–18 febbraio	Aquarius
♓	pesci	acqua	timido, simpatico, sensibile	19 febbraio–20 marzo	Pisces

Like a Fish to Water

Imagine you are reading the horoscopes for some very well-known *personaggi storici* (historical figures). With the names is a brief description of who they were and their key accomplishments. You might want to go back to Chapter 10 to review some adjectives to help you describe the different characteristics that make up each sign.

Are there some signs that stand out more than others? Did the individuals in Table 14.11 live up to their astrological inclinations?

Table 14.11 Historical Figures

Personaggio Storico	Descrizione	Data di Nascità	Segno Astrologico
Caterina de' Medici	(moglie di Enrico II è patrona delle arti)	13 aprile 1519	ariete
Leonardo da Vinci	(l'uomo del Rinasciamento) "Mona Lisa"	15 aprile 1452	ariete
Galileo (fisico)	"pendolo"	15 febbraio 1564	capricorno
Giuseppe Garibaldi	(l'unificazione d'Italia 1860)	4 luglio 1807	cancro
Niccolò Machiavelli	(politico) "Il Principe"	3 maggio 1469	toro
Michelangelo	(pittore/scultore/architetto) "La Cappella Sistina"	5 marzo 1475	pesci
Benito Mussolini	(dittatore; fascista)	28 luglio 1883	leone
Luigi Pirandello	(drammaturgo) "Sei Personaggi in Cerca d'Autore"	28 giugno 1867	cancro
Giacomo Puccini	(compositore) "La Boheme"	22 dicembre 1858	capricorno

The Least You Need to Know

➤ Use the third person of the verb *fare* ("fa") to express weather conditions and the temperature.

➤ To express the date, use the number of the day plus the month and the year.

➤ Use the words *dopo Cristo* to describe a historical event that occurred after the death of Christ but before the beginning of the second millennium and *avanti Cristo* to describe an event before the birth of Christ.

Did You Know?
The Medici family was enormously influential during the Renaissance. Having settled in Florence during the 12th century, its reign of power lasted well into the 17th century. These powerful merchants and bankers later developed strong ties to royalty, bringing two popes and two queens into power, including Caterina de' Medici (1519–1589), who became the wife of Henry II of France and was mother to Charles IX.

Bella!

I Can't Believe My Eyes!

You're in Rome, the eternal city. What to see first? Rome is such a big *città*, and there are so many places to go. You want to see *la Cappella Sistina*, and of course, there's *il Colosseo*, and *il Foro*. Your guidebook says that *la Villa Borghese* has just reopened after extensive renovations, and then, you want to take your picture with your hand in the *Bocca della Verità*, just like Audrey Hepburn did in that film you saw so long ago. There are so many things to do—but how? Read on; this chapter will give you the tools to set your own agenda.

Seeing Is Believing

A lifetime wouldn't be long enough to see all there is in *Italia*. The choices outlined in Table 15.1 are endless. Sometimes it can be a little overwhelming; each *città* has its own charm and specialties. Italy is a country filled with more art from more periods of history than just about any place in the world. Overload is possible, so take it slow and stick with your list of "must-sees," but allow yourself to *scoprire* (discover) something you hadn't anticipated. There's a mystery to Italy and the people who live there that plucks at the strings of every heart. And just as Rome wasn't built in a day, nor should it be seen in one.

Table 15.1   Where to Go and What to Do

Il Luogo	L'Attività	The Place	The Activity
l'acquario	vedere i pesci	the aquarium	see the fish
l'azienda vinicola	fare un "picnic"	the winery	have a picnic
il castello	fare le foto	the castle	take pictures
la cattedrale	vedere le vetrate colorati	the cathedral	see the stained-glass windows
la chiesa	vedere l'architettura, accendere una candela	the church	see the architecture, light a candle
il cinema	vedere un film	the cinema	see a film
il circo	vedere lo spettacolo	the circus	see the show
la discoteca	danzare/ballare	the discotheque	dance
l'enoteca	assaggiare il vino	the wine bar	taste the wine
la fontana	fare il bagno	the fountain	go swimming (just kidding!)
il giardino	sentire i profumi dei fiori	the garden	smell the flowers
il mercato	guardare la merce	the market	look at the merchandise
il museo	vedere le opere d'arte	the museum	see the art
l'opera	ascoltare la musica	the opera	listen to the music
il parco	fare una passaggiata	the park	take a stroll
la piazza	guardare la gente	the public square	look at the people

Il Luogo	L'Attività	The Place	The Activity
lo stadio	guardare una partita	the stadium	watch a game
il teatro	vedere una commedia	the theatre	see a play
lo zoo	guardare gli animali	the zoo	look at the animals

I See You See Me

When you see something wonderful, you say, "It is a feast for the eyes." If this is the case, Italy will feed you until you are absolutely gorged. There are two verbs used to describe the act of using your eyes: *vedere* (to see) and *guardare* (to look at/watch). Both are regular verbs, described in Tables 15.2 and 15.3, that follow the rules of their particular verb family.

Table 15.2   Vedere (to See)

Singular	Plural
io vedo (I see)	*noi vediamo* (we see)
tu vedi (you see)	*voi vedete* (you see)
lui/lei/Lei vede (he/she sees; You see)	*loro vedono* (they see)

Table 15.3   Guardare (to Look at)

Singular	Plural
io guardo (I look)	*noi guardiamo* (we look)
tu guardi (you look)	*voi guardate* (you look)
lui/lei/Lei guarda (he/she looks; You look)	*loro guardano* (they look)

Let's Go Visit, Find, See, Look At...

In the last chapter, you learned about verbs that require a preposition when followed by an infinitive. There are so many ways of saying something that it would take a lifetime to learn all of them. If you find something that works for you, stick with it. But if you want to expand a little, or simply understand what someone else is saying to you, the terms in

Table 15.4 will give you the edge you need. Many of these have already been presented and should sound familiar.

Table 15.4 Verbs for Sightseeing

Verbi and Espressioni	Verbs and Expressions
andare*	to go
andare a trovare	to go visit
andare a vedere	to go (to) see
fare* un giro	to take a spin/to go around
fare una passeggiata	to take a walk
fare vedere	to show (literally, "to make see")
girare	to go around
passeggiare	to stroll
passare a	to pass by
restare	to rest/stay
rimanere*	to remain
ritornare	to return
uscire*	to go out/exit
venire*	to come
visitare	to visit

Note: These verbs are irregular.

Perché non facciamo un giro della città?	Why don't we take a spin around the city?
Vado a vedere lo spettacolo a teatro.	I am going to see the show at the theatre.
Fammi vedere le tue foto!	Show me your photos!
Passa a trovarmi!	Pass by to visit me!

More Irregular Verbs

There are a few more verbs you should learn before you strap on a camera and put on those walking shoes. You've already learned a few of the irregular verbs. By now, you should have the subject pronouns memorized, especially the *Lei* form (you, polite). When reading the following verbs, read aloud to yourself: see it, say it, write it, and you'll have it.

Uscire (to Go Out/Exit)

You're ready to paint the town red and you're dying to go out. *Uscire*, which is fully conjugated in Table 15.5, will get you out of your hotel room and into the heart of the action. By the way, you'll see this verb used above any exit: *Uscita*.

As a Rule

Remember your pronunciation rules: *sco* is pronounced like *sk* in the word "sky." *Sci* is pronounced like *sh* in the word "she."

Table 15.5   Uscire (to Go Out/Exit)

Singular	Plural
io esco (I go out)	*noi usciamo* (we go out)
tu esci (you go out)	*voi uscite* (you go out)
lui/lei/Lei esce (he/she goes out; You go out)	*loro escono* (they go out)

Stefano esce ogni sera.	Stefano goes out every evening.
(Noi) Usciamo alle tre e un quarto.	We're going out at 3:15.

Venire (to Come)

Eventually, you have to come down to earth. The irregular verb *venire*, shown in Table 15.6, may help you find your way.

Table 15.6   Venire (to Come)

Singular	Plural
io vengo (I come)	*noi veniamo* (we come)
tu vieni (you come)	*voi venite* (you come)
lui/lei/Lei viene (he/she comes; You come)	*loro vengono* (they come)

Vieni con noi?	Are you coming with us?
Sì, vengo fra cinque minuti.	Yes, I'm coming in five minutes.

Rimanere (to Remain)

Like the verb *venire*, *rimanere* has similar endings (but not exactly the same). Keep in mind as you look at Table 15.7 that it is an *-ere* verb.

Table 15.7   Rimanere (to Remain)

Singular	Plural
io rimango (I remain)	*noi rimaniamo* (we remain)
tu rimani (you remain)	*voi rimanete* (you remain)
lui/lei/Lei rimane (he/she remains; You remain)	*loro rimangono* (they remain)

Rimango in albergo stasera.	I'm remaining in the hotel this evening.
Rimangono in campagna.	They are remaining in the country.

Your Turn

How are you doing with the verbs? Check out your progress by filling in the appropriate conjugations for the following verbs. Keep in mind that some may be irregular.

1. Trovare: to find/visit

   Singular   *Plural*

   io _____   noi _____

   tu _____   voi _____

   lui/lei/Lei _____   loro _____

2. Andare: to go (irregular)

   Singular   *Plural*

   io _____   noi _____

tu _____ voi _____

lui/lei/Lei _____ loro _____

3. Passare: to pass

Singular *Plural*

io _____ noi _____

tu _____ voi _____

lui/lei/Lei _____ loro _____

4. Fare: to do/make (irregular)

Singular *Plural*

io _____ noi _____

tu _____ voi _____

lui/lei/Lei _____ loro _____

5. Ritornare: to return

Singular *Plural*

io _____ noi _____

tu _____ voi _____

lui/lei/Lei _____ loro _____

Practice Makes Perfetto

Use your new skills to describe where you, or someone else, might be going. It's much easier than you will probably make it, so remember to keep it simple. There are no tricks here.

Example: (noi) *andare* a vedere/il Colosseo

Answer: Andiamo a vedere il Colosseo.

Did You Know?
Vatican City is considered its own, separate entity even though it lies in the heart of Rome. The Vatican has its own postal system and citizens carry separate passports.

1. (Pasquale) *fare* una passeggiata/in piazza

2. (Io) *andare* a vedere/un film

3. (Noi) *andare* ad ascoltare/l'opera

4. (Giuseppe and Maria) *fare*/una foto del castello

5. (Voi) *fare* un giro/in macchina

6. (Tu) *prendere*/l'autobus

Dire (to Say/Tell)

You've already seen the phrase, *Come si dice...in italiano*? in Chapter 3 and know it means, "How do you say...in Italian?"

Dire is another irregular verb that can come in handy. Note in Table 15.8 that the stem changes to *dic* in all persons except the second plural.

Table 15.8   Dire (to Say)

Singular	Plural
io dico (I say)	*noi diciamo* (we say)
tu dici (you say)	*voi dite* (you say)
lui/lei/Lei dice (he/she says; You say)	*loro dicono* (they say)

Dico di restare qui.	I say to stay here.
Che cosa dici?	What do you say?
Che ne dici?	What do you think? (idiomatic)

The Power of Suggestion

The gorgeous Italian you sat next to on the plane phoned you at your *albergo* and you've made a date to go sightseeing. You've got your itinerary all set for the day, and you know exactly which sights you want to see. You're a take-charge kind of person, but you don't want to dominate a situation. Rather than tell someone what you want to do, there's a more subtle way; you can suggest by dropping a couple of hints, such as "Why don't we take a trip?" or "Why don't you go jump in a lake?"

The easiest way to make a suggestion is to ask this simple question using the words *perché non...* (why not...):

Perché non + the verb in the second person plural form (noi)?

For example:

Perché non andiamo in Italia?	Why don't we go to Italy?
Perché non partiamo domani?	Why don't we leave tomorrow?

If you want to make someone think they actually have a choice in the matter, you can ask them what they think of the idea.

Che ne pensi/pensa?	What do you think (of it)?
Che ne dici/dice?	What do you say (about it)?

To suggest the English "Let's...," use the second person plural form (noi):

Andiamo in Italia.	Let's go to Italy.
Andiamo a mangiare.	Let's go eat.
Mangiamo.	Let's eat.
Partiamo stasera.	Let's leave this evening.

Other Useful Phrases Expressing Suggestion

Without getting into a lot of grammatical gobbly-gook, you can shape all of the phrases in Table 15.9 to whatever you want to suggest doing. The second column shows you what verb is used. Just add the infinitive of any verb you want to use after each expression.

Table 15.9   Getting Suggestive

Frase	Verbo	Phrase
Ti va di...? (tu)	Le va di...? (Lei)	*andare* Are you in the mood to...? (idiomatic; literally, does it go with you?)
Ti interessa...? (tu)	Le interessa...? (Lei)	*interessare** Are you interested in...? (literally, is it interesting to you?)
Ti piacerebbe...? (tu)	Le piacerebbe...? (Lei)	*piacere** (conditional) Would you like...? (literally, would it please you to...?)

Note: Both these verbs require the use of object pronouns. You'll learn more about these in Chapter 16. The verb piacere *is covered in Chapter 17 and the conditional tense will be covered in Chapter 23. Stay tuned.*

Notice how the examples you just saw in Table 15.9 apply in the following suggestions:

Ti va di andare al cinema?	Are you in the mood to go to the movies?
Ti interessa fare un viaggio in Italia?	Does a trip to Italy interest you?

If you really want to be passive-aggressive, add the word *non* in front of your sentence.

Non ti piacerebbe...vedere il castello?	Wouldn't you like to see the castle?
Non Le piacerebbe...guardare la partita?	Wouldn't you like to see the game?

Yes or No

Petulant teenagers give abrupt yes or no answers to questions. Most of the rest of us say, "Yes, but..." or "No, because..." If you want to elaborate on your answer, here's what you have to do: Change the pronoun *Le* or *ti* from the question to *mi* in your answer. Check out the examples in Table 15.10.

Table 15.10   Elaborating

Affirmativo	Negativo
Sì, mi va di andare al cinema.	No, non mi va di andare al cinema.
Sì, mi interessa fare un viaggio in Italia.	No, non mi interessa fare un viaggio in Italia.
Sì, mi piacerebbe vedere il castello.	No, non mi piacerebbe vedere il castello.

Of course, you can always state what you want by using the verb *volere*, using both the present indicative and the conditional tenses.:

Vuoi/vorresti andare in Italia?	Do you want (would you like) to go to Italy?
Sì, voglio/vorrei andare in Italia.	Yes, I want (would like) to go to Italy.

Expressing Your Honest Opinion

Chapter 9 offered you a sampling of nationalities along with adjectives you can use to describe the world you live in. A few exclamations, as shown in Table 15.11, might come in handy when you're truly moved or utterly disgusted.

Table 15.11 Exclamations

Aggettivo	La Pronuncia	Meaning
Che bello!	*kay beh-loh*	How beautiful!
Che brutto!	*kay bRoo-toh*	How ugly!
Che disastro!	*kay dee-zahz-tRoh*	What a disaster!
Eccellente!	*eh-cheh-len-teh*	Excellent!
Fantastico!	*fahn-tahs-tee-koh*	Fantastic!
Favoloso!	*fah-voh-loh-zoh*	Fabulous!
Magnifico!	*mahg-nee-fee-koh*	Magnificent!
Meraviglioso!	*meh-Rah-vee-lyoh-zoh*	Marvelous!
Orribile!	*oh-Ree-bee-leh*	Horrible!
Ridicolo!	*Ree-dee-koh-loh*	Ridiculous!
Stupendo!	*stoo-pen-doh*	Stupendous!
Terribile!	*teh-Ree-bee-leh*	Terrible!

The Big, Blue Marble

The world isn't flat (and you know your belly isn't either after eating all that pasta). Table 15.12 tells you how to say the different countries and continents in Italian.

As a Rule

All geographical terms, including continents, countries, cities, states, towns, islands, and so on, require the definite article:

Quest'estate, noi visitiamo l'Italia, la Spagna, la Francia, e la Grecia.

The only exception occurs when the term comes after the preposition *in* and *is* feminine, singular:

Noi andiamo in Italia, in Albania, e in Africa.

All countries, regions, states, towns, and so on are capitalized.

Nationalities are not capitalized.

Table 15.12   Countries

Paese	Nationalità	Country	Nationality
Il Belgio	belga	Belgium	Belgian
La Cina	cinese	China	Chinese
La Città del Vaticano	Vaticana	Vatican City	—
La Corea del sud/ del nord	coreano/a	North/South Korea	Korean
La Danimara	danese	Denmark	Danish
L'Egitto	egiziano/a	Egypt	Egyptian
L'Etiopa	etiope	Ethiopia	Ethiopian
La Finlandia	finlandese	Finland	Finnish
La Francia	francese	France	French
La Germania	tedesco/a	Germany	German
Il Giappone	giapponese	Japan	Japanese
La Grecia	greco/a	Greece	Greek
L'Inghilterra/La Gran Bretagna	inglese	England/Great Britain	English

Paese	Nationalità	Country	Nationality
L'Irlanda	irlandese	Ireland	Irish
L'Israele	israeliano/a	Israel	Israeli
L'Italia	italiano/a	Italy	Italian
Il Libano	libanese	Lebanon	Lebanese
La Libia	libico/a	Libya	Libyan
Il Messico	messicano/a	Mexico	Mexican
La Norvegia	norvegese	Norway	Norwegian
La Polonia	polacco/a	Poland	Polish
Il Portogallo	portoghese	Portugal	Portuguese
La Spagna	spagnolo/a	Spain	Spanish
Gli Stati Uniti d'America	americano/a	U.S.A.	American
Il Sud Africa	sud africano/a	South Africa	South African
La Svezia	svedese	Sweden	Swedish
La Svizzera	svizzero/a	Switzerland	Swiss
La Turchia	turco/a	Turkey	Turkish

The following countries all have the same name (or almost exactly) in Italian. Be sure to pronounce them using Italian phonetics:

Afghanistan	Bolivia	Ghana	Iraq
Albania	Botswana	Guinea	Kenya
Algeria	Bulgaria	Grenada	Kuwait
Angola	Canada	Guatemala	Liberia
Antigua	Colombia	Haiti	Liechtenstein
Argentina	Congo	Honduras	Madagascar
Australia	Costa Rica	India	Malesia
Austria	Cuba	Indonesia	Nepal
Belize	El Salvador	Iran	Nicaragua

211

Pakistan	Scandinavia	Sudan	Vietnam
Panama	Senegal	Taiwan	Zaire
Romania	Sierra Leone	Tunisia	Zambia
Russia	Siria	Uruguay	Zimbabwe
San Marino*	Somalia	Venezuela	

San Marino has the honor of being the longest surviving republic in the world.

Attenzione!
Don't forget to use the preposition *in* before the name of a country and the preposition *a* before the name of a city.

It's also easy to figure out which continents are which:

L'Africa	L'Asia
L'America del Nord	L'Australia
L'America del Sud	L'Europa
L'Antartide	

Once Upon a Time

Did You Know?
In 1492, Cristofero Colombo bumped into North America, thinking he had found a route to India. The Florentine Amerigo Vespucci (1454–1512), a skilled navigator and cartographer commissioned by King Ferdinand of Spain to do some fact checking, realized that Columbus had not reached India but in fact had "discovered" a new continent, thus named, "The New World." The letters that Vespucci wrote describing what he had seen became very popular, leading the new continent to be named after him and not Columbus.

The peninsula now known as Italy was once a cluster of city states. Powerful families struggled to maintain power, often trying to outdo one another by supporting the creation of many of today's landmarks in the form of magnificent cathedrals, fortresses, and works of art. Today, Italy is unified; however, each of its 20 regions still has its own flavor and is run by locally elected officials. Refer to Appendix D to see these regions.

The regions are

L'Abruzzo	Il Molise
La Basilicata	Il Piemonte
La Calabria	La Puglia
La Campania	La Sardegna
L'Emilia-Romagna	La Sicilia
Il Friuli-Venezia Giulia	La Toscana
Il Lazio	Il Trentino-Alto Adige
La Liguria	L'Umbria

La Lombardia	La Val D'Aosta
Le Marche	Il Veneto

A Refresher

In Chapter 9, you learned all about the verb *essere* and showing possession with *di*. It might be a good idea to go back and review this chapter. Remember that nationalities are considered to be adjectives, often must change to reflect gender, and always must reflect number. Tell someone you are from the following countries and what your nationality is. To say you have a particular origin, you must use *Sono d'origine* + the nationality in its feminine form:

> **Did You Know?**
> In the region of Trentino-Alto Adige just outside the Austrian border, the majority of people speak German, which is taught in schools and is one of two official languages (Italian being the other).

Sono d'origine italiana.	I'm of Italian origins.
Sono d'origine tedesca.	I'm of German origins.
Sono d'origine irlandese.	I'm of Irish origins.

Example: Italia

Answer: Sono italiano. Sono d'origine italiana.

1. Gli Stati Uniti d'America
2. La Francia
3. La Spagna
4. La Grecia
5. L'Irlandia

The Least You Need to Know

➤ To suggest an activity ("Let's…"), use the first person plural (*noi*) form of the verb.

➤ Express your opinion using simple exclamations. (*Fantastico! Orribile!*)

➤ Countries and other geographical locations always take the definite article and are capitalized. Nationalities are not capitalized and are considered adjectives and must agree in gender and number.

➤ The verbs *venire* (to come), *uscire* (to go out), *rimanere* (to remain), and *dire* (to say/tell) are all irregular.

Shop 'Til You Drop

The word *Italian* is synonymous with style, and whether you bring back handblown Murano wine glasses, a Gucci or Fendi bag, an Armani suit, or an expressive cameo made in Florence, Italy is a place you definitely want to shop.

Stores Galore

Anything in a foreign country, no matter how simple, can have a special kind of appeal. As you meander, you find some licorice lozenges in a small *tabaccheria*, a silk scarf gently blowing in the wind at the *mercato*, a small hand-painted porcelain doll in a *vetrina*. The appeal might go back to when we were hunters and gatherers, but there's no question about it: Shopping for new delights is one of life's greatest pleasures. Table 16.1 will help you find your way to the stores that carry the merchandise you're looking for.

Table 16.1   Stores

Il Negozio	La Merce	The Store	The Merchandise
la bottega	tutto	shop	everything
il negozio di scarpe	le scarpe	shoe store	shoes
la cartoleria	la carta, le cartoline, giochi, sigarette	stationery store	paper, postcards, toys, cigarettes
la farmacia	le medicine	pharmacy	medicine
la fioraio	i fiori, le piante	florist	flowers, plants
la gioielleria	i gioielli	jewelry store	jewelry
il giornalaio	i giornali, le riviste, le cartoline	newspaper stand	newspapers, magazines, postcards
il grande magazzino	i gioielli, i giochi, i mobili, i profumi, i vestiti	department store	jewelry, toys, furnishings, perfumes, clothing
la libreria	i libri	bookstore	books
il mercato	tutto	market	everything
il negozio d'abiglia-mento	l'abbligliamento/ i vestiti	clothing store	clothing
il negozio d'arredamento	i mobili	furniture store	furniture
la pasticceria	le paste, le torte, i biscotti	pastry shop	pastries, cakes, cookies
la pelletteria	le giacche, le borse, le valigie	leather store	jackets, purses, luggage
la profumeria	i profumi, i cosmetici	cosmetics shop	perfumes, cosmetics
la tabaccheria	le sigarette, i sigari, i fiammifferi	tobacco shop	cigarettes, cigars, matches

If you can't remember the name of the kind of store you want to find, simply ask for *il negozio di* (the store of) and the object you're looking for.

Diamonds Are a Girl's Best Friend

It could be a sapphire ring, a gold watch, or a silver chain that trips your trigger. What-ever your fancy, Italy has a long tradition of fine gold- and silversmiths, and some of the finest jewelry in the world can be found there. Table 16.2 shows you how to ask for it.

Table 16.2   Jewelry

Oggetto	La Pronuncia	Meaning
l'acquamarina	*lah-kwah-mah-Ree-nah*	aquamarine
l'ametista	*lah-meh-tees-tah*	amethyst
l'anello	*lah-neh-loh*	ring
l'argento	*laR-jen-toh*	silver
il braccialetto	*eel bRah-chah-leh-toh*	bracelet
il cammeo	*eel kah-meh-oh*	cameo
la catena	*lah kah-teh-nah*	chain
il ciondolo	*eel chon-doh-loh*	pendant
il diamante	*eel dee-ah-mahn-teh*	diamond
la giada	*lah jah-dah*	jade
i gioielli	*ee joh-yeh-lee*	jewelry
la madreperla	*lah mah-dReh-peR-lah*	mother-of-pearl
l'onice	*loh-nee-cheh*	onyx
gli orecchini	*ylee oh-Reh-kee-nee*	earrings
l'oro	*loh-Roh*	gold
le perle	*leh peR-leh*	pearls
la pietra preziosa	*lah pee-eh-tRah pRe-zee-oh-zah*	precious stone
il rubino	*eel Roo-bee-noh*	ruby
il topazio	*eel toh-pah-zee-oh*	topaz
il turchese	*eel tooR-keh-zeh*	turquoise
lo zaffiro	*loh zah-fee-Roh*	sapphire

It's in the Jeans

Italians are born knowing how to dress. It's a gene that has been passed from generation to generation (well, almost!), but that doesn't mean that those less fortunate shouldn't have the opportunity *essere di moda* (to be in fashion). Table 16.3 gives you some helpful words to get you started.

Table 16.3 L'Abbigliamento (Clothing)

Clothing Item	Italian	Pronunciation
article	l'articolo	*lahR-tee-koh-loh*
bathing suit	il costume di bagno	*eel kohs-too-meh dee bahn-yoh*
belt	la cintura	*lah cheen-too-Rah*
boots	gli stivali	*ylee stee-vah-lee*
bra	il reggiseno	*eel Reh-jee-seh-noh*
coat	il cappotto	*eel kah-poh-toh*
dress	l'abito	*lah-bee-toh*
jeans	i jeans	*ee jeens*
gloves	i guanti	*ee gwahn-tee*
hat	il cappello	*eel kah-peh-loh*
jacket	la giacca	*lah jah-kah*
lining	la fodera	*lah foh-deh-Rah*
model	il modello	*eel moh-deh-loh*
overcoat	il cappotto	*eel kah-poh-toh*
pajamas	il pigiama	*eel pee-jah-mah*
pants	i pantaloni	*ee pahn-tah-loh-nee*
pullover	il golf	*eel golf*
raincoat	l'impermeabile	*leem-peR-mee-ah-bee-leh*
robe	l'accappatoio	*lah-kah-pah-toh-yoh*
sandals	i sandali	*ee sahn-dah-lee*
scarf	la sciarpa	*lah shaR-pah*
shoes	le scarpe	*leh skaR-peh*
skirt	la gonna	*lah goh-nah*
slippers	le pantofole	*leh pahn-toh-foh-leh*
sneakers	le scarpe da tennis	*leh skaR-peh dah teh-nees*
suit	il vestito	*eel veh-stee-toh*
sweat suit	la tuta da ginnastica	*lah too-tah dah jee-nah-stee-kah*
sweater	la maglia	*lah mah-lyah*
pullover T-shirt	la maglietta	*lah mah-lyeh-tah*

Clothing Item	Italian	Pronunciation
umbrella	l'ombrello	*lohm-bReh-loh*
underwear	gli slip	*ylee sleep*
	le mutandine (f.)	*leh moo-tahn-dee-neh*
	le mutande (m.)	*leh moo-tahn-deh*

The helpful expressions in Table 16.4 will make your shopping even more enjoyable. Remember to modify adjectives when appropriate.

As a Rule

The verb used to try something on is the regular verb *portare*, meaning, to carry or to wear.

Singular	Plural
io porto (I wear)	*noi portiamo* (we wear)
tu porti (you wear)	*voi portate* (you wear)
lui/lei/Lei porta (he/she wears; You wear)	*loro portano* (they wear)

Gina porta la taglia quarantaquattro.   Gina wears size 44.

Porto il numero 39 di scarpe.   I wear a size 39 shoe.

Table 16.4 Phrases for Shopping 'Til You Drop

Espressione	Expression
Che taglia porta?	What size do you wear?
Porto la misura…	I wear size…
Che numero di scarpe?	What size shoe?
Porto il numero…	I wear a size…
caro/economico	expensive/cheap
classico	classical
il commesso/la commessa	sales clerk
essere di moda	to be in fashion
fare compere/fare le spese	to go shopping*
fare un affare	to make a deal

continues

Table 16.4 Continued

Espressione	Expression
fuori stagione	out of season
la misura	the size
il numero di scarpe	shoe size
il prezzo	the price
la svendita	sale
la taglia: piccola, media, grande	size: small, medium, large
la vetrina	shop window
lo sconto	discount
Questo è troppo…	This is too…
corto	short
lungo	long
stretto	tight
grande	big

*la spesa *refers to food shopping;* le spese *refers to shopping, as in "shop 'til you drop."*

One Size Does Not Fit All

Attenzione!
Keep in mind that there are two ways to express size in Italian: *la misura* (as in "measure") or *la taglia* (as in "cut").

Sizes vary, so make sure to try on something before you spend any of your hard-earned money. You should also make sure you have a basic knowledge of size lingo. Let's begin with the basics:

Piccolo	small
Medio	medium
Grande	large

Table 16.5 will help you determine what *taglia* you are.

Table 16.5 Conversion Tables for Clothing Sizes

Italian	American	Italian	American
Women – Clothing		*Men – Clothing*	
38	4	44	34
40	6	46	36
42	8	48	38
44	10	50	40
46	12	52	42
48	14	54	44
50	16	56	46
52	18	58	48
		60	50
Women – Shoes		*Men – Shoes*	
35	5	38	5
36	6	39	6
37	7	40	7
38	8	41	8
39	9	42	9
40	10	43	10
41	11	44	11
		45	12
		46	13

As a Rule

To convert centimeters into inches, divide by .39.

To convert inches into centimeters, multiply by 2.54.

By the way, in Italy, don't expect to be waited on hand and foot when you go into a store. Salespeople will be attentive to your needs and always treat you with respect, but don't expect a new best friend. In smaller, neighborhood stores, the atmosphere is more friendly. Incidentally, the first thing an Italian notices is your feet; shoes indicate a great deal about where a person is from. Americans tend to wear sneakers—a dead giveaway.

I Colori

As you saw in Chapter 10, colors are adjectives and must agree with the noun they are describing, whether masculine or feminine, singular or plural. Review Chapter 10 to see how adjectives work.

To describe any color as light, simply add the adjective *chiaro* to the color to form a compound adjective, as in *rosso chiaro* (light red).

What's What
Go back to Chapter 10 and study the demonstrative adjectives/ pronouns for this and that (*questo/quello*). It'll be helpful when you want to say, "I'll take this" (or that, these, and those).

To describe any color as dark, add the word *scuro*, as in *rosa scuro* (dark pink). (*Rosa* is masculine unless you are talking about *la rosa*, the flower.)

Smooth as Silk

Italian cloth is as fine as fine can be. Silks, cashmeres, wools, cottons, chiffons…rather than spend a fortune on designer clothing, you might consider buying the fabrics and having a *sarto* (tailor) sew something custom-made to your style and fit. Table 16.6 will give you the ability to describe just what you want.

Table 16.6 Fabrics

Fabric	Italian	La Pronuncia
acetate	l'acetato	*lah-cheh-tah-toh*
cashmere	il cachemire	*eel kah-sheh-mee-Reh*
chiffon	lo chiffon	*loh shee-fohn*
cotton	il cotone	*eel koh-toh-neh*
flannel	la flanella	*lah flah-neh-lah*
gabardine	il gabardine	*eel gah-baR-dee-neh*
knit	la maglia	*lah mahl-yah*
lace	il merletto, il pizzo	*eel meR-leh-toh, eel pee-tsoh*
leather	il cuoio, la pelle	*eel kwo-yoh, lah peh-leh*

Fabric	Italian	La Pronuncia
linen	il lino	*eel lee-noh*
rayon	la viscosa	*lah vee-skoh-sah*
silk	la seta	*lah seh-tah*
suede	il camoscio	*eel kah-moh-shoh*
taffeta	il taffetà	*eel tah-feh-tah*
velvet	il velluto	*eel veh-loo-toh*
wool	la lana	*lah lah-nah*

Objection!

Back in Chapter 7, you learned about different kinds of objects. In this chapter, you've learned all about shopping and how to ask for what you want. Since we're on the subject of precious objects, this is as good an opportunity as any to introduce the subject of object pronouns. As a reminder: An object pronoun replaces the object in a sentence. Because there is no neuter in Italian, all object pronouns must reflect gender and plurality.

Direct and indirect object pronouns replace objects in order to avoid repetition, as in the following examples:

What's What
The **direct object** asks what or whom the subject is acting upon.

The **indirect object** asks for what or whom the subject is acting.

> *Direct Object:*
>
> Kim   eats   an apple.   She eats it.
>
> subject–verb–direct object

Ask yourself the question: What does Kim eat? An apple/it.

> *Indirect Object:*
>
> Fulvio offers   Grazia   a glass of wine.   He offers her a glass of wine.
>
> Subject–verb–indirect object–direct object

To whom does Fulvio offer the glass of wine? Grazia/her.

The Object Pronouns

Table 16.7 outlines the object pronouns in Italian.

Table 16.7   Direct and Indirect Object Pronouns

Direct Object Pronouns		Indirect Object Pronouns	
Pronoun	Meaning	Pronoun	Meaning
Singular			
mi	me	mi	to/for me
ti	you (familiar)	ti	to/for you
lo	him/it	gli	to/for him
la	her/it	le	to/for her
La	You (formal)	Le	to/for You (formal)
Plural			
ci	us	ci	to/for us
vi	you (plural)	vi	to/for you (plural)
li	them (m. and f.)	loro	to/for them
le	them (f.)	(gli)	to/for them (spoken language)*

Note: Gli is commonly used to replace loro primarily in the spoken language. Although it is not considered correct grammar, it is widely used.

What sometimes makes the object pronouns confusing for the non-native speaker is their similarity to each other as well as to the articles and other words in Italian. This is why it is so important to listen to the context of a sentence. One trick is to remember that direct and indirect object pronouns are all the same *except in the third person singular and plural forms*.

The following rules will make it easier to know when you should use object pronouns:

1. All object pronouns agree in gender and number with the nouns they replace:

   Direct Object Pronoun:

   ***Lo** vedo ogni giorno. (mio fratello)*   I see **him** every day. (my brother)

   ***Li** vedo ogni settimana. (miei fratelli)*   I see **them** every week. (my brothers)

   Indirect Object Pronoun:

Gli offro una mano. (a mio fratello)	I offer **him** a hand. (to my brother)
Ti mando un bacio. (a te)	I send **you** a kiss. (to you)

2. Both direct and indirect object pronouns are usually placed immediately before a conjugated verb:

Leopoldo compra il giornale e lo legge a Mario.	Leopoldo buys the newspaper and reads it **to Mario.**
Giulia gli legge una storia.	Giulia reads (**to him**) a story.
Quando vedo i biscotti, li mangio.	When I see cookies, I eat **them.**
Ti voglio accompagnare al cinema.	I want to accompany **you** to the movies.

3. When the infinitive depends on the verbs *dovere* (to have to), *volere* (to want), or *potere* (to be able to), the object pronoun can also be attached to the infinitive:

Voglio accompagnarti al cinema.	I want to accompany you to the movies.

When to Use the Direct Object Pronoun

"My friend Sofia asked me to buy a present for Sofia." Huh? You would never say something so awkward and confusing, right? You'd probably say something like "My friend Sofia asked me to buy a present for *her*." As you can see, direct object pronouns can make your life a lot easier when you use them to replace the direct object in a sentence:

Bacio il ragazzo. I kiss the boy. → *Lo bacio.* I kiss him.

Leggo i libri. I read the books. → *Li leggo.* I read them.

Easy, right? You don't even have to add a preposition (as in "to look *at*" or "to wait *for*"). In Italian, verbs such as *guardare* (to look at), *cercare* (to look for), and *aspettare* (to wait for) have a built-in preposition:

Cerco il teatro. I am searching for the theatre. → *Lo cerco.* I am searching for it.

Guardo la ragazza. I am looking at the girl. → *La guardo.* I am looking at her.

Aspetto le mie amiche. I am waiting for my friends. → *Le aspetto.* I am waiting for them.

When to Use Indirect Object Pronouns

"Congratulations! If you have the winning number, a check for 1 billion dollars will be sent *to you*!" Lucky you—you're the indirect object of the billion-dollar sweepstakes. As you can see here, the indirect object of a sentence tells to whom or for whom the action is done. They are often replaced by indirect object pronouns:

Sandro writes to his parents. → Sandro writes to *them*.

I send a letter to Donna. → I send a letter to *her*.

Herb gives Sandy a book every Christmas. → Herb gives (to) *her* a book every Christmas.

Some verbs that take a direct object in English take an indirect object in Italian:

Telefono a Dario stasera. (I am calling Dario this evening) → *Gli telefono stasera.* (I am calling him this evening.)

The following are verbs that may use an indirect object or its pronoun in Italian:

chiedere	insegnare	portare	rispondere
dare	leggere	preparare	scrivere
dire	mandare	presentare	telefonare
domandare	mostrare	prestare	vendere
donare	offrire	regalare	
fare sapere*	parlare	rendere	

*to let know

Mark offre un bicchiere di vino *a Marina*. → *Le* offre un bicchiere di vino.

Elisabetta scrive *a Gabriele* una lettera. → *Gli* scrive una lettera.

Joel telefona *ai suoi amici*. → Joel telefona *loro*.

Faccio sapere *a Silvia* la data. → *Le* faccio sapere la data.

The indirect object pronoun follows a command when you use the *tu, noi,* or *voi* form of the verb. In certain cases, such as with the verbs *dare* and *fare*, you add an extra "m" when using the familiar form (*tu*):

Compra il libro *per Giovanni*! Compra**gli** il libro!

Da un bacio *a me*! Dam**mi** un bacio!

Fa un favore *a me*! Fam**mi** un favore!

Offrite *a Carlo e Gianni* i soldi. Date **loro** i soldi *or* Date**gli** i soldi.

The indirect object pronoun precedes a negative command except with *loro*:

Non comprare il libro *per Giovanni*! Non **gli** comprare il libro!

Non dare un bacio *a Giorgio*! Non **gli** dare un bacio!

Non date una risposta *a Carlo e Carlotto*. Non date **loro** la risposta.

Attenzione!
The indirect object pronoun *loro* is often replaced with *gli* in modern Italian:

Giovanni telefona loro or *Giovanni gli telefona.*

Chiede loro di uscire or *Gli chiede di uscire.*

In an imperative, *gli* is attached to the end of the verb:

Telefona loro! Telefonagli!

Who's Who

Replace the direct object in each sentence with the direct object pronoun. Translate the sentences.

Example: Leggo il giornale.

Answer: Lo leggo.

1. Mangiamo la pasta.

2. Dante e Boccaccio vogliono mangiare la pizza.

3. Prendo l'autobus.

4. Mario scrive un libro.

5. Vedo Giuseppe e Mario.

6. Giovanni bacia la sua ragazza.

7. Comprate una macchina.

8. Lei capisce la materia?

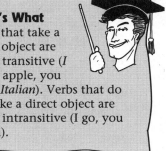

What's What
Verbs that take a direct object are called transitive (*I eat* an apple, you speak *Italian*). Verbs that do not take a direct object are called intransitive (I go, you return).

As a Rule

All object pronouns agree in gender and number with the nouns they replace.

In a negative sentence, the word *non* always comes before the object pronoun:

Non la voglio.	I don't want it.
Non lo bacio.	I don't kiss him.

When object pronouns are attached to the end of an infinitive, the final *-e* is omitted:

Devo darti un bacio.	I must give you a kiss.
Vorrei invitarli alla festa.	I'd like to invite them to the party.

Singular object pronouns can be contracted in front of verbs that begin with a vowel:

Li aspetto da un'ora. (i miei amici)	I've been waiting for them for an hour. (my friends)
L'ascolto. (la musica)	I'm listening to it. (the music)

Who's Who II

Just replace the indirect object with its appropriate pronoun. You get to double object pronouns later.

Example: Beatrice scrive una lettera a Dante.

Answer: Beatrice gli scrive una lettera.

1. Desideriamo parlare a voi.

2. Maria e Giorgio danno un regalo a te.

3. Carlo telefona a Anna.

4. Lo studente fa una domanda al professore.

5. Offro un caffè a Caterina.

6. Danno una cioccolatina ai bambini.

7. Offro una birra a Dominick.

8. Augurano (to wish well) una buona notte a noi.

Who's Who—Final Round

Determine which kind of object pronoun should go in the following sentences where it is *italicized*.

1. Guardate *il film.*

2. Regalo a Lorenzo *un mazzo di fiori.* (bunch of flowers)

3. Vede *la bella ragazza*?

4. Regalo *a Lorenzo* un mazzo di fiori.

5. Danno i libri *ai bambini.*

6. Conosco *il signor Spadone* molto bene.

7. Danno *i libri* ai bambini.

8. Accettiamo *l'invito* volentieri (gladly).

> **Did You Know?**
> In Chapter 8 you learned about the expression *Ecco!* To say, "Here it is!" or "Here they are!" simply attach the appropriate object pronoun to *ecco,* as in "*Eccolo!*" (*Ecco il libro*) or "*Eccoli!*" (*Ecco i pantaloni*).

The Least You Need to Know

➤ Italians use the metric system, so make sure you know what your proper *misura* is.

➤ The verb *portare* is used to express "to wear."

➤ A direct object pronoun answers the question, "*What* or *whom* is the subject acting upon?"

➤ An indirect object pronoun answers the question, "*To what* or *to whom* is the subject acting for?"

➤ Use object pronouns to replace the object in a sentence. Object pronouns are usually placed before the conjugated verb, except in an affirmative command when they come after.

Chapter 17

Bread, Wine, and Chocolate

In This Chapter

➤ Different foods and where to buy them

➤ Using *ne* and how to express quantity

➤ The verb *piacere* (to be pleasing to)

➤ Reflexive verbs

Food. Italy. The two are inseparable. It's *gastronomia* brought to the level of art. What makes Italy so special is the *attenzione* it gives to the everyday elements of successful living; therefore, it's natural that food plays an important *ruolo* in the Italian lifestyle. Italians know that fine cuisine is a precursor to living *la dolce vita*.

Many different kinds of stores cater to food, although a great deal of crossover occurs. Make sure you eat something before reading this chapter or you won't be able to *concentrare* on anything. *Buon Appetito!*

Verbs That Go with Any Meal

You remember the verbs *mangiare* (to eat) and *bere* (to drink). Because eating is a favorite pastime of most self-respecting Italians, you're going to need a few more verbs to get through any decent meal: *assaggiare* (to taste), *cenare* (to dine), *comprare* (to buy), *cucinare* (to cook), *pranzare* (to eat lunch), and *preparare* (to prepare). Don't forget the irregular verb *fare* used in the idiomatic expressions *fare la colazione* (to eat breakfast) and *fare la spesa* (to go food shopping) or the verb *andare* (to go).

To Market, to Market

Did You Know?

The word *carnevale* (meaning "carnival" and source of the English word carnal) is no different from the infamous Mardi Gras (in Italian, *Martedì Grasso*—literally, "fat Tuesday"). This was the last night one was permitted to eat meat before beginning the period of Lent. In Italy, two of the most famous *carnevale* celebrations take place in Venice and Viareggio where tens of thousands show up to participate in the festivities and watch the parades.

An increasingly popular way for families to vacation abroad and a new form of *turismo* in general is called *agriturismo*. Guests stay in the countryside on working farms or vineyards, which are usually equipped with all the amenities while maintaining a rustic, natural feel. It's a great way to experience Italy as it has existed for centuries, close to the land, but near enough to the sites that you can have the best of both worlds.

Imagine you are staying with your family in a rented villa for a month. The tomatoes are ripe and the basil is fresh. The words in Table 17.1 should help you on your next shopping expedition. To tell someone you would like to take something, use the verb *prendere* (to take), as in *Prendo un chilo di pomodori.* (I'll take a kilo of tomatoes.)

Table 17.1   Dal Negozio

Negozio	Il Prodotto	Store	The Product
il bar	il caffè, i liquori, gli alcolici	bar	coffee, liquors, alcohol
la drogheria	tutto	neighborhood store	everything
l'enoteca	il vino	wine bar	wine

Negozio	Il Prodotto	Store	The Product
il fornaio	il pane	bakery	bread
la gelateria	gelato	ice cream shop	ice cream
la latteria	il formaggio, il latte, le uova	dairy store	cheese, milk, eggs
la macelleria	la carne, il pollo	butcher	meat, chicken
il mercato	tutto	the market	everything
il negozio di frutta e verdura	la frutta, le verdure, i legumi	fruit and vegetable store	fruit, vegetables, legumes
la pasticceria	la pasta, i dolci	pastry shop	pastry, sweets
la pescheria	il pesce	fish store	fish
il supermercato	tutto	supermarket	everything
il vinaio	il vino	wine store	wine

Dal Negozio di Frutta e Verdura

In Italy, you should never pick out your own fruits or vegetables unless you're told that it's okay to do so. The *commessa* will carefully choose the best, ripest, most succulent produce you could want. Table 17.2 gives you the terms so you know what you're getting.

Table 17.2   Le Verdure

Vegetable	La Verdura	La Pronuncia
anise	l'anice	*lah-nee-cheh*
artichoke	il carciofo	*eel kahR-choh-foh*
asparagus	gli asparagi	*ylee ah-spah-Rah-ghee*
beans	i fagioli	*ee fah-joh-lee*
cabbage	il cavolo	*eel kah-voh-loh*
carrots	le carote	*leh kah-Roh-teh*
cauliflower	il cavolofiore	*eel kah-vohl-oh-fee-yoh-Reh*
corn	il mais	*eel mayss*
eggplant	la melanzana	*lah meh-lan-zah-neh*

continues

233

Table 17.2 Continued

Vegetable	La Verdura	La Pronuncia
garlic	l'aglio	*lah-lyoh*
green beans	i fagiolini	*ee fah-joh-lee-nee*
legumes	i legumi	*ee leh-goo-mee*
lettuce	la lattuga	*lah lah-too-gah*
mushrooms	i funghi	*ee foon-ghee*
olive	l'oliva	*loh-lee-vah*
onion	la cipolla	*lah chee-poh-lah*
peas	i piselli	*ee pee-zeh-lee*
potato	le patate	*leh pah-tah-teh*
rice	il riso	*eel Ree-zoh*
spinach	gli spinaci	*ylee spee-nah-chee*
tomatoes	i pomodori	*ee poh-moh-doh-Ree*
vegetables	la verdura	*lah veR-doo-Rah*
zucchini	gli zucchini	*ylee zoo-kee-nee*

In Rome, a favorite summertime treat is *il cocomero* (watermelon), which can be bought at brightly lit *bancarelle* (stands). It's as red as a pepper, so sweet your teeth will hurt, and as wet as a waterfall (get extra napkins). Somehow, the Italians manage to eat the thickly sliced pieces with a plastic spoon (good luck!). Another piece of fruit advice: Italians rarely bite into an apple. They peel it with a knife in one long curl and then slice it into bite-sized chunks, which they then share with everyone at the table. Table 17.3 provides a list of the Italian for various fruits and nuts.

Table 17.3 La Frutta e La Nocciola

English	Italian	La Pronuncia
almond	la mandorla	*lah mahn-doR-lah*
apple	la mela	*lah meh-lah*
apricot	l'albicocca	*lal-bee-koh-kah*
banana	la banana	*lah bah-nah-nah*
cherries	le ciliegie	*leh chee-lay-jay*

English	Italian	La Pronuncia
chestnut	la castagna	*lah kah-stahn-yah*
date	il dattero	*eel dah-teh-Roh*
figs	i fichi	*ee fee-kee*
fruit	la frutta	*lah fRoo-tah*
grapefruit	il pompelmo	*eel pom-pehl-moh*
grapes	l'uva	*loo-vah*
hazelnut	la nocciola	*lah noh-choh-lah*
lemon	il limone	*eel lee-moh-neh*
melon	il melone	*eel meh-loh-neh*
orange	l'arancia	*lah-Rahn-chah*
peach	la pesca	*lah pes-kah*
pear	la pera	*lah peh-Rah*
persimmon	il caco	*eel kah-koh*
pineapple	l'ananas	*lah-nah-nas*
pistachio nut	il pistacchio	*eel pee-stah-kee-yoh*
pomegranate	la melagrana	*lah meh-lah-gRah-nah*
raisin	l'uva sultanina	*loo-vah sool-tah-mee-nah*
walnut	la noce	*lah noh-cheh*

As a Rule

Fruit is usually feminine, with a few exceptions. The fruit tree is masculine. *La mela* (the apple) becomes *il melo* (the apple tree), *l'arancia* becomes *l'arancio* (the orange tree), *la pera* becomes *il pero* (the pear tree), and so on.

La frutta refers to all fruit in general. *Un frutto* refers to a piece of fruit, as in, *Vuole un frutto?* (Do you want a piece of fruit?)

In Macelleria

One of the reasons Italian food is so scrumptious is its freshness. Most perishables are bought and cooked immediately. Meats and poultry are best when selected by your local *macellaio* (butcher) who will ask you how you would like it cut. In Italy, if you order a *fettina*, you are given a thinly sliced portion of meat, usually either *di manzo* (beef) or *di vitello* (veal). *Il filetto* is thicker. You find the terms for different types of meat in Table 17.4.

Table 17.4 La Macelleria

Meat and Poultry	La Carne e Pollame	La Pronuncia
beef	il manzo	*eel mahn-zoh*
chicken	il pollo	*eel poh-loh*
cold cuts	i salumi	*ee sah-loo-mee*
cutlet	la costoletta	*lah koh-stoh-leh-tah*
duck	l'anatra	*lah-nah-tRah*
fillet	il filetto	*eel fee-leh-toh*
ham	il prosciutto	*eel pRoh-shoo-toh*
lamb	l'agnello	*lah-nyeh-loh*
liver	il fegato	*eel feh-gah-toh*
meat	la carne	*lah kaR-neh*
meatballs	le polpette	*leh pol-peh-teh*
pork	il maiale	*eel mah-yah-leh*
pork chop	la braciola	*lah bRah-choh-lah*
quail	la quaglia	*lah kwah-lyah*
rabbit	il coniglio	*eel koh-nee-lyoh*
salami	il salame	*eel sah-lah-meh*
sausage	la salsiccia	*lah sal-see-chah*
steak	la bistecca	*lah bee-steh-kah*
turkey	il tacchino	*eel tah-kee-noh*
veal	il vitello	*eel vee-teh-loh*
veal shank	l'osso buco	*loh-soh boo-koh*

La Latteria

The only real *parmigiano* comes from Parma, Italy. There are so many wonderful cheeses in Italy that you'll want to grab some *pane, una bottiglia di vino*, and good company, go sit in a *parco*, and watch people. The simple pleasures are often the best. Most *supermercati* carry a wide selection of cheeses and wines, but you can check your neighborhood stores as well for the products described in Table 17.5.

Table 17.5   La Latteria

Dairy Product	Il Prodotto	La Pronuncia
butter	il burro	*eel boo-Roh*
cheese	il formaggio	*eel foR-mah-joh*
cream	la panna	*lah pah-nah*
eggs	le uova	*leh woh-vah*
milk	il latte	*eel lah-teh*
yogurt	lo yogurt	*loh yoh-guRt*

They've Got a Million of 'Em

The Italians have a saying for everything. Some idiomatic expressions related to food and eating are outlined in Table 17.6.

Table 17.6   Expressions to Dine By

L'Espressione	Expression	Direct Translation
Bere come una spugna.	To drink like a fish.	To drink like a sponge.
Rimanere sullo stomaco.	Not to agree with.	To remain in the stomach.
Di bocca buona.	A good eater.	A good mouth.
Una ciliegia tira l'altra.	One thing leads to the other.	One cherry pulls the other.
Non me ne importa un fico secco.	I don't give a damn.	I don't care one dry fig's worth.
Fare la frittata.	To make a mess of.	To make an omelette of things.

continues

Table 17.6   Continued

L'Espressione	Expression	Direct Translation
Fino al midollo.	To the bone.	To the marrow.
Liscio come l'olio.	Smooth as silk.	Smooth as oil.
Un osso duro.	A hard nut to crack.	A hard bone.
Dire pane al pane e vino al vino.	To call a spade a spade.	To call bread bread and wine wine.
Mangiare pane e cipolla.	To live on bread and water.	To eat bread and onion.
Togliersi il pane di bocca.	To give the shirt off your back.	To give bread from the mouth.
Di pasta buona.	Good natured.	Of good pasta.
Avere lo spirito di patata.	To have a poor sense of humor.	To have the spirit of a potato.
Essere un sacco di patate.	To be a klutz.	To be a sack of potatoes.
Fare polpette di…	To make mincemeat of…	To make meatballs of…
Rosso come un peperone.	Red as a beet.	Red as a pepper.

La Pescheria

Ahh, *i frutti di mare*! Go to any seaside village in Italy and you're guaranteed to eat some of the best seafood you've ever had. Table 17.7 gives you a little taste.

Table 17.7   La Pescheria

Fish and Seafood	I Pesci e Frutti di Mare	La Pronuncia
fish	il pesce	*eel peh-sheh*
squid	i calamari	*ee kah-lah-mah-Ree*
shrimp	i gamberetti	*ee gahm-beh-Reh-tee*
tuna	il tonno	*eel toh-noh*
trout	la trota	*lah tRoh-tah*
swordfish	la pesce spada	*lah peh-sheh spah-dah*
flounder	la passera	*lah pah-seh-Rah*
crab	il granchio	*eel gRan-kee-yoh*

Fish and Seafood	I Pesci e Frutti di Mare	La Pronuncia
halibut	l'halibut	*lah-lee-boot*
herring	l'aringa	*lah-Reen-gah*
lobster	l'aragosta	*lah-Rah-gohs-tah*
mussel	la cozza	*lah koh-tsah*
oyster	l'ostrica	*loh-stRee-kah*
salmon	il salmone	*eel sahl-moh-neh*
sardines	le sardine	*leh saR-dee-neh*
scallops	le cappesante	*leh kah-peh-sahn-teh*
cod	il merluzzo	*eel meR-loo-stoh*
sole	la sogliola	*lah soh-lyoh-lah*
anchovies	le acciughe	*leh ah-choo-gheh*
whities	i bianchetti	*ee bee-ahn-keh-tee*

Pasta Anyone?

A chapter about Italian cuisine that did not include the different kinds of pasta wouldn't be a chapter about food. In Italian, the same word for pasta is what is used for pastry. If you're in a *ristorante*, you won't have to distinguish; they'll know what you mean.

i rigatoni

le penne

i fusilli

le farfalle (bow ties)

i capellini
(angel hair—like the word, *i capelli*)

le linguine

i tortellini

i cannelloni

le orecchiette (ear-shaped)

gli gnocchi (potato dumplings)

le tagliatelle/le fettuccine
(*tagliare*/to cut; *fetta*/a slice)

i ravioli

This Drink's on Me

As is the Italian way, certain times befit certain beverages. *Il cappuccino* is generally consumed in the morning with a *cornetto* (similar to a croissant). *L'espresso* can be consumed any time of the day but is usually taken after meals (never *cappuccino*). To whet your appetite, you can have an *aperitivo*, and to help you digest, a *digestivo* or *amaro*. As an

239

afternoon pick-me-up, you can indulge in a *spremuta* (freshly squeezed juice). Table 17.8 lists different kinds of things you can drink. You should be able to pronounce these words without the guide—just sound them out like you see them.

Table 17.8   I Bibiti

Drinks	Le Bibite
beer	la birra
coffee	il caffè
freshly squeezed juice	la spremuta
freshly squeezed grapefruit	la spremuta di pompelmo
freshly squeezed orange	la spremuta d'arancia
fruit juice	il succo di frutta
hot chocolate	la cioccolata calda
iced tea	il tè freddo
lemon soda	la limonata
milk	il latte
mineral water	l'acqua minerale
sparkling mineral water	l'acqua minerale gassata/frizzante
non-carbonated mineral water	l'acqua minerale naturale
orange soda	l'aranciata
sparkling wine	lo spumante
tea	il tè
wine	il vino

Dappertutto (Everywhere)

Do you have a sweet tooth? Italians love their *caramelle*, and if you're a chocolate addict, you definitely want to check out Perugina's Baci (kisses), which come in a silver wrapper and always include a fortune. Unwrap them carefully! Table 17.9 lists a number of treats.

Table 17.9 For Your Sweet Tooth

The Candy	La Caramella
candy	la caramella
chocolate	la cioccolata
cough drop	una caramella per la tosse
gum	la gomma americana
licorice	la liquirizia
mint	la menta

It's the Quantity That Counts

Different measurements can lead to confusion. Table 17.10 will help make the metric system much easier to follow. These comparisons are approximate but close enough to get roughly the right amount.

Table 17.10 Measuring

Solid Measures		Liquid Measures	
U.S. System	Metrico	U.S. System	Metrico
1 oz.	28 grammi	1 oz.	30 millilitri
1/4 lb.	125 grammi ("un etto")*	16 oz. (1 pint)	475 millilitri
1/2 lb.	250 grammi	32 oz. (1 quart)	circa un litro
3/4 lb.	375 grammi	1 gallon	3.75 litri
1.1 lbs.	500 grammi		
2.2 lbs.	1 chilogrammo ("un chilo")		

Prices are often by the etto *(a hectogram).*

It might be just as easy to indicate a little of this, a little of that, and then say when enough is enough using the expression, *Basta così.* Table 17.11 gives you some helpful ways of expressing quantity.

Table 17.11 Quantities

Amount	La Quantità	Amount	La Quantità
a bag of	un saccetto di	a jar of	un vasetto di
a bottle of	una bottiglia di	a pack of	un pacchetto di
a box of	una scatola di	a piece of	un pezzo di
a can of	una lattina	a slice of	una fetta di
a container of	un barattolo di	a little of	un po' d400f
a dozen (literally, "few of")	una decina di	a quarter pound (about)	un etto di
a drop of	una goccia di	a lot of	un sacco di
a kilo of	un chilo di	enough	basta/sufficiente
		too much	troppo

You Asked for It; You Got It!

You're out on your own, hoping to prepare a wonderful meal. You're planning to start with a light *brodo di tortellini* (tortellini in broth), then you want to roast a *pollo*, and for dessert, some *fragole fresche*, covered with *panna*. Here are some useful verbs and expressions you can use to make your meal:

Vorrei del/della/etc...	I would like some...
Per favore mi dia...	Please give me... (interrogative)
Mi può dare...	Can you give me...
Prendo...	I'll take...
Ne voglio...	I want some...
Dove posso trovare (la tua richiesta)?	Where can I find (your request)?
Quanto viene?	How much does it come to?
Quanto ne serve per (numero delle persone)?	How much is necessary for (number of people)?
Quanto pesa?	How much does it weigh?
Avete un sacchetto di plastica?	Do you have a plastic bag?

The Use of the Pronoun Ne

You've learned how to indicate some or any by using the preposition *di* plus *l'articolo*. The pronoun *ne* comes in handy when used to ask for a "part of" or "some of" a greater quantity. It can be translated to mean *some, any, of it, of them, some of them, any of it*, and *any of them*.

Like most object pronouns, *ne* usually precedes the verb but follows if the verb is in the infinitive form. It often replaces phrases beginning with *di*.

Imagine that someone asks you whether you want some ice cream. You're stuffed to the gills and if you eat one more bite, you think you'll explode, so you say, "Nah, I don't want any, thanks." It is assumed that *any* refers to the ice cream:

Question: *Vuole della frutta?*	Would you like some fruit?
Answer: *No grazie, non ne voglio.*	No, thanks; I don't want any.
Non voglio mangiarne.	No, thanks; I don't want to eat any.
Question: *Quante sorelle hai?*	How many sisters do you have?
Answer: *Ne ho due.*	I have two of them.

Answer the following questions using the pronoun *ne* using the affirmative and the negative:

Example: Vuoi una sigaretta?

Answer: Sì, ne voglio.

No, non ne voglio.

1. Hanno dei soldi? (Do they have money?)

2. Avete pane? (Do you have bread?)

3. Bevi vino? (Do you drink wine?)

4. C'è del gelato? (Is there any ice cream?)

5. Vogliamo comprare del formaggio? (Do we want to buy cheese?)

What's Your Pleasure? The Verb Piacere

There is no verb "to like" in Italian. You must always use *piacere* (to be pleasing to). Instead of "I like chocolate," you say, "Chocolate is pleasing to me." In Italian, the subject of the verb (that which determines which person should be used), is the thing that is liked. This is quite different from English. You'll need to know your indirect object pronouns to use this verb.

Piacere is rarely used in anything other than the third person singular and plural. See how it conjugates:

Piacere (to be pleasing)

Piace (it is pleasing)   *Piacciono* (they are pleasing)

Some rules about the verb *piacere*:

1. *Piacere* is almost always used in third person (singular and plural) and is always used with an indirect object or indirect object pronoun (to me, to you, to him/her, to us, to them):

Mi piace la cioccolata.	I like chocolate; chocolate is pleasing to me.
Mi piacciono i cioccolatini.	I like chocolates; chocolates are pleasing to me.
A loro piace la cioccolata.	They like chocolate; chocolate is pleasing to them.
Vi piace la cioccolata?	Do you like chocolate; is chocolate pleasing to you?
Sì, ci piace la cioccolata.	Yes, we like chocolate; chocolate is pleasing to us.

2. If the subject is an infinitive, it is considered singular:

Ti piace mangiare la cioccolata?	Do you like to eat chocolate; is eating chocolate pleasing to you?
Sì, mi piace mangiare la cioccolata.	Yes, I like to eat chocolate.

Attenzione!
Even when what is liked is an infinitive with a plural object, the verb *piacere* is used in the singular:

Ti piace mangiare i dolci? Does eating sweets please you?

Gli piace bere l'espresso e il cappuccino. Drinking espresso and cappuccino is pleasing to him.

3. If the subject of the verb *piacere* is a noun (and not a pronoun), you must use the preposition *a* (or *a* and *article*) before the noun:

A Marcello piace bere il vino.	Marcello likes to drink wine.
Ai bambini piace la cioccolata.	The children like chocolate.

4. The verb *dispiacere* means "to be sorry" (and not "to be displeasing") as well as "to mind." It is used exactly like the verb *piacere*:

Mi dispiace.	I'm sorry.
Le dispiace attendere un momento?	Do you mind holding for a moment?

What's What

The indirect object pronouns are used with the verb *piacere*, as in, *Gli piacciono i dolci* (sweets are pleasing to him).

Singular	Plural
mi (to/for me)	*ci* (to/for us)
ti (to/for you)	*vi* (to/for you)
gli/le/Le (to/for him/her/You)	*loro* (to/for them)

Using the Verb Piacere

Ask someone if he or she likes the following. Remember that the thing that is liked is the subject and the verb *piacere* must reflect number.

Example: Le _____ il vino bianco?

Answer: Le piace il vino bianco?

1. Ti _____ la frutta?

2. Signora, Le _____ il vino?

3. Vi _____ gli spaghetti?

4. Ti _____ cucinare?

5. Mamma, ti _____ le caramelle?

6. A loro _____ l'Italia?

Using the Verb Piacere II

Imagine you are asking your partner if they like something from the following list. Give both an affirmative and negative response.

Example: Ti piacciono i biscotti?

Answer: Sì, mi piacciono i biscotti.

No, non mi piacciono i biscotti.

1. i dolci
2. la pasta
3. gli spaghetti
4. le acciughe
5. i fichi
6. il fegato

245

A Special Treat

There's nothing like good old-fashioned cooking. Here's an opportunity to apply your new Italian skills with a special recipe. The following words will help your dish turn out *perfetto*:

aggiungere	to add
bollire	to boil
cuocere	to cook
girare	to mix
mettere	to put
versare	to pour

Minestra di Riso e Limone

Ingredienti:

8 tazze di brodo

1 tazza di riso Arborio

3 tuorli di uova

1/4 tazza formaggio Parmigiano-Reggiano, grattugiato

1 cucchiaino di scorza di limone grattugiata

1 cucchiaino di succo di limone

1. *Mettete il brodo in un tegame e portatelo al punto di ebollizione. Aggiungete il riso, coprite il tegame e fatelo cuocere 20 minuti.*

2. *Nel frattempo battete le uova, aggiungete il formaggio, il limone grattugiato e il succo di limone.*

3. *Quando il riso è cotto, versate le uova nella minestra, sbattendo in continuazione. Riscaldate la minestra e servitela subito.*

Per 4 persone.

You've Got Good Reflexes

Are you having fun yet? In Italian, when you enjoy yourself, get dressed, or comb your hair, you are using a reflexive verb. When you introduce yourself by saying, "Mi chiamo...," you are using the reflexive verb *chiamarsi*, meaning, "to call oneself."

Reflexive verbs are easily identified by the *-si* attached at the end of the infinitive. Conjugation of the reflexive verbs follows the same rules as any other Italian verb with one exception: Reflexive verbs require the use of *reflexive pronouns*. These pronouns show that the subject is performing an action upon itself. In other words, the subject and the reflexive pronoun both refer to the same persons or things, as in the phrases, "We enjoyed ourselves" and "I hurt myself." Don't get confused by the similarity these pronouns have to other pronouns but keep in mind that they only differ from the direct-object pronouns in the third-person singular and plural.

Table 17.11   Reflexive Pronouns

Singular	Plural
mi (myself)	*ci* (ourselves)
ti (yourself)	*vi* (yourselves)
si (Yourself, himself/herself)	*si* (themselves)

Look at the reflexive verb *chiamarsi* in Table 17.12 to see how reflexive pronouns work.

Table 17.12   Chiamarsi (to call oneself)

Singular	Plural
mi chiamo (I call myself)	*ci chiamiamo* (we call ourselves)
ti chiami (you call yourself)	*vi chiamate* (you call yourselves)
si chiama (he/she calls him/herself; You call yourself)	*si chiamano* (they call themselves)

Come ti chiami?	How do you call yourself?
Mi chiamo Gabriella.	I call myself Gabriella.

Attenzione

It's interesting that the verb *annoiarsi* (to be bored) is reflexive, literally translating to "I bore myself." In Italian, you are responsible for your own boredom! The verb *truccarsi* means "to make up." It's interesting to note that the noun *trucco* means "trick" in Italian.

Look at some common reflexive verbs in Table 17.13.

Table 17.13   Reflexive Verbs

Il Verb Riflessivo	La Pronuncia	Meaning
accorgersi	*ah-koR-jeR-see*	to notice
addormentarsi	*ah-doR-men-taR-see*	to fall asleep
alzarsi	*ahl-zaR-see*	to get up
annoiarsi	*ah-noh-yaR-see*	to be bored
arrabbiarsi	*ah-Rah-bee-aR-see*	to get angry
conoscersi	*koh-noh-sheR-see*	to know each other
chiamarsi	*kee-ah-mahR-see*	to call
diplomarsi	*dee-ploh-mahR-see*	to obtain a diploma
divertirsi	*dee-veR-teeR-see*	to enjoy
fermarsi	*feR-mahR-see*	to stop
laurearsi	*lau-Reh-ahR-see*	to graduate
lavarsi	*lah-vahR-see*	to wash
mettersi	*meh-teR-see*	to put on
pettinarsi	*peh-tee-nahR-see*	to comb
rendersi	*Ren-dehR-see*	to realize
ricordarsi	*Ree-koR-dahR-see*	to remember/to remind
sentirsi	*sen-teeR-see*	to feel
sposarsi	*spoh-zahR-see*	to get married
svegliarsi	*sveh-lyahR-see*	to get up
truccarsi	*tRoo-kahR-see*	to make up
vestirsi	*veh-steeR-see*	to get dressed

Vi conoscete da molto tempo?	Do you know each other for a long time?
Federico si laurea a giugno.	Federico is graduating in June.
Ricorda di lavarti la faccia!	Remember to wash your face!
I bambini si divertono al parco.	The children enjoy themselves in the park.
Come ti chiami?	What do you call yourself?

Some rules applying to reflexive verbs might make them a little easier to master:

1. When talking about parts of the body or clothing, a possessive adjective is not required when using a reflexive verb:

Mi lavo il viso.	I wash my face.
Si toglie la giacca.	He/she takes off the jacket.

2. The reflexive pronoun can be placed before the verb or after the infinitive when preceded by a form of the verb *potere, dovere,* or *volere*:

Non voglio alzarmi troppo presto.	I don't want to wake up too early.
Devo lavarmi i capelli.	I must wash my hair.

Attenzione!

Because reflexive pronouns are not gender specific, if you want to specify who is doing what, you'll have to use a proper name or noun:

Si lava il viso. → *Isabella si lava il viso.*

Si alzano alle otto. → *I ragazzi si alzano alle otto.*

As a Rule

Reflexive verbs follow the same rules of conjugation as any other *-are*, *-ere*, or *-ire* verb, but can always be identified by the *-si* that follows the infinitive. Some verbs, such as *sentire*, can mean two different things depending on whether or not they are reflexive. As a regular *-ire* verb, it can mean "to hear," as in *Sento la musica* (I hear the music), or "to smell," as in *Sento il profumo* (I smell the perfume). As a reflexive verb, *sentirsi* means "to feel," as in *Mi sento bene* (I feel well).

3. Many verbs can be made into reflexive verbs. In some cases, the meaning changes dramatically. Table 21.9 shows you some of these verbs.

Table 17.14 What's in a Name

Verb	English	Reflexive Verb	English
annoiare	to annoy	annoiarsi	to get bored
battere	to beat	battersi	to fight
chiedere	to ask	chiedersi	to wonder
comportare	to entail	comportarsi	to behave
giocare	to play	giocarsi	to risk
infuriare	to infuriate	infuriarsi	to get angry
licenziare	to dismiss/to fire	licenziarsi	to resign/to quit
offendere	to offend	offendersi	to take offense (at)
onorare	to honor	onorarsi	to take pride (in)
perdere	to lose	perdersi	to get lost
scusare	to excuse	scusarsi	to apologize
vincere	to win	vincersi	to master oneself

Mi perdo nelle città nuove.	I get lost (I lose myself) in new cities.
Giovanni si annoia quando va all'opera.	Giovanni is bored when he goes to the opera.

Test Your Reflexes

Use the reflexive verbs in parentheses in the following sentences with the appropriate reflexive pronoun:

Example: Noi _____ spesso. (vedersi)

Answer: Noi ci vediamo spesso.

1. Io _____ alle nove. (alzarsi)

2. Luciano e Marcello _____ da nove anni. (conoscersi)

3. Tu _____ in palestra? (divertirsi)

4. Giulia deve _____ i capelli ogni giorno. (lavarsi)

5. Tu, come _____ ? (chiamarsi)

6. Noi _____ una volta la settimana. (telefonarsi)

7. Come _____ la nonna di Sandra? (sentirsi)

8. Antonella e Marco _____ lunedì prossimo. (sposarsi)

Reciprocity

Every time you say to someone *Arrivederci!* you are using a reflexive. The expression literally translates as "to re-see each other." The same goes for the expression, *Ci vediamo!* (We'll see one another), which comes from the infinitive *vedersi*.

You have seen all of the verbs in Table 17.15 as non-reflexive verbs. By simply being made reflexive, these verbs can all express reciprocity.

Table 17.15   Do Unto Others

Reflexive Verb	English
abbracciarsi	to hug one another
baciarsi	to kiss one another
capirsi	to understand one another
conoscersi	to know one another
guardarsi	to look at one another
incontrarsi	to meet one another/to run into
salutarsi	to greet each other
vedersi	to see one another

Ci abbracciamo ogni volta che ci vediamo.

We hug one another every time we see each other.

Madre e figlia si capiscono senza parole.

Mother and daughter understand one another without words.

The Least You Need to Know

➤ You need to do two things to eat well in Italy: work up a good appetite and learn a few gastronomical verbs: *mangiare* (to eat), *bere* (to drink), *assaggiare/gustare* (to taste), *cenare* (to dine), *comprare* (to buy), *cucinare* (to cook), *pranzare* (to eat lunch), and *preparare* (to prepare).

➤ The pronoun *ne* is used to express that you want a "part of" or "some of" a greater quantity.

➤ To say that you like something, you must use the verb *piacere*—to be pleasing.

➤ You must use indirect object pronouns with *piacere*.

➤ Reflexive verbs, identified by the pronoun *-si* attached to the end of the infinitive, require the use of one of the reflexive pronouns: *mi, ti, si* (singular), *ci, vi,* and *si* (plural).

➤ Reflexive pronouns may appear similar to other pronouns, but be careful; their meanings are different.

➤ Many regular verbs can become reflexive. In some cases, however, the meaning changes dramatically.

Shall We Dine?

You have certainly enjoyed roaming through *il mercato* checking out the fresh produce. Your nostrils are in love with the mingling aromas at *la panetteria* and you successfully cooked your first Italian meal in Italian without killing anyone.

Cooking at home is nice, but you're on vacation. You don't want to do dishes. Why not take a break? Sit back, relax, and let someone else do the running around for a change. If you want to understand the menu or if you have special needs, this chapter will help you ask for what you want.

So Many Restaurants

There are restaurants for every palate and every pocket. You don't need to go to a five-star restaurant to eat well in Italy. Some of the smaller, family-run joints have the best food in town. Choose the place that best fits your needs:

il bar: apart from serving drinks of all kinds, bars serve *panini* (sandwiches), *tramezzini* (snacks), and assorted *paste* (pastries).

la caffeteria: pick and choose from whatever you see behind the glass counter, find an empty table, and eat. Inexpensive and nourishing, not exactly date material.

la mensa: like a cafeteria, wholesome food on a fixed-price basis; usually frequented by students.

l'osteria: no different from a tavern, it's often family-run and frequented by locals.

la paninoteca: sandwiches and beverages, good "on-the-go" food.

la pizzeria: just like it sounds, here you get your pizza and calzones (literally meaning, "big socks").

il ristorante: can range in quality and cost; usually a more formal atmosphere.

self-service: increasingly popular with young people; like a cafeteria, you grab a tray and pick your plate.

la tavola calda: "hot table"—ready-to-eat food that you can take out as well.

la tavola fredda: "cold table"—appetizers usually set up in a restaurant where you pay per plate based on how much food you eat.

Two for Dinner, Please

When you call a restaurant (and after you arrive), you may hear the following:

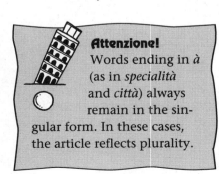

Attenzione!
Words ending in *à* (as in *specialità* and *città*) always remain in the singular form. In these cases, the article reflects plurality.

A che ora vorrebbe* mangiare?	At what time would you like to eat?
Per quante persone?	For how many people?
Va bene questo tavolo?	Is this table all right?
Tutto bene?	Is everything all right?
Le specialità del giorno sono...	Today's specials are…
Si accomodi.	Make yourself comfortable.

*Third-person conditional tense of volere *(to want).*

The expressions in Table 18.1 will help you ask for what you want.

Table 18.1   Dal Ristorante

L'Espressione	Expression
Cameriere	Waiter
Vorrei fare una prenotazione…	I'd like to make a reservation…
…per stasera	…for this evening
…per domani sera	…for tomorrow evening
…per sabato sera	…for Saturday evening
…per due persone	…for two people
…alle otto	…for 8:00
Possiamo sederci…	May we sit…
…vicino alla finestra?	…near the window?
…sul terrazzo?	…on the terrace?
C'è una zona per non fumatori?	Is there a non-smoking section?
Quanto tempo si deve aspettare?	How long is the wait?
Qual è la specialità della casa?	What is the house special?
Qual è il piatto del giorno?	What is the special for the day?
Che cosa ci consiglia?	What do you recommend?
Vorrei una porzione di…	I'd like one portion of…
Il conto, per favore.	The check, please.
Abbiamo mangiato* molto bene.	We ate very well.

*Past participle of mangiare.

A Table Setting

Prior to the 15th century, most food was eaten with the hands or from the point of a knife. Although it did not come to be commonly used until the 17th century, it appears that *i napoletani* created the four-pronged fork to aid them in eating spaghetti. Nowadays, it is considered *maleducato* (rude) to eat with your hands unless you're eating bread. Table 18.2 provides terms for the eating implements and other useful items.

Did You Know?
Il tavolo refers to a table in a restaurant; *la tavola* refers to a table at home.

Table 18.2 At the Table

At the Table	Alla Tavola	La Pronuncia
bowl	la scodella	*lah skoh-deh-lah*
carafe	la caraffa	*lah kah-Rah-fah*
cup	la tazza	*lah tah-tsah*
dinner plate	il piatto	*eel pee-ah-toh*
fork	la forchetta	*lah foR-keh-tah*
glass	il bicchiere	*eel bee-kee-yeh-Reh*
knife	il coltello	*eel koh-teh-loh*
menu	il menù	*eel meh-noo*
oil	l'olio	*loh-lee-yoh*
napkin	il tovagliolo	*eel toh-vahl-yoh-loh*
pepper	il pepe	*eel peh-peh*
salt	il sale	*eel sah-leh*
spoon	il cucchiaio	*eel koo-kee-ay-yoh*
table	il tavolo	*eel tah-voh-loh*
tablecloth	la tovaglia	*lah toh-vahl-yah*
teaspoon	il cucchiaino	*eel koo-kee-ay-ee-noh*
vinegar	l'aceto	*lah-cheh-toh*

Il Bar

In Italy, the bar is a place to meet friends, have a coffee, grab a *panino* (sandwich, which literally comes from the word *pane*, meaning "little bread"), or have an *amaro* after dinner. You must go to the *cassa* (cashier), pay for your choice, take your *scontrino* (receipt) to the bar, and order. It is customary to leave 100 lire or so as a gesture of good will, and don't forget to take your *scontrino* with you; it's the law. If you don't, the bar might get in trouble, and you could be fined (although this is uncommon). There is no drinking age in Italy because alcohol doesn't play a central role in leisure time. Wine flows easily and children drink a little from their parents' cups, but it is not considered entertainment to go out and "get juiced."

Did You Know?
One toasts (*fare un brindisi*) another to celebrate victory or an important accomplishment. (In *italiano, si dice*, "*Salute!*" or "*Cin cin!*")

In Italy, they take their coffee very seriously, and it is served in a variety of manners. Traditionally, Italians drink their coffee *in piedi* (standing up). Anytime you sit down for service, you're going to pay up to four times the amount. Some establishments have courtesy tables, and it's polite to bring your cup back up to the bar after you've finished drinking. If you must drink American coffee, which by Italian standards is considered weak and without flavor, you must ask for *un caffè americano*. If you are in a small town, you should indicate this as *un caffè molto lungo*. Table 18.3 illustrates the different kinds of *caffè* you can order. Practice reading your Italian. Remember to use the verb *prendere* (to take) to ask for what you want, as in *Prendo un espresso*.

Table 18.3 Coffee, Coffee Everywhere

Il Tipo di Caffè	La Descrizione
un espresso	caffè con molta acqua
un espresso lungo	caffè concentrato
un espresso ristretto	caffè nero
un cappuccino	un espresso con latte vaporizzato (steamed)
un latte macchiato	molto latte, poco caffè
un caffè macchiato	caffè con una goccia (a drop) di latte
un caffè latte	caffè fatto (made) a casa con latte
un caffè corretto	caffè con un liquore
un caffè decaffeinato	caffè senza caffeina
un caffè Hag	caffè senza caffeina come (like) la Sanka
un caffè freddo	caffè freddo

Etiquette for Idiots

Italians are not big snackers; when they eat, they really eat. Although nothing is written in stone, to enhance your dining *esperienza* a few guidelines won't hurt.

For example, in Italy, almost everything is *alla carta*, that is, ordered individually. If you want *un contorno* (a side) of veggies, you'll get a separate *piattino* because Italians almost never have more than one kind of food on a plate unless you're eating from a buffet, called a *tavola fredda*.

Did You Know?
Contrary to popular belief, Marco Polo wasn't the first to introduce spaghetti to Italy. Evidence that the Romans had various forms of pasta pre-dates Marco Polo's adventure.

It's *possibile* to mix and match *antipasti* or *contorni*, which is often a great solution to vegetarians or people who don't want to eat pasta all the time. Generally, you order a *primo piatto* (first course), which is usually a pasta dish or soup, and then you eat your *secondo piatto* (main course). *L'insalata* is usually eaten with *il secondo piatto*. Finally, when you order *un caffè*, it is assumed you mean *espresso*. (Remember, Italians never drink cappuccino after a meal and grated cheese is never offered for pasta dishes that include fish.) Table 18.4 outlines the different courses.

Table 18.4   Courses

L'Italiano	La Definizione	English	The Definition
l'antipasto	un assaggio per stimolare l'appetito	appetizer	a taste to stimulate the appetite
il primo piatto	la pasta, il risotto, o la zuppa	first course	a pasta, risotto, or soup
il secondo piatto	la carne, il pollo, o il pesce	second course	meat, chicken, or fish
il contorno	di solito le verdure: gli spinaci, i fagioli, le melanzane, etc.	side dish	usually vegetables: spinach, beans, eggplant, and so on

What's on the Menu?

Italian food can be found in restaurants all over the world. You are probably already familiar with a lot of *piatti*. Tables 18.5 through 18.7 help you interpret some of what you might find.

Table 18.5   I Primi Piatti

Il Primo Piatto	What It Is
lasagna	lasagna
minestrone	vegetable soup
brodo	broth
gnocchi al sugo di pomodoro	potato pasta with tomato sauce
pasta e fagioli	pasta with beans
linguine alle vongole	spaghetti in clam sauce
spaghetti alla bolognese	spaghetti in meat sauce
penne alla vodka	tubes of pasta with tomato, vodka, cream, and hot peppers
spaghetti alla carbonara	spaghetti with bacon, egg, and Parmesan
stracciatella	eggdrop soup
zuppa di verdura Toscana	Tuscan country soup
orecchiette ai broccoli e aglio	ear-shaped pasta with broccoli and garlic
tortellini prosciutto e piselli	tortellini with prosciutto and peas

Il Primo Piatto	What It Is
ravioli di zucca e ricotta	pumpkin ravioli with ricotta cheese
risotto di mare	seafood risotto

Table 18.6   I Secondi Piatti

Il Secondo Piatto	What It Is
pollo al limone	lemon chicken
pollo ai funghi	chicken with mushrooms
polpette al ragù	meatballs in tomato sauce
cotoletta alla milanese	breaded cutlet
pollo alla francese	chicken cooked in wine and lemon sauce
involtini di vitello	veal rolls cooked in wine with mushrooms
calamari alla marinara	squid in tomato sauce
salsicca affumicata	smoked sausage
pollo alla griglia	grilled chicken
bistecca	steak
ossobuco alla Milanese	oxtail or veal shanks with lemon, garlic, and parsley
agnello arrosto al rosmarino	roast lamb spiced with rosemary
anatra con vin santo	duck with holy wine (sherry)
coda di rospo con carciofi	monkfish with artichokes

Table 18.7   I Contorni e Gli Antipasti

Il Contorno/L'Antipasto	What It Is
la bruschetta lucchese	bruschetta with tomatoes, beans, and herbs
i calamari fritti	fried calamari
i cuori di carciofo marinati	marinated artichoke hearts
i fagioli alla veneziana	beans, anchovies, and garlic
i finocchi al cartoccio	baked fennel (literally "in a bag")
i formaggi vari	various cheeses
i funghi trifolati	sautéed mushrooms, garlic, onion, and parsley
il prosciutto con melone	prosciutto with melon
l'insalata di pomodoro e cipolla	tomato and onion salad
l'insalata verde	green salad

continues

Table 18.7 Continued

Il Contorno/L'Antipasto	What It Is
le melanzane alla griglia	grilled eggplant
le patate bollite	boiled potatoes
gli spiedini di gamberi alla griglia	skewered grilled shrimp
gli spinaci saltati	spinach tossed with garlic
gli zucchini fritti	fried zucchini

Ho Una Fame Da Lupo (I'm as Hungry as a Wolf)

There's no better way to understand what's on a menu than to look at one. Take a look and see how much you can understand:

Ristorante Gabriella

La Carta

Le Specialità del Giorno:

Gli Antipasti: Insalata di Sedano, Funghi e Formaggio 6.000

Frutti di Mare 7.500

Bruschetta al pomodoro 3.000

Carpaccio con arugola e parmigiano 8.000

I Primi Piatti: Vongole con Vermicelli 12.000

Polenta con Porcini 9.000

Spaghetti alla Bolognese 10.000

Minestrone 8.000

I Secondi Piatti: Spiedino Misto 15.000

Bistecca marinata alla griglia 20.000

Coniglio alla Contadina 18.000

Fruitti di mare 17.000

I Contorni: Insalata mista 5.000

Melanzane alla griglia 5.000

Finocchio con prosciutto 6.000

Fiori di Zucca Ripieni 6.000

Pane e Coperto 3.000

Per gruppi di oltre sei persone l'8% sarà aggiunto di servizio.

La Pizza e Il Formaggio

Italians like to have their own pizza, which are about as big as a plate and ordered individually. The crust is crunchy, and the pizza lightly covered with melted cheeses ranging from *gorgonzola*, a sharp cheese; *mozzarella*, a soft delicate cheese made from the milk of water buffalo; *Parmigiano-Reggiano*, a sharp cheese and one of Italy's finest (bring some back—you'll be glad you did); *pecorino*, a sharp cheese made from sheep milk; *provolone*, a sharp cheese often grated; and *ricotta* (literally meaning "recooked"), which is made from the whey produced in the cheese-making process, producing a soft, almost sweet cheese. Table 18.8 describes some of the pizza you can order.

> **Did You Know?**
> In Italy, each region has its own bread. For example, *il pane toscano* is found throughout Tuscany and Umbria; here the bread has no salt, stemming back to the 13th century when a salt tax was imposed on the people.

Table 18.8   Le Pizze

La Pizza	English
Bianca	"White" pizza; plain (no tomato, no cheese; just crust)
Ai Funghi	Tomato, mozzarella, and mushrooms
Margherita	Tomato and mozzarella
Napoletana	Tomato, mozzarella, anchovies, capers, and olives
Quattro Formaggi	Four cheeses: mozzarella, fontina, Swiss, and gorgonzola
Quattro Stagioni	Represents the four seasons: artichokes (spring), olives (summer), mushrooms (autumn), prosciutto (winter)
Alle Verdure	Vegetables: tomato, mozzarella, zucchini, spinach, eggplant, and mushrooms

That's the Way I Like It

Being able to express how you want something prepared avoids undesirable surprises, so consult Table 18.9 for the proper terminology. If you are looking for a lumberjack breakfast with eggs, pancakes, sausage, orange juice, and coffee, stay home. Italians eat eggs for lunch or dinner as a *secondo piatto*.

Table 18.9 Proper Preparation of Meats and Vegetables—La Carne e La Verdure

Preparation	La Preparazione	La Pronuncia
baked	al forno	*ahl foR-noh*
boiled	bollito	*boh-lee-toh*
breaded	impanato	*eem-pah-nah-toh*
broiled	alla fiamma	*ah-lah fee-ah-mah*
fried	fritto	*fRee-toh*
grilled	alla griglia	*ah-lah gReel-yah*
marinated	marinato	*mah-Ree-nah-toh*
medium	normale	*noR-mah-leh*
poached	in camicia	*een kah-mee-chah*
rare	al sangue	*ahl sahn-gweh*
steamed	al vapore	*ahl vah-poh-Reh*
well-done	ben cotto	*ben koh-toh*
fried (eggs)	uova fritte	*woh-vah fRee-teh*
hard-boiled (eggs)	uova bollite	*woh-vah boh-lee-teh*
poached (eggs)	uova in camica	*woh-vah een kah-mee-chah*
scrambled (eggs)	uova strapazzate	*woh-vah stRah-pah-tsah-teh*
soft-boiled (eggs)	uova alla coque	*woh-vah ah-lah koh-kay*
omelette	l'omelette	*loh-meh-leh-teh*

Spice Up Your Life

If you want it hot, ask for *piccante*, but keep in mind that Italian food is generally flavored with a variety of spices that are subtly blended to create the dishes you love. Table 18.10 describes some of the spices you'll encounter while eating Italian cuisine.

Table 18.10 Spices

Spices	Le Spezie
basil	il basilico
bay leaf	la foglia di alloro
caper	il cappero

Spices	Le Spezie
chives	le cipolline
dill	l'aneto
garlic	l'aglio
ginger	il ginger
honey	il miele
ketchup	il ketchup
mint	la menta
mustard	la senape
nutmeg	la noce moscata
oregano	l'origano
paprika	la paprika
parsley	il prezzemolo
pepper	il pepe
rosemary	il rosamarino
saffron	lo zafferano
salt	il sale
sugar	lo zucchero

Special People Have Special Needs

You're in great shape and have eliminated certain things from your diet. There's no reason to destroy all your hard work with one visit to Italy. The phrases in Table 18.11 will help you get what you need.

Table 18.11 Special Needs

Phrase	La Frase
I am on a diet.	Sto in dieta. (stare in dieta) Faccio la dieta. (fare la dieta)
I'm a vegetarian.	Sono vegetariano/a.
Do you serve Kosher food?	Servite del cibo kosher?
I can't eat anything made with…	Non posso mangiare niente che contenga…

continues

Table 18.11   Continued

Phrase	La Frase
I can't have any...	Non posso prendere...
...dairy products	...latticini
...alcohol	...alcol
...saturated fat	...grassi saturi
...shellfish	...frutti di mare
I'm looking for a dish...	Cerco un piatto...
...high in fiber	...con molta fibra
...low in cholesterol	...con poco colesterolo
...low in fat	...con pochi grassi
...low in sodium	...poco salato
...without preservatives*	...senza conservanti

Be sure to use the Italian word conservanti *and not the false cognate* preservativi, *which means "prophylactics"!*

You Call This Food?

You asked for a rare steak, but you received what looks like a shoe. There's a small nail in your pizza (don't worry, you won't be charged extra), a hair in your spaghetti, or cheese in the pasta (when you specifically asked for none). Keep your calm and ask the waiter to bring it back to the kitchen using the Italian outlined in Table 18.12.

Table 18.12   Take It Away!

English	L'Italiano
This is...	Questo è...
...burned	...bruciato
...dirty	...sporco
...overcooked	...troppo cotto
...spoiled/not right	...andato male
...too cold	...troppo freddo
...too rare	...troppo crudo
...too salty	...troppo salato

English	L'Italiano
...too spicy	...troppo piccante
...too sweet	...troppo dolce
...unacceptable	...inaccettabile

Fine Wine

Italian wines are among the best in the world, fulfilling one fifth of the total production. Italian standards for wine are very high, and finer wines are classified as *denominazione di origine controllata (DOC)* or *denominazione di origine controllata e garantita (DOCG)*, which you'll see on the wine label. Other wines are simply classified as *vino da tavola* (table wine), can range in quality, and are served by many restaurants as *il vino della casa* (the house wine). Some wines you might order are mentioned in Table 18.13.

Table 18.13 Bottle o' Wine, Fruit of the Vine

Wine	Il Vino
red wine	il vino rosso
rosé wine	il rosè
white wine	il vino bianco
dry wine	il vino secco
sweet wine	il vino dolce
sparkling wine	lo spumante

One of Italy's most popular cocktails is the Bellini, created by Giuseppe Cipriani of Harry's Bar in Venice. This light, refreshing drink is perfect before a meal:

Bellini

> *2/3 tazza (160 ml.) di purè di pesca (peach purée)*
>
> *1 cucchiaino di purè di lampone (raspberry purée)*
>
> *1 bottiglia di Prosecco (o Asti Spumante o champagne)*
>
> *In ogni bicchiere di vino o spumante, versate 7 cucchiaini di purè di pesca. Aggiungete 2—3 gocce di purè di lampone. Mettete il vino e servite subito.*

What's Your Fancy?

Gli aperitivi (aperitifs) and *gli amari* (digestives) are a lovely part of a meal. Try something new, and bring back a bottle of Cynar (made from artichokes) to share with your friends. A common practice is to drink Sambucca with a couple of coffee beans (*grani di caffè*). In some parts, they are called *le mosche* (flies) because of their resemblance to the little pests. Word has it that this controls garlic breath (and you're going to be eating *a lot* of garlic). You'll find many drinks to try in Table 18.14.

Table 18.14   Gli Alcolici

Gli Aperitivi	Gli Amari
Aperol	Fernet
Campari (bevuto con/senza acqua minerale frizzante)	Jeigermaister (Germania)
Cynar (a base carciofo)	Lucano
Martini (bianco o rosso)	Petrus (Olanda)
Negroni	Averna

Pastries, cakes, and cookies share one key ingredient—*lo zucchero* (sugar)—which is why they are simply called *i dolci* (sweets) in Italian. Because most *dolci* are peculiar to a particular region, many cannot be found elsewhere. The following brief list mentions some of the *dolci* you can find in Italy. If baked goods, such as *biscotti* (cookies, literally meaning "twice baked") and *torte* (cakes), don't trip your trigger, dip into *un gelato* (ice cream) at a *gelateria* where you are given up to three flavors in any *porzione* (portion). If you're not sure of a flavor, ask for *un'assaggio* (a taste).

Le paste	Il millefoglie (literally, 1000 sheets)
La avarese (as in "Bavarian")	Il panettone
Il biscotto di mandorle (almond cookies)	Il panforte (Tuscan)
Il cannolo (Sicilian)	Il profiterole
La colomba	I ricciarelli (Tuscan)
Il cornetto/la brioche	La sfogliatella della nobilità (noble's pastry)
La crostata (pie)	La torta di frutta fresca (fresh fruit tart)
Il danese ("Danish")	Il tiramisù (literally, "pick me up")
Il diplomatico (literally, "diplomat")	Il ventaglio
La macedonia di frutta (fruit cup)	La zuppa inglese (English trifle)
Il maritozzo	

It Was Delicious

Your meal was *delizioso*, so why not tell someone? Use the exclamations you learned in Chapter 15 to describe your meal or a restaurant.

Give It to Me

Suppose you're in a restaurant and the waiter suggests you try the evening special, *Pasta Primavera*. He describes it as a nice, light sauce with fresh vegetables. You're so hungry you could eat a horse. Rather than saying "Bring me the *pasta primavera*," you want to tell him, "Bring it to me," using the imperative (command) form of the verb. This would require that you use two object pronouns: "it" (referring to the pasta) and "to me."

Double Object Pronouns

When you say, "Bring me the pasta primavera," you are using the imperative form of the verb with a direct object (the pasta) and an indirect object (me). Remember that a direct object is the direct recipient of the verb. In English, that sentence would read, "Bring it to me." In Italian, it would look like this: "*Mi porti la pasta primavera*," which would in turn become "*Mela porti*."

In Italian, unlike English, it is possibile to join the object pronouns together to form one word. In Table 18.15, notice how the indirect object pronouns *mi, ti, ci,* and *si* change to *me, te, ce,* and *se*. Also note that the indirect object pronouns *gli, le,* and *Le* change to *glie-* before direct object pronouns, creating one word.

Table 18.15   Double Object Pronouns

	Indirect Object		Direct Object		
Pronoun	lo	la	li	le	ne
mi	me lo	me la	me li	me le	me ne
ti	te lo	te la	te li	te le	te ne
gli, le, Le	glielo	gliela	glieli	gliele	gliene
ci	ce lo	ce la	ce li	ce le	ce ne
si	se lo	se la	se li	se le	se ne

Attenzione!
When dealing with double object pronouns, it is assumed the speaker has already referred to the object of the sentence. In certain cases, the gender of the indirect object is not always obvious:

Presti la macchina a Silvia? Sì, gliela do.

Are you lending the car to Silvia? Yes, I'm lending it to her.

Keep in mind the following: When the same verb has two object pronouns, the indirect object always precedes the direct object.

Mandi la lettera al signor Rossi? Sì, gliela mando.

Are you sending the letter to Mr. Rossi? Yes, I'm sending it to him.

Restituiscono i soldi alla signora? Sì, glieli restituiscono.

Are they giving back the money to the woman? Yes, they are giving it back to her.

After an infinitive, the final *-e* is dropped and the double object pronoun is attached to the end of the infinitive forming one word:

Posso spedirtela?   Can I send it to you?

Vuole darcelo.   He wants to give it to us.

The Least You Need to Know

➤ You can read an Italian menu if you know the right terms for the food you love (and hate). Everything in Italy is ordered *alla carta*, and Italians traditionally enjoy an *espresso* after their meal.

➤ Ask to make a reservation using the expression *Vorrei fare una prenotazione* or *Vorrei prenotare un tavolo*. Do not use the cognate, *riservare*, which means "to keep" or "to put aside."

➤ There are several parts to an Italian meal: *gli antipasti, i contorni, i primi piatti, i secondi piatti,* and *i dolci*.

➤ When dealing with double object pronouns, the indirect object pronoun always precedes the direct object pronoun.

Chapter 19

Having Fun Italian Style

In This Chapter

➤ Sports and games

➤ Cinema, music, and art

➤ Adverbs

➤ The past tense

➤ Using double object pronouns in the past

You've rented a car, seen the sights, and eaten wonderful food. That's all fine and dandy for a tourist, but you're a traveler; you want to come back with more than a photograph and some souvenirs. Now is the time to dig a little deeper, stretch your cultural muscles, and learn something firsthand about how the Italians enjoy themselves.

This chapter covers many of the pastimes that make up the Italian lifestyle. If you're a sports fan, learn a bit more about the Italian's passion: soccer. If you are a music fanatic, see how much you already know. If art is your shtick, you'll gain a useful vocabulary to discuss the various implications an individual artist had in mind. Let's not forget film, where the Italians have surpassed average standards. You'll also learn how to tell anyone you meet what you did and saw by using the past tense. Let the games begin!

Name Your Game

Don't get confused when you hear the word *football*. It means soccer, also known as *il calcio*. Someone once said that there are three things you should never dare take away from an Italian: *la mamma*, *la pasta*, and *il calcio*. Expect anarchy if you dare. Many sports require the use of the verbs *fare* and *andare*.

Table 19.1 Game Time

Sport	Lo Sport	La Pronuncia
aerobics	l'aerobica	*lay-eh-Roh-bee-kah*
baseball	il baseball	the same as in English
basketball	la pallacanestra	*lah pah-lah-kah-neh-stRah*
bicycling	andare in bicicletta	*ahn-dah-Reh een bee-chee-kleh-tah*
boating	andare in barca	*ahn-dah-Reh een baR-kah*
diving	fare il subacqueo	*fah-Reh eel soo-bah-kweh-oh*
fishing	pescare	*peh-skah-Reh*
football	il football americano	*… ah-meh-Ree-kah-noh*
game	la partita	*lah paR-tee-tah*
golf	il golf	the same as in English
hockey	l'hockey	the same as in English
horseback riding	andare a cavallo	*ahn-dah-Reh ah kah-vah-loh*
jogging	fare footing	*fah-Reh footing*
karate	fare karate	*fah-Reh kah-Rah-teh*
rock climbing	l'alpinismo	*lahl-pee-nee-zmoh*
inline skating	fare pattinaggio	*fah-Reh pah-tee-nah-joh*
rowing	il canottaggio	*eel kah-noh-tah-joh*
skating	pattinare	*pah-tee-nah-Reh*
skiing	lo sciare	*loh shee-ah-Reh*
soccer	il calcio	*eel kahl-choh*
sport	lo sport	the same as in English
surfing	fare il surf	*fah-Reh eel surf*
swimming	fare il nuoto, nuotare	*fah-Reh eel nwoh-toh, nwoh-tah-Reh*
team	la squadra	*lah skwah-dRah*
tennis	il tennis	the same as in English
volleyball	la pallavolo	*lah pah-lah-voh-loh*
wind surfing	il windsurf	the same as in English

You're Playing with My Head

Looking for less exertion? Table 19.2 mentions a few games that allow you to use more brain power than brawn.

Table 19.2 Deal Me In

The Game	Il Gioco
backgammon	il backgammon
briscola (a popular card game)	la briscola
cards	le carte
checkers	la dama
chess	gli scacchi
dice	i dadi
gambling	giocare d'azzardo
hide-and-seek	Cu-cù
poker	il poker
scopa (a popular card game)	scopa
solitaire	il solitario
tarot	i tarocchi

Wanna Play?

In Italian, there are two verbs that signify "to play": *giocare* and *suonare*. *Giocare* is used when playing sports or games. (It may seem silly, but associating with the word "joker" might help you remember this verb.) *Suonare* is used when playing an instrument; think about the word *suono*, meaning "sound." Each verb is regular and shouldn't be confused with each other.

When participating in a sport, the verb *fare* is often used, as in

Mi piace fare sport.	I like doing sports.
Facciamo una partita di calcio.	Let's play a game of soccer.

Out in Left Field

Each sport or activity has its own particular playing field, as shown in Table 19.3.

Table 19.3   Beach Blanket Bingo

The Place	Il Posto	La Pronuncia
beach	la spiaggia	*lah spee-ah-jah*
casino	il casinò	*eel kah-see-noh*
court/field	il campo	*eel kam-poh*
golf course	il campo da golf	*eel kam-poh dah golf*
gym	la palestra	*lah pah-leh-stRah*
mountain	la montagna	*lah mohn-tan-yah*
ocean	l'oceano	*loh-sheh-ah-noh*
park	il parco	*eel paR-koh*
path	il sentiero	*eel sen-tee-eh-Roh*
pool	lah piscina	*lah pee-shee-nah*
rink	la pista da pattinaggio	*lah pees-tah dah pah-tee-nah-joh*
sea	il mare	*eel mah-Reh*
slope	la pista da sci	*lah pees-tah dah shee*
stadium	lo stadio	*loh stah-dee-yoh*
track	la corsa	*lah koR-sah*

Make a Date

Review Chapter 14 to remember how to *fissare un'appuntamento* (make an appointment) so that you can ask someone if she wants to meet you tomorrow at the court for *una partita* of tennis. If you still don't remember the conjugation of the verb *volere*, review Chapter 13. Translate the following sentences into Italian:

1. Why don't we meet at 3:00 tomorrow?
2. Are you in the mood to go swimming? (idiomatic; a hint: *Ti va di…*)
3. Let's go to the mountains next week.
4. Why not visit the museum?
5. Do you want to play tennis with me?

Il Cinema

The word *cinema* is an abbreviated version of *cinematografo*. Italy has spawned some of the best film makers in the world. Spaghetti westerns first brought Cinecittà in Roma (the Hollywood of Italy) into the foreground, as well as noted actors such as Sofia Loren, Marcello Mastroianni, Giancarlo Giannini, Gina Lollobrigida, and Alberto Sordi, to mention a few.

In the end, everyone is a film critic. Did you like it or was it contrived? Did the story engage you or did you find yourself squirming in your seat? The terms in Table 19.4 can help you discuss what aspects of the film worked and determine whether a film deserves the thumb's up or thumb's down.

Table 19.4   Movie Talk

The Cinema	Il Cinema
actor	l'attore
camera	la cinepresa
cinema	il cinema
close-up	primo piano
director	il regista
dissolve	dissolvenza
film	il film, la pellicola
long-shot	campo lungo
panning	panoramica
plot	la trama
producer	il produttore
scene	la scena
screen	lo schermo
theater	la sala cinematografica
to hear	sentire, udire
to listen	ascoltare
to look	guardare
to see	vedere
video camera	la telecamera

The Arts

It's almost presumptuous to even try to list an Idiot's Who's Who of the arts; there are so many notable Italians whose contributions to the arts have made an impact through time. From the Romans to the Renaissance to right now, the Italians have been influencing the world for over 2,000 years. The following sections are meant as a taster, or *antipasto*, to whet your appetite.

La Musica

Nothing soothes the savage breast like music. Is there a musical instrument that makes you swoon every time you hear it? Find it in Table 19.5 or find your favorite Italian composer in the timeline.

Did You Know?

Wendy Keyes, Executive Producer of Programming at the Film Society of Lincoln Center, New York City, offered her expertise and came up with the following "must sees" of Italian cinema. Here are her top 15 favorites. (The director is in parentheses next to the movie title.)

The White Sheik (Fellini)

Bicycle Thief (De Sica)

Roma: Open City (Rossellini)

Kaos (Taviani Brothers)

Caro Diario (Moretti)

The Human Voice (Rossellini)

L'Amerika (Amelio)

Big Deal on Madonna Street (Monicelli)

The Conformist (Bertolucci)

Ossessione (Visconti)

La Dolce Vita (Fellini)

Seven Beauties (Wertmuller)

Hands Over the City (Rosi)

L'Avventura (Antonioni)

Before the Revolution (Bertolucci)

Table 19.5 The Sound of Music

Instrument	Lo Strumento
accordion	la fisarmonica
cello	il violoncello
clarinet	il clarineto
drum	il tamburo, la batteria
flute	il flauto
guitar	la chitarra
harp	l'arpa
horn	il corno
oboe	l'oboe
piano	il pianoforte
piccolo	il piccolo
saxophone	il sassofono
trombone	il trombone
trumpet	la tromba
viola	la viola
violin	il violino

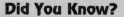

Did You Know?

The 16th through 18th centuries brought music to an entirely different level, and much of this occurred in Italy. In Venezia emerged Giovanni Gabrielli (1557–1612), one of the first composers to use the term *concerto* ("bringing into agreement"), for it was in classical music that many different voices were brought to form one. From Cremona came the great violin maker Antonio Stradivari (1644–1747). Later came Giuseppe Verdi (1813–1901), who at the age of 20 was already heard at Milano's famous opera house La Scala. By the time he died, the patriotic composer had written 26 operas including *Otello*, *Rigoletto*, and *La Traviata* (meaning "the corrupted"). Giacomo Puccini (1858–1924) wrote *Tosca* when *opera verismo* was at its height.

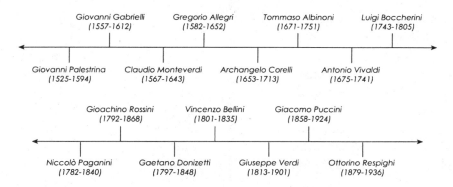

An Educated Idiot

Most of the terminology used in classical music is of Italian derivation. The following words all relate to music. Some are adjectives; others are nouns and verbs, usually in the gerund form, such as *accelerando* (*accelerare*), *diminuendo* (*diminuire*), and *morendo* (*morire*).

a cappella	animato	diminuendo	intermezzo
accelerando	aria	dolce	legato
adagio	arpeggio	fantasia	lento
adagissimo	bel canto	finale	mezzo-forte
agitato	castrato	forte	morendo
alla breve	concerto	grave	opera
allegro	crescendo	grazioso	operetta
alto	da capo	impresario	piano

Life Imitates Art

Le belle arti (the visual arts) attempt to interpret the real world, glorify God (or gods), or express something without words. As ideas about the world have changed, so has the art that depicts these notions. Ultimately, you know what you like and what you don't, and that is often the only criterion necessary to appreciate a piece.

Table 19.6 Adding to Your Palette

English	Italian	English	Italian
abstract	astratto	mosaic	il mosaico
acrylic	acrilico	oil	olio
architecture	l'architettura	painter	il pittore
background	lo sfondo	painting	il quadro
Baroque	Barocco	perspective	la prospettiva
bronze	il bronzo	picture	la pittura
ceramic	la ceramica	pigments	i colori
classical	classico	portrait	il ritratto
cubism	il cubismo	realism	realismo
depth	la profondità	restoration	il restauro
Etruscan	etrusco	sculptor	lo scultore
figure	la figura	sculpture	la scultura
foreground	il primo piano	shadow	l'ombra
fresco	l'affresco	sketch	lo schizzo
futurism	il futurismo	statue	la statua
geometric	geometrico	symbol	il simbolo
granite	il granito	the Middle Ages	il Medioevo
human figure	la figura umana	the Renaissance	il Rinascimento
landscape	il paesaggio	to paint	dipingere
light	la luce	to sculpt	scolpire
marble	il marmo	visual arts	le belle arti
master	il maestro	work of art	un'opera d'arte
masterpiece	il capolavoro		

Adverbs

Every time you utter, *"Ancor!"* you're not only speaking in Italian, but you are also using an adverb (in this case, *ancora* means "again"). As you recall from Chapter 2, adverbs describe verbs or adjectives and tell how well you do something, such as, "She plays the piano *beautifully*," or "You are *sincerely* the *most* beautiful person I've ever met."

Most adverbs in English end in **-ly**. In Italian, they generally end in *-mente*, although a few exceptions exist. (So what's new?) You can form most Italian adverbs by adding *-mente* to the end of the feminine form of the adjective:

seria (serious)	*seriamente* (seriously)
profonda (profound)	*profondamente* (profoundly)
chiara (clear)	*chiaramente* (clearly)

Adjectives ending in *-le* or *-re* drop the final *-e* before adding *-mente*:

facile (easy)	*facilmente* (easily)
gentile (kind)	*gentilmente* (kindly)
Puoi imparare facilmente l'italiano.	You can easily learn Italian.
Siete gentilmente pregati di lasciare un messaggio.	You are kindly asked to leave a message.

Adverbs are usually placed after the verb, although some may come before:

Probabilmente vado domani.	I'm probably going tomorrow.
Ti parlo seriamente.	I'm speaking to you seriously.
Quel film è profondamente triste.	That film is profoundly sad.
Chiaramente la situazione è grave.	Clearly the situation is serious.

Several adverbs are irregular and must be memorized:

appunto	exactly
meglio	better
bene	well
neanche	not even
forse	maybe
nemmeno	by no means

in fretta	in a hurry
piano	softly/slowly

Sto bene, grazie.	I am well, thanks.
Non abbiamo neanche tempo di fare la doccia.	We don't even have time to take a shower.
Parli lentamente per favore.	Speak slowly please.

When talking about quantity, you might want less or more, depending on your mood:

abbastanza	enough
non più	not, any more, no more
appena	hardly, scarcely
piuttosto	rather, somewhat
meno	less
poco	not very
molto	a lot, much, very
troppo	too
parecchio	quite a lot of

Many adverbs relating to time and place aren't formed from an adjective.

Table 19.7 Adverbs of Time and Place

Adverbs of Place		Adverbs of Time	
altrove	(elsewhere)	adesso	(now)
dappertutto	(everywhere)	allora	(then)
davanti	(in front of)	ancora	(still, again)
dentro	(inside)	di solito	(usually)
dietro	(in back, behind)	domani	(tomorrow)
dovunque	(anywhere)	dopo	(after)
fuori	(outside)	ieri	(yesterday)
giù	(down)	mai	(never)
là, lì	(there)	oggi	(today)
laggiù	(down there)	ora	(now)
lontano	(far)	poi	(after)
qui, qua	(here)	presto	(quickly, early)
quassù	(up here)	prima	(before)

Adverbs of Place		Adverbs of Time	
sopra	(above, on)	quando	(when)
sotto	(beneath)	sempre	(always)
su	(up; on top)	spesso	(often)
vicino	(near)	subito	(soon, immediately)

As a Rule

It's possible to use the preposition *con* and a noun in lieu of an adverb:

Guidate con attenzione.   Drive attentively. (Drive with attention.)

Parla con sincerità.   He speaks sincerely. (He speaks with sincerity.)

The More Things Change

Make the following adjectives into adverbs. Many of these adjectives will require that you make them feminine before converting them to adverbs.

Example: breve *(brief)*

Answer: brevemente *(briefly)*

1. dolce (sweet)
2. sincero (sincere)
3. intelligente (intelligent)
4. necessario (necessary)
5. veloce (fast/quick)
6. regolare (regular)
7. difficile (difficult)
8. probabile (probable)
9. solo (only)
10. gentile (kind)

Il Passato Prossimo (The Present Perfect)

Like English, there are several ways of expressing the past in Italian. For now, you're going to learn about the *passato prossimo*, equal in meaning to the simple past tense in English, as in "I forgot," "I ate," and the present perfect, as in "I have forgotten," "I have eaten."

The *passato prossimo* requires the use of the helping (or auxiliary) verbs *avere* and *essere* (Chapter 9). You already saw how the verb *stare* is used in the present progressive tense (also in Chapter 9). You use a compound tense whenever you say that you have done something. In Italian, all transitive verbs (verbs that take a direct object) require the use of the auxiliary verb *avere*. All intransitive verbs (verbs taking an indirect object) require the use of *essere*.

Constructing the Past Participle

When you use the *passato prossimo*, you need a past participle. For example, in English you use the helping verb have plus the participle (wished/finished/studied). Most of the time, this is regular, but English, also has several irregular past participles (had/been/sang). The same goes for Italian.

As you recall from Chapter 8, Italian has three principal verb families (*-are*, *-ere*, and *-ire*). To make the past participle from an infinitive, you hold onto the stem and add the appropriate ending, as shown in Table 19.8.

Table 19.8   Endings for the Past Participle

Endings			Infinitive		Participle
-are	→	-ato	lav/are	→	lavato
-ere	→	-uto	pot/ere	→	potuto
-ire	→	-ito	cap/ire	→	capito

Forming the Past with Avere

The good news is that when used with transitive verbs, the past participle doesn't change (unless accompanied by a direct object pronoun, which I discuss in a bit). The only thing you need to conjugate is your helping verb. Look at the verb *lavare* (to wash) in Table 19.10 to better understand how this works. Just in case you forgot about *avere*, here it is one more time in Table 19.9.

Table 19.9   Avere

Singular	Plural
io ho	noi abbiamo
tu hai	voi avete
lui/lei/Lei ha	loro hanno

Table 19.10   The Present Perfect Using Avere: Lavare

Singular	Plural
ho lavato (I have washed)	*abbiamo lavato* (we have washed)
hai lavato (you have washed)	*avete lavato* (you have washed)
ha lavato (You/he/she has washed)	*hanno lavato* (they have washed)

As a Rule

Transitive verbs (verbs that take a direct object) use *avere* as an auxiliary verb, whereas intransitive verbs use *essere*.

Many *-ere* verbs have irregular past participles.

All reflexive verbs requires *essere* as their auxiliary verb.

One trick to remember which auxiliary verb to use is this: Verbs of locomotion such as *andare* (to go), *venire* (to come), *uscire* (to go out/exit), and *entrare* (to enter) are intransitive and take *essere*. Verbs such as *mangiare* (to eat) and *studiare* (to study) are transitive and take *avere*.

When negating something in the past, the word *non* comes before the helping verb:

Non ho mangiato molto.	I didn't eat much.

Adverbs related to time are placed between the auxiliary verb and the past participle:

Hai già mangiato?	Have you already eaten?
Non ho mai visto il film Cinema Paradiso.	I have never seen the movie *Cinema Paradiso.*
Abbiamo sempre passato l'estate al mare.	We always passed the summer by the sea.

Some commonly used irregular past participles with *avere* are shown in Table 19.11.

Table 19.11 Commonly Used Irregular Past Participles with Avere

Verb	Past Participle	Meaning
aprire	aperto	to open
bere	bevuto	to drink
chiedere	chiesto	to ask
chiudere	chiuso	to close
conoscere	conosciuto	to know someone
correre	corso	to run
decidere	deciso	to decide
dire	detto	to say
leggere	letto	to read

continues

Table 19.11   Continued

Verb	Past Participle	Meaning
mettere	messo	to put/to place/to wear
offrire	offerto	to offer
perdere	perso	to lose
prendere	preso	to take
rispondere	risposto	to respond
rompere	rotto	to break
scrivere	scritto	to write
spendere	speso	to spend
togliere	tolto	to take from
vedere	visto	to see
vincere	vinto	to win

Abbiamo vinto la partita.	We won the game.
Hai scritto alla Mamma?	Did you write to Mom?
Il ristorante ha chiuso presto.	The restaurant closed early.
Ci hanno chiesto un favore.	They asked us for a favor.

Forming the Past with Essere

Intransitive verbs always require the use of *essere* as their auxiliary. How can you remember what those verbs are? Think of a squirrel living in a tree and imagine all the motions he does in and around his home, high up in the branches of a great old oak tree: up, down, in, out, coming, going, staying, remaining, and leaving.

Whenever *essere* is used as the auxiliary verb, the participle is still formed by adding the appropriate ending to the stem of the verb. However, the participle must reflect both gender and plurality with the subject.

Table 19.12   Essere

Singular	Plural
io sono	noi siamo
tu sei	voi siete
lui/lei/Lei è	loro sono

It's a lot easier to visualize how something works than it is to over-analyze it with a bunch of rules. Think of a relationship where things have been talked up and down, inside and out. You can't see the forest from the trees! Take a step back to gain perspective. This concept works even when talking about something as mundane as grammar. Now, for your viewing pleasure, take a look at how the verb *andare* is used in Table 19.13.

Table 19.13   The Present Perfect Using Essere: Andare

Singular	Plural
sono andato/a (I went)	*siamo andati/e* (we went)
sei andato/a (you went)	*siete andati/e* (you went)
è andato/a (You/he/she went)	*sono andati/e* (they went)

La ragazza è andata all'università di Bologna.	The girl went to the university of Bologna.
Enrico V (quinto) è diventato matto.	Henry V went crazy.

As a Rule

The verb *avere* takes itself as an auxiliary verb.

Ho avuto un'idea buonissima.	I had a great idea.

The verb *essere* also takes itself as an auxiliary verb.

Sono stata in Italia in estate.	I was in Italy for the summer.

Many adjectives can be formed by simply using the past participle of a verb. Take the verb *stupire* (to be amazed), which is often used as an adjective.

As an adjective:

Luisa è stata stupita.	Luisa was amazed.

As a verb:

Mi ha stupito.	It amazed me.

Another verb commonly used as an adjective is *perdersi* (to lose oneself). Look at the difference between the following two sentences.

As an adjective:

Mi sono perso.	I am lost.

As a verb:

Ho perso la mia borsa.	I lost my bag.

Table 19.14 contains a list of the most commonly used intransitive verbs conjugated with *essere*.

Table 19.14 Intransitive Verbs Commonly Used with Essere

Verb	Past Participle	Meaning
andare	andato	to go
apparire	apparso*	to appear
arrivare	arrivato	to arrive
bastare	bastato	to be enough
cadere	caduto	to fall
dispiacere	dispiaciuto	to be sorry
diventare	diventato	to become
entrare	entrato	to enter
esistere	esistito	to exist
essere	stato*	to be
ingrassare	ingrassato	to gain weight
morire	morto*	to die
nascere	nato*	to be born
partire	partito	to leave
piacere	piaciuto*	to be pleasing
restare	restato	to stay
rimanere	rimasto*	to remain
ritornare	ritornato	to return
salire	salito	to go up/to get on
scendere	sceso*	to get off
sembrare	sembrato	to seem
stare	stato*	to stay
succedere	successo*	to happen
tornare	tornato	to return
uscire	uscito	to go out
venire	venuto	to come
vivere	vissuto*	to live

Irregular participle.

Sono uscita alle otto.	I went out at 8:00.
Roberto è nato nel 1967.	Roberto was born in 1967.

Siamo stati svegli tutta la notte.   We were awake all night.

Le studentesse sono partite per le vacanze.   The students have left for vacation.

Reflexive verbs always take *essere* as their auxiliary verb:

Ci siamo baciati.   We kissed each other.

Mi sono alzata prestissimo.   I woke up very early.

As a Rule

In the simple past, the verb *piacere* is used in the same way as the present. In this case, the object that is doing the pleasing determines the tense of the verb. Because *piacere* is used with the helping verb *essere*, the object doing the pleasing must be reflected in the participle:

Ti piace lo spettacolo? →Ti è piaciu**to** lo spettacolo?

Mi piaciono gli animali. →Mi sono piaciu**ti** gli animali.

Ci piace l'Italia. →Ci è piaciu**ta** l'Italia.

Vi piacciono le macchine.→ Vi sono piaciu**te** le macchine.

Wait a Minute, Il Postino

Imagine that you are writing *una lettera* to someone back in Italy. Using the past participle, you want to tell her about the things you saw and did while you were on vacation. Start your letter with *Caro* or *Cara* (Dear) and end it with *Sinceramente* (sincerely).

Direct Object Pronouns and the Passato Prossimo

As you recall, transitive verbs take a direct object and are conjugated with the verb *avere*. When forming the *passato prossimo* with a direct object pronoun, the ending of the participle must reflect gender and plurality. Note that the singular direct object pronouns meaning "it" (*lo/la*) drop the final vowel and join with the auxiliary verb *avere*. The plural object pronouns don't change.

Table 19.15 Passato Prossimo with Direct Object Pronouns

Sentence	Direct Object	Direct Object Pronoun	Example
Hai spedito la lettera?	*la lettera* →	*la*	*Sì, l'ho spedita.*
Did you send the letter?	the letter →	it	Yes, I sent it.
Hai mangiato il pane?	*il pane* →	*lo*	*Sì, l'ho mangiato.*
Did you eat the bread?	the bread →	it	Yes, I ate it.
Hai ricevuto le lettere?	*le lettere* →	*le*	*No, non le ho ricevute.*
Did you receive the letters?	the letters →	them	No, I didn't receive them.
Hai letto i libri?	*i libri* →	*li*	*Sì, li ho letti.*
Did you read the books?	the books →	them	Yes, I read them.

Indirect Object Pronouns and the Passato Prossimo

Both transitive and intransitive verbs can take an indirect object pronoun, but the participle doesn't have to agree.

Table 19.16 Passato Prossimo with Indirect Object Pronouns

Sentence	Indirect Object	Indirect Object Pronoun	Example
Hai parlato alla ragazza?	*la ragazza*	→ *le*	*Sì, le ho parlato.*
Did you speak to the girl?	the girl	→ (to her)	Yes, I spoke to her.
Hai spedito la lettera a Paolo?	*Paolo*	→ *gli*	*Sì, gli ho spedito la lettera.*
Did you send the letter to Paolo?	Paolo	→ (to him)	Yes, I sent him a letter.
Hai offerto ai signori un caffè?	*i signori*	→ *loro/gli**	*Sì, ho offerto loro un caffè. (Sì, gli ho offerto un caffè.)*
Did you offer the men a coffee?	the men	→ (to them)	Yes, I offered them a coffee.
Hanno mandato un pacco noi?	*noi*	→ *ci*	*Sì, ci hanno a mandato un pacco.*
They sent a package to us?	us	→ (to us)	Yes, they sent us a package.

*Both of these are correct. If you recall, loro *can be replaced with the pronoun* gli.

As a Rule

As with single object pronouns, the past participle must still reflect the gender and number of the direct object. *Lo* and *la* become *l'* before a verb beginning with a vowel or with *h*:

> *Ti ho detto la verità→ Te l'ho detta.* (I told it to you.)

> *Ci hanno dato i libri. → Ce li hanno dati.* (They gave them to us.)

The Passato Prossimo and Double Object Pronouns

Everything here is detail. If you don't always remember to make things agree, you won't be locked into a tower and fed stale bread until you die. However, if you want to be a master, you've got to pay special attention to the little things.

Attenzione!

When dealing with object pronouns, it is assumed the speaker has already referred to the object of the sentence. With double object pronouns, the gender of the indirect object will not always be obvious.

> *Hai dato la lettera al padrone? → Sì, **gliel'ho data**.*

> Did you give the letter to the landlord? → Yes, I gave it to him.

> *Hai prestato la macchina a Silvia? → Sì, **gliel'ho prestata**.*

> Did you lend the car to Silvia? → Yes, I lent it to her.

You may recall that when the same verb has two object pronouns, the indirect object pronoun always precedes the direct object pronoun. The following examples illustrate how double object pronouns work with the *passato prossimo*.

Hai mandato la lettera al signor Rossi?	Did you send the letter to Mr. Rossi?
*Sì, **gliel'ho mandata**.*	Yes, I sent it to him.
Hanno restituito i soldi alla signora?	Did they give back the money to the woman?
*Sì, **glieli** hanno restituiti.*	Yes, they gave it back to her.

The Least You Need to Know

➤ The verb *fare* is often used to describe participation in a sport.

➤ Use the verb *giocare* to play games and the verb *suonare* to play an instrument.

➤ Adverbs are formed by adding *-mente* to many feminine adjectives. Many adverbs of time and place are irregular and must be memorized.

➤ The past participle is created by adding the appropriate ending to the stem of a verb. The three regular forms are *-ato*, *-uto*, and *-ito*.

➤ The two helping verbs used to form the *passato prossimo* are *essere* and *avere*.

➤ Intransitive verbs and reflexive verbs require *essere* as their auxiliary verb.

➤ The past participle must agree in gender and number with the preceding direct object pronoun.

➤ Double object pronouns often form one word and are used to refer to something already mentioned.

Part 4
Trouble in Paradise

By now, you should be able to pronounce the Italian without everything being spelled out for you. This section deals with the darker side of traveling and the problems that often crop up when you least expect it. You told them to stay home when you were packing, but the tenacious little pests somehow managed to slip into your luggage when you weren't looking. Little did you know that you were opening Pandora's box when you unclicked the latch on your brand new suitcase.

It's not a bad idea to be a little Zen about problems when you're abroad. If you go with the flow and don't have too many expectations, you'll not only have room for unexpected treats, but you also won't be too dismayed when life gets in the way of your plans.

You'll also learn some more complicated elements of the language, which at first may seem unnecessarily difficult. It's like learning algebra for the first time. Initially, it's all a blur, but slowly, or sometimes immediately, a light bulb goes off and Eureka! you get it. Visit a bookstore and pick up a book or two that specializes in Italian grammar or verbs if you want to get all the variations of a particular theme. Borrow tapes from your local library (they're free!), and start from scratch to see how much you really have learned. Don't be dismayed if you listen to the Italian news and can't understand a word; stick with films and friends for now.

Chapter 20

You're Not Having Un Buon Giorno

In This Chapter

➤ Personal services

➤ Describing your needs

➤ Stressed pronouns

➤ Making comparisons

➤ *Ci* and *vi*

Everyone fantasizes about getting away from it all, but somehow problems manage to slip into your luggage and follow you wherever you go. Your e-mail isn't working on your laptop computer and you need help fast. Your perfect black pumps can't handle the cobblestone streets and you need to have the heel replaced. You just spilled tomato sauce all over your favorite silk tie, the one with The Beatles on it. Your camera has suddenly developed mechanical problems. One lens in your glasses just popped out, and you forgot to bring along your miniature screwdriver set. This chapter helps you solve life's little nuisances.

Get Down to the Basics

Before you can get anything done, you must be able to find someone who can help you. Your guidebook probably won't help, but a copy of *le pagine gialle* (the Yellow Pages) might. To locate one, ask your concierge or visit any TELECOM (phone center). Speaking on the telephone is elaborated on in Chapter 23, but for now, a couple of tips might help.

Tip #1: Know what your needs are and write down the appropriate questions before you make the call. Having something written in front of you will help you focus.

As a Rule

When calling any establishment open to the public, whether a *parrucchiere* (hair dresser), *sarto* (tailor), or a *calzolaio* (shoemaker), it is often appropriate to use the second person plural (*voi*) form of the verb:

Avete...?	Do you have...?
Potete...?	Are you able to...?
A che ora aprite?	At what time do you open?
A che ora chiudete?	At what time do you close?

Tip #2: Let the establishment know that you do not speak Italian very well and ask the person to speak slowly. If you want to take the easy way out, ask if they speak English:

Non parlo l'italiano molto bene.	I don't speak Italian very well.
Parlate lentamente, per favore.	Speak slowly, please.
Parlate l'inglese?	Do you speak English?

Tip #3: Keep it simple. Basic statements such as *Ho bisogno...* (I need) can go a long way.

The following sentences in Table 20.1 will help you find out *if* someone can help you, *when* they are open, *how* to get there, and *what* your needs are. Go back to Chapter 11 to remember how to ask for directions.

Table 20.1 Help!

La Frase	The Phrase
Ho bisogno di...	I need...
Mi potete aiutare?	Can you help me?
Siete aperti	Are you open
...adesso?	...now?
...fino a che ora?	...until what time?
...la domenica?	...Sundays?
Dov'è...	Where is...
Conosce...	Do you know...
...un buon parrucchiere?	...a good hairdresser?
...un buon sarto?	...a good tailor?
...un buon calzolaio?	...a good shoemaker?
...una buona tintoria?	...a good dry cleaner?

Mirror Mirror on the Wall...

Between packing, notifying your credit card companies, bringing the dog to the pound, paying your bills, and making sure your passport is valid, you didn't have time to make it to the hairdresser for a little shampoo, cut, and tint. Now your roots are showing and every time you venture out, you find yourself wrapping your head with a scarf or plunking on a hat. Women in Italy usually go to the *parrucchiere*, whereas men visit the *barbiere*. While you're at it, you decide to go for the works, maybe even a mud bath.

Some verbs and idiomatic expressions you might find useful appear in Table 20.2. You see *farsi*, which is a reflexive verb (*fare + si*) used when one is having something done to themselves. You'll learn more about reflexive verbs in Chapter 21.

Table 20.2 Getting Gorgeous (the Italian Way)

English	L'Italiano
to blow-dry	asciugare i cappelli
to color	tingere i capelli
to curl	fare i riccioli
to cut	tagliare
to get a haircut	farsi tagliare i capelli
to get a manicure	farsi fare il manicure
to get a pedicure	farsi fare il pedicure
to get a permanent	farsi la permanente
to shampoo	farsi lo shampoo
to shave	farsi la barba
to wax	farsi la ceretta

Build up your grooming vocabulary with the terms in Table 20.3.

Table 20.3 Well Groomed

English	L'Italiano
bald	calvo
bangs	la frangia
beard	la barba
brush	la spazzola
comb	il pettine
conditioner	il balsamo
cut	il taglio
face	il viso
facial	la pulizia del viso
gel	il gel
hair	i capelli
hairspray	la lacca
head	la testa

English	L'Italiano
mud	il fango
mustache	i baffi
nail	l'unghia
nail file	la limetta
nail polish	lo smalto per le unghie
razor	il rasoio
shampoo	lo shampoo

Do Blondes Really Have More Fun?

There's a revolution happening inside as the "real" you comes forth: Maybe you'd rather be a bobbed redhead, a permed brunette, or a cropped blond. Maybe you want every hair on your head shaved off. If you don't like it, it'll grow back—but to avoid any misunderstandings, look at Table 20.4 to get the lowdown on stylists' lingo. Remember that the word *capelli* is plural, and your adjectives (given here in the masculine, plural form) must agree:

Preferisco i miei capelli…   I prefer my hair…

Li vorrei…   I'd like them…

Table 20.4   Get Rid of That Gray

Style	Lo Stile
auburn	castani
black	mori
blond	biondi
brunette	bruni
curly	ricci
darker	più scuri
layered	scalati
lighter	più chiari
like this photo	come questa foto

continues

Table 20.4 Continued

Style	Lo Stile
long	lunghi
medium	medi
red	rossi
retouched	ritoccati
straight	lisci
the same	uguali
trimmed	spuntati
wavy	ondulati
with highlights	con i colpi di sole

Just a Little off the Top, Per Favore

Pretend you're in Italy, going for an afternoon of pampering at a nearby spa. Practice telling someone what your needs are. Tell them what you want done (a facial, a manicure, a cut, and so on) and then describe what you want your new look to be.

In Tintoria (at the Dry Cleaners')

You've taken care of your physical needs, but your appearance wouldn't be complete without clean clothes. Because the concept of an automated laundromat is still in the developmental stage in Italy, travelers must either wash their own clothes in the bathtub or have someone else do the job. (It's not a bad idea to bring detergent with you, as well as a couple of clothes pins.) Chapter 16 gave you the names of stores and clothing. Perhaps you went out last night, and had one too many and now your favorite silk shirt has Chianti spilled on it. There's a grass stain on your pants from that lovely picnic you had in the *parco* the other day. When you bring your clothing to the laundry, you'll be asked, *Qual è il problema*? (What's the problem?), or *Mi dica* (Tell me). You'll probably have to use the demonstrative pronouns *this* or *these*, so review Chapter 10 if you don't remember them.

Table 20.5   The Dirt on Dirt (and Other Mishaps)

English	L'Italiano
È...	It is...
...una macchia	...a stain
...una bottone che manca	...a missing button
...uno strappo	...a tear
Mi potete lavare a secco questo (questi...)?	Can you dry clean this (these) for me?
Mi potete rammendare questo (questi...)?	Can you mend this (these) for me?
Mi potete stirare questo (questi...)?	Can you iron this (these) for me?
Mi potete inamidare questo (questi...)?	Can you starch this (these) for me?
Quando sarà pronto?	When will it be ready?
L'ho bisogno il più presto possibile.	I need it as soon as possible.

Dal Calzolaio (at the Shoemaker's)

You've never walked this much before, and every step takes you deeper into the mystery of *Italia*. What were you thinking when you decided to buy new shoes right before your trip? Instead of breaking them in, your feet have been destroyed and you've got blisters on top of your blisters. Maybe you want to have your *scarpe* stretched, a heel replaced, or a new shoelace added. The phrases in Table 20.6 will help you.

Table 20.6   If the Shoe Fits

English	L'Italiano
shoe	la scarpa
boot	lo stivale
heel	il tacco
sole	la suola
to stretch	allargare
to shine	lucidare
to repair	riparare
shoelace	laccio da scarpe

Dall'Ottica (at the Optician's)

You just sat on your glasses and need to have them repaired. Perhaps you want to invest in designer frames. Maybe you want a new look and you have decided to splurge on a beautiful pair of sunglasses.

Table 20.7   The Better to See You With

English	L'Italiano
astigmatism	l'astigmatismo
contact lens	le lenti a contatto
eyes	gli occhi
far-sighted	presbite
frame	la montatura
glasses	gli occhiali
lens	le lenti
near-sighted	miope
prescription	la ricetta medica
sunglasses	gli occhiali da sole

Dal Negozio di Fotografia (at the Camera Shop)

You bought what you thought was enough film for your camera, but now you need more. You want to buy a filter for your lens before it gets scratched, which could also use a good cleaning.

Table 20.8   Say Mozzarella

English	L'Italiano
battery	la batteria
camera	la macchina fotografica
exposure	l'esposizione
film	la pellicola
flash	il "flash"
lens	l'obiettivo
to develop	sviluppare

In Gioielleria (at the Jeweler's)

Maybe your watch came off during a gondola ride and you need to get another, or perhaps the battery just ran out of juice. If you need to go the jeweler to have something fixed or replaced, the words in Table 20.9 will help you get things ticking again. Refer back to Chapter 16 for a list of jewelry terms. If you've broken a chain and need it repaired, or have lost a stone and want to have it replaced, ask the salesperson, *Può riparare questo?* (Can you fix this?).

What's What
Is your watch fast? Tell the repair person, *Va avanti*. Is it slow? Tell him, *Va indietro*.

Table 20.9   Fix It Again, Tony

English	L'Italiano
battery	la batteria
chain	la catena
clasp	il gancio
watch	l'orologio
watch band	il cinturino

Nel Negozio Elettronica (at the Electronics Store)

You've brought over your laptop computer and have been furiously tapping away at the keys, trying to recall every detail for the book you're going to write about Italy; maybe you're just trying to stay in touch with friends or colleagues back home, and your e-mail doesn't work. Perhaps the battery has died and you need to replace it. If your computer just won't work, you'll have to bring it in and explain, *Il mio computer non funziona*, and pray you haven't lost any material. A few of the terms in Table 20.10 might also help you get your point across.

Table 20.10   Vocabulary for the Information Superhighway

English	L'Italiano
battery	la batteria
computer	il computer
disks	i dischetti

Table 20.10 Continued

English	L'Italiano
e-mail	la posta electronica
keyboard	la tastiera
laptop computer	il computer portatile
mouse	il mouse
screen	lo schermo

Help, I Lost My Passport!

It could happen to anyone, so don't feel like a total idiot if you lose your passport. Hopefully, you have written down the number, or better yet, made a photocopy of the front page with all your vital statistics. You'll want to advise the embassy as soon as *possibile*, and it wouldn't hurt to let the police know where you are staying in case the missing passport miraculously turns up. Don't lose your head; some helpful vocabulary might make it a little easier to describe your situation.

Table 20.11 Don't Leave Home Without It (But If You Do...)

English	L'Italiano
Where is...?	Dov'è...?
...police station	...il posto di polizia
...the American embassy	...l'ambasciata americana
...the American consul	...il console americano
I lost...	Ho perso...
...my passport	...il mio passaporto
...my wallet	...il mio portofoglio
...my purse	...la mia borsa
...my head	...la mia testa

Stressed Out

And you thought you were finished with pronouns. Disjunctive, or stress pronouns are used to emphasize certain facts and highlight or replace certain nouns or pronouns.

Table 20.12 Disjunctive Pronouns

Singular		Plural	
Pronoun	Meaning	Pronoun	Meaning
me	me	noi	us
te	you (familiar)	voi	you (plural)
lui	him/it	loro	them (m. and f.)
lei	her/it	sé	themselves
Lei	You (formal)		
sé	himself/herself		

Disjunctive pronouns are used when you want to emphasize either a direct or indirect object in a sentence. The following examples compare the difference between emphatic and unemphatic object pronouns:

English	Emphatic	Unemphatic
I'm waiting **for him**.	*Aspetto **lui**.*	*Lo aspetto.*
I give **you** a gift.	*Do un regalo **a te**.*	*Ti do un regalo.*
Call (telephone) **me**.	*Telefona **a me**.*	*Mi telefona.*

The following points may help you remember when to use a disjunctive pronoun:

1. Disjunctive pronouns must always follow a verb or preposition:

*Vuoi venire **con** me?*	Do you want to come with me?
*Aspetto una telefonata **da** lei.*	I am waiting for a phone call from her.
*Sono orgoglioso **di** te.*	I am proud of you.
*Questi fiori sono **per** voi.*	These flowers are for you.
*Lui parte prima **di** me.*	He is leaving before me.

2. The disjunctive pronoun *sè* is used to indicate *oneself, himself, herself,* and *themselves* as well as *itself*:

Caterina parla sempre di sé.	Caterina always talks about herself.
La luce si spegne da sé.	The light goes out by itself.
Anna lavora per sé.	Anna works for herself.

301

3. The disjunctive pronoun is most commonly used when there are two direct or indirect objects in a phrase:

*Daniela scrive **a me** e **a te**.*   Daniela writes to me and to you.

*Telefonano **a lui** e **a lei**.*   They are telephoning him and her.

Stressful Exercise

Use the appropriate stressed pronoun in the following sentences:

1. Senza di ____, non posso vivere. (you, informal)

2. Mario parla sempre di ___. (himself)

3. Vuole parlare a ____? (me)

4. Questa lettera è per ____. (Cristina)

5. Passiamo la sera alla casa di ____. (me and Steven)

6. Viene con ____ o con ____? (me, her)

Comparatives and Superlatives

You use adjectives and adverbs all the time to compare things. Often, you can add **-er** or **-est** to an adjective in English to indicate that something is more (or less) beautiful, big, sweet, tall and so on, as in, "She is sweeter than honey; in fact, she is the sweetest person I have ever met." Use Table 20.13 to help you compare things:

Table 20.13 Comparison of Adjectives: Inequality

	Adjective	Meaning
POSITIVE	triste	sad
COMPARATIVE	più triste	sadder
	meno triste	less sad
SUPERLATIVE	il/la* più triste	the saddest
	il/la* meno triste	the least sad

Note: The same rules apply using the plural articles i, gli, and le.

As a Rule

The comparative and superlative forms of the adjectives must agree in gender and number with the nouns they describe:

Maschile:

Quel bambino è il più piccolo.	That baby is the smallest.
I tuoi occhi sono i più belli.	Your eyes are the most beautiful.

Femminile:

Quella bambina è la più bella.	That baby is the most beautiful.
Le mie figlie sono le più simpatiche.	My daughters are the nicest.

To compare one thing as being either more or less than another, place the word *più* (more) or *meno* (less) before the adjective::

Questo ristorante è più caro.	This restaurant is more expensive.
Quel ristorante è meno caro.	That restaurant is less expensive.

To express the English "than," use the preposition *di* (or its contraction) in front of nouns and pronouns.

Ho più amici di te.	I have more friends than you.
Il gatto è più piccolo del cane.	The cat is smaller than the dog.
I cani sono più grandi dei gatti.	Dogs are bigger than cats.

The comparative and superlative forms of the adjectives must agree in gender and number with the nouns they describe:

La luna è meno grande della terra.	The moon is smaller than the earth.
I pianeti sono più piccoli del sole.	The planets are smaller than the sun.

Che is used when making comparisons of quantity, when comparing two qualities pertaining to the same person or thing, or when comparing two infinitive verbs:

Più...di (che)	more...than
meno...di (che)	less...than
Tu sei più alto di me.	You are taller than I.

Io sono meno alta di te.	I am less tall than you.
Di sera fa più freddo che di giorno.	The evening is colder than the day.
Meglio tardi che mai.	Better late than never.
È più facile giocare che studiare.	It's easier to play than study.

To make a relative comparison between two things, simply add *più* (more) or *meno* (less) before the adjective or adverb.

Questo è il ristorante più caro.	This restaurant is the most expensive.
Quello è il ristorante meno caro.	That restaurant is the least expensive.

Attenzione

You've seen *che* used as an interrogative adjective meaning "what." It is also used with the subjunctive signifying "that" and "than." Look for clues in a sentence that can help you determine its meaning. The following examples illustrate the different uses of this word:

Che significa?	What does it mean?
È più bello cantare che urlare.	Singing is more beautiful than shouting.
Penso che Giulia sia simpatica.	I think that Giulia is nice.

Better than the Best

In addition to having regular forms, some adjectives have irregular comparative and superlative forms. Are you good? Getting better? Or the best?

Table 20.14 Irregular Adjective Comparatives and Superlatives

Adjective	Comparative	Relative Superlative
buono (good)	migliore (better)	il/la migliore (the best)
cattivo (bad)	peggiore (worse)	il/la peggiore (the worst)
grande (big/great)	maggiore (bigger/greater)	il/la maggiore (the biggest/greatest)
piccolo (small)	minore (smaller/lesser)	il/la minore (the smallest/least)

What's What

Maggiore and *minore* are often used to reference family members, such as younger sister or older brother. The superlative is used to indicate "the oldest" or "the youngest."

The superlatives *migliore, peggiore, maggiore,* and *minore* drop the final *-e* before nouns, except with nouns beginning with *s* + consonant or *z*:

Mio fratello minore si chiama Roberto.	My younger brother is called Robert.
Tu sei la mia miglior amica!	You are my best friend.

How are you doing? Well? A perfect illustration of an irregular adverb is the word *well*. In Italian, irregular adverbs are easily learned. Table 20.15 outlines some of the most commonly used adverbs:

Table 20.15 Irregular Adverb Comparatives and Superlatives

Adverb	Comparative	Absolute Superlative
bene (well)	meglio (better)	benissimo (best)
male (badly)	peggio (worse)	malissimo (worse)
molto (much/a lot)	più, di più (more)	moltissimo (very much)
poco (little)	meno, di meno (less)	pochissimo (very little)

Oggi sto meglio.	I am better today.
Devi studiare di più.	You must study more.
Anna lavora moltissimo in questi giorni.	Anna is working very much these days.

To make the relative superlative, simply add the definite article in front of the comparative:

Arrivo il più presto possibile.	I'm arriving as soon as possible.
Faccio del mio meglio.	I'm doing my best.

Comparisons of Equality

To say that something is as good as another is called a comparison of equality. Follow this formula to say that two things are equal:

(tanto)...quanto + adjective or adverb	*as...as*
(così)...come + adjective or adverb	*as...as*

Tanto and *cosè* can also be omitted.

Jessica ì (tanto) alta quanto Gabriella.	Jessica is as tall as Gabriella.
Tu sei (così) bello come tuo padre.	You are as handsome as your father.
Mi piace sciare (tanto) quanto giocare a tennis.	I like skiing as much as playing tennis.
L'insegnante impara (tanto) quanto insegna.	The teacher learns as much as she teaches.

Personal pronouns following *come* or *quanto* are always stressed:

Io sono intelligente come te.	I am as intelligent as you are.
Tu sei come me.	You are like me.

Absolutely, Totally Superlative

If something is really extraordinary, you can use the adverb *veramente* (truly) or *molto* (very) in front of your adjective or adverb. Or, to show the extreme of something, a poetic, commonly used ending is *-issimo*. Table 20.16 looks at a few adjectives (which must always reflect gender and number) used in this manner:.

Table 20.16   Above Average

Adjective	"Very"	"Extremely"
bello	molto bello	bellissimo
buono	molto buono	buonissimo/ottimo*
cattivo	molto cattivo	cattivissimo/pessimo*
grande	molto grande	grandissimo
piccolo	molto piccolo	piccolissimo
vecchio	molto vecchio	vecchissimo
veloce	molto veloce	velocissimo

Irregular

As a Rule

Ottimo is often used in addition to *buonissimo* when something is really great, as in the best. *Pessimo* is used to describe something that is as bad as bad can get, as in *Questo ristorante è pessimo* (This restaurant is the worst).

Sto benissimo!	I am very well!
La macchina è velocissima.	The car is really fast.

Ci and Vi

In Chapter 9 you learned about the adverb *ci* and saw how it works with the verb *essere*. Besides being object pronouns, *ci* and *vi* are used as adverbs of place, meaning "here" and "there." Modern Italian tends to use *ci* more often, although the two are interchangeable.

They often replace nouns or prepositional phrases preceded by *a*, *in*, and *su*, saving the speaker unnecessary repetition.

Denoting place:

Vai spesso in piazza?	Do you often go to the piazza?
Sì, ci vado.	Yes, I go there.
Abiti a New York?	Do you live in New York?
No, non ci abito.	No, I don't live there.

Denoting things or ideas:

Credi in Dio?	Do you believe in God?
Sì, ci credo.	Yes, I do.
Pensi ai tuoi genitori?	Do you think about your parents?
Sì, ci penso.	Yes, I do.

Go On and Brag a Little

Translate the following sentences into Italian.

1. You are the most beautiful woman in the world.

2. The view is gorgeous.

3. He is as nice as he is handsome.

4. I'm feeling better, thank you.

5. Are you going to Italy this summer? Yes, I'm going there.

The Least You Need to Know

➤ Asking for what you need starts with being able to describe your problem.

➤ Use stress pronouns when you want to emphasize a point or after the preposition *a*.

➤ Use *meno* (less) or *più* (more) before adjectives and adverbs to make comparisons or express the superlative.

➤ Use *(tanto) quanto* or *(così) come* to express that things are equal.

➤ Use the ending *-issimo* to form the absolute superlative of adverbs and adjectives.

➤ Use *ci* or *vi* in lieu of a prepositional phrase.

Chapter 21

Is There a Doctor in the House?

You're probably more prone to getting sick while in a foreign country than any other time. You're in a new environment, eating different foods, your daily rituals have been altered, and you're having a great time. Those little bugs know just when to crash a party. Sickness can be especially exasperating in a foreign country where you don't know the names of your medicines and you have to explain to a *dottore* or *farmacista* exactly what the problem is. In this chapter, you'll learn how to feed your cold, starve your fever, and get back on your feet. You'll also learn about the imperfect tense, another way to talk about the past.

What a Bod!

When you were little, you were probably asked silly questions such as "Where's your nose? Where are your ears?" and because you were a brilliant child, you pointed, much to everyone's joy and delight. Now you're going to need that genius to identify those parts in Italian. If a kid can do it, so can you. Use the word *che* plus the appropriate form of *bello* plus the body part to give a compliment, as in *Che begli occhi!* (What beautiful eyes!) Irregular plural forms are provided in parentheses. Start at your toes and work up.

Table 21.1   The Sum of Your Parts

The Body	Il Corpo	The Body	Il Corpo
ankle	la caviglia	head	la testa
arm	il braccio (le braccia)	heart	il cuore
back	la schiena	knee	il ginocchio (le ginocchia)
blood	il sangue	leg	la gamba
body	il corpo	mouth	la bocca
bone	l'osso (le ossa)	nail	l'unghia
brain	il cervello	neck	il collo
buttock	il sedere	nose	il naso
chest	il petto	skin	la pelle
chin	il mento	shoulder	la spalla
ear	l'orecchio	stomach	lo stomaco
eye	l'occhio	throat	la gola
face	il viso	toe	il dito
finger	il dito (le dita)	tongue	la lingua
foot	il piede	tooth	il dente
hand	la mano (le mani)	wrist	il polso

The verb *farsi* is used to describe something that is done, as well as what we use to say when something hurts. In this case, the subject of the sentence is the troublesome body part (or parts). If what is hurting you is singular—for example, your head—so is your verb; if your feet hurt you, because they are plural, your verb must also be plural. You may want to refer back to Chapter 16 to review your indirect object pronouns again.

Mi fa male la testa.	My head hurts. (My head is hurting me.)
Mi fanno male i piedi.	My feet hurt. (My feet are hurting me.)

A doctor or pharmacist will ask you what hurts by changing the indirect object pronoun. The verb stays the same.

Ti fa male il braccio?	Does your arm hurt?
Le fa male lo stomaco?	Does your stomach hurt?
Le fanno male i piedi?	Do your feet hurt?

Express Yourself

In Chapter 5, you saw the verb *avere* as it is used in idiomatic expressions. You can use this verb to describe any kind of ache, whether it's in your head or your stomach. You'll also use the reflexive verb *sentirsi* (to feel) to describe your various ailments, as in, *Mi sento male* (I feel badly). When using the idiomatic expression *avere mal di*, the final *-e* is dropped from the word *male*. The following expressions will help you describe your discomfort or pain.

Ho...	I have...
...mal di testa	...a headache
...mal di stomaco/pancia	...a stomachache
...mal di gola	...sore throat
Mi fa male...	(the body part)... hurts me...
Mi fa male il ginocchio	My knee hurts.
Mi fanno male i piedi.	My feet hurt.
Mi sento male.	I feel bad.
Non mi sento bene.	I don't feel well.

As a Rule

The preposition *da* is used in the present tense to indicate an action that began in the past that is still occurring in the past, much like the word "since."

Da quanto tempo soffre?	(For) How long have you been suffering?
Soffro da due giorni.	I've been suffering for (since) two days.

What Ails You?

There's no need to be shy about what you're experiencing—if you want to get better, that is. Are you constipated? Do you have diarrhea? Got your period? Italians are people too, and they experience the same kinds of ailments you do. The doctor may ask you a few questions, some of which are included here. Naturally, the *Lei* form of the verb is used to maintain a professional relationship.

Qual è il problema?	What is the problem?
Come si sente?	How do you feel?
Quanti anni ha?	How old are you?
Da quanto tempo soffre?	(For) How long have you been suffering?
Prende delle medicine?	Are you taking any medications?
Ha delle allergie?	Do you have any allergies?
Soffre di…?	Do you suffer from…?
Ha avuto…?	Have you had…?
Che cosa Le fa male?	What hurts you?

Tell Me Where It Hurts

Imagine you are telling a doctor what your aches and pains are. If you are using the expression *Mi fa male*, don't forget to account for number if what hurts you is plural.

Example: your head

Answer: Mi fa male la testa. *or* Ho mal di testa.

1. your knee
2. your shoulders
3. your feet

4. your throat
5. your tooth
6. your ankle

As a Rule

If you want the indirect object pronoun to clearly and specifically express who is in pain, you may add the preposition *a* plus the name of the person or a prepositional phrase:

A Fabio fanno male le braccia.   Fabio's arms hurt.

It is not necessary to use the possessive adjective before a body part because it is already indicated by the indirect object pronoun.

This Isn't Funny Anymore

You may have a serious medical condition that warrants immediate attention. Don't hesitate to contact a doctor or call for *un'ambulanza* should you feel the need for one. You may think you've taken care of everything by bringing your own little medicine chest filled with leftover pills from prescriptions for one thing or another, but self-medicating could make things worse, especially in a foreign country. The words in Table 21.2 will help you describe what's going on.

Table 21.2 Symptoms and Conditions

Symptom	Il Sintomo	Symptom	Il Sintomo
abscess	l'ascesso	dizziness	le vertigini
blister	la vescica	exhaustion	l'esaurimento
broken bone	un osso rotto	fever	la febbre
bruise	il livido	fracture	la frattura
bump	la tumefazione	headache	il mal di testa
burn	la scottatura	indigestion	l'indigestione
chills	i brividi	insomnia	l'insonnia
constipation	la stitichezza	lump (on the head)	il bernoccolo
cough	la tosse	migraine	l'emicrania
cramps	i crampi	nausea	la nausea
diarrhea	la diarrea	pain	il dolore

continues

Table 21.2   Continued

Symptom	Il Sintomo	Symptom	Il Sintomo
rash	un'irritazione	swelling	il gonfiore
sprain	la distorsione	toothache	il mal di denti
stomachache	il mal di stomaco	wound	la ferita

Some particularly unattractive verbs and other useful phrases describing conditions are outlined in Table 21.3.

Table 21.3   How Are You Feeling?

Italian	English	Example	English
avere la nausea	to be nauseous	Ho la nausea.	I am nauseous.
avere la tosse	to cough	Ho la tosse.	I am coughing.
essere esaurito	to be exhausted	Sono esaurito/a.	I am exhausted.
sanguinare	to bleed	Sanguino.	I am bleeding.
starnutire	to sneeze	Starnutisco.	I am sneezing.
vomitare	to vomit	Vomito.	I am vomiting.

This Is What You Have

The word *disease* literally means "not at ease." Should you have to visit the doctor, he or she is going to ask you to fill out a form, tell about any medications you're taking, and answer questions about pre-existing medical conditions. Table 21.4 offers you some helpful, if unpleasant, terms to describe health.

Table 21.4   Conditions and Diseases

Illness	La Malatia	Illness	La Malatia
angina	l'angina	cancer	il cancro
appendicitis	l'appendicite	cold	il raffreddore
asthma	l'asma	diabetes	il diabete
bronchitis	la bronchite	drug addiction	la tossicodipendenza

Illness	La Malatia	Illness	La Malatia
dysentry	la dissenteria	pneumonia	la polmonite
flu	l'influenza	polio	la poliomielite
German measles	la rosolia	smallpox	il vaiolo
gout	la gotta	stroke	il colpo apoplettico
heart attack	l'infarto	sunstroke	il colpo di sole
hemophilia	l'emofilia	tetanus	il tetano
hepatitis	l'epatite	tuberculosis	la tubercolosi
measles	il morbillo	whooping cough	la pertosse
mumps	gli orecchioni		

Your doctor may give you a *ricetta medica* (prescription) to be filled at the *farmacia* or *drogheria*.

Alla Farmacia (at the Pharmacy)

You're a trooper, willing to suffer through the minor inconveniences of having too much fun. Although not life threatening, sometimes you need a little something to take the edge off a headache. Maybe you've been eating richer foods than your stomach is accustomed to. Perhaps you've been sampling a few too many glasses of wine during your tour through Tuscany's vineyards. The Mediterranean sun can be rough on tender skin and you need a nice, cool cream to soothe your burn.

A visit to the *farmacia* can solve many of your problems as well as provide prescriptions, vitamins, and assorted sundries. Pick up some *vitamina C* to get your system back in sync, buy some *aspirina* for your head, or smooth some moisturizer all over your body.

Table 21.5 Drugstore Items

English	L'Italiano
ace bandage	la fascia elastica
antibiotics	gli antibiotici
antiseptic	l'antisettico
aspirin	l'aspirina

continues

Table 21.5 Continued

English	L'Italiano
Band-Aids	i cerotti
body lotion	la lozione
baby bottle	il biberon
castor oil	l'olio di ricino
condoms	i preservativi
cotton balls	i batuffoli di ovatta
cotton swabs (for ears)	i tamponi per le orecchie
cough syrup	lo sciroppo per la tosse
deodorant	il deodorante
depilatory wax	la ceretta depilatoria
diapers	i pannolini
eye drops	le gocce per gli occhi
floss	il filo interdentale
gauze bandage	la fascia
heating pad	l'impacco caldo
ice pack	la borsa del ghiaccio
laxative	il lassativo
mirror	lo specchio
needle and thread	l'ago e filo
nose drops	le gocce per il naso
pacifier	il ciuccio
pills	le pastiglie
prescription	la ricetta medica
razor	il rasoio
safety pin	la spilla di sicurezza
sanitary napkins	gli assorbenti
scissors	le forbici
shaving cream	la crema da barba

English	L'Italiano
sleeping pill	il sonnifero
soap	il sapone
syringe	la siringa
talcum powder	il talco
tampons	i tamponi
thermometer	il termometro
tissues	i fazzoletti
toothbrush	lo spazzolino da denti
toothpaste	il dentifricio
tweezers	le pinzette
vitamins	le vitamine

Suppose you can't find what you're looking for or they're out of stock. The following sentences all express possible questions you may have for the pharmacist:

Mi serve una ricetta?	Do I need a prescription?
Sa dove posso trovare...?	Do you know where I can find...?
C'è un'altra farmacia qui vicino?	Is there another pharmacy nearby?
C'è una farmacia notturna?	Is there an all-night pharmacy?

I Was What I Was: The Imperfect

L'imperfetto (the imperfect) tense describes repeated actions that occurred in the past. Whenever you refer to something that used to be or describe a habitual pattern, you use the imperfect. *Mentre* (while), *quando* (when), *sempre* (always), *spesso* (often), and *di solito* (usually) are all key words you can look for to identify when the imperfect is being used. Take a look at the following example in English:

Many years ago, when I was a student in Italy, I studied all the time. Studying wasn't difficult because I considered the time passed in *piazza* part of my cultural experience. Fridays, my friends and I usually went to the discotheque where we danced all night long. Saturdays, we often slept in late. Sundays, we always stayed at home because we had to do homework for Monday's lessons.

Attenzione
When using the past tense, be careful to use the appropriate tense. At times it may not always be clear whether you should use the present perfect or the imperfect.

Now look at the translation:

Molti anni fa, quando **ero** una studentessa in Italia, **studiavo** sempre. Studiare non **era** difficile perché **consideravo** il tempo passato in piazza una parte della mia esperienza culturale. Il venerdì i miei amici ed io **andavamo** in discoteca dove **ballavamo** tutta la notte. Spesso il sabato **dormivamo**. La domenica **rimanevamo** sempre a casa perché **dovevamo** fare i compiti per le lezioni di lunedì.

The imperfect also expresses actions we were doing when something else happened. For example, "I was studying when the telephone rang." The phone interrupted your studies, which you had been doing for an indefinite amount of time.

As a Rule

Which tense should you use? The present perfect expresses an action that was completed at a specific time in the past; you did it once and now it's over and done with. The imperfect represents an action that continued to occur, that was happening, that used to happen, or that would (meaning used to) happen.

Andavamo al mare ogni estate.   We used to go to the sea every summer.

Formation of the Imperfect

The imperfect tense is one of the easiest tenses to remember. With the exception of the verb *essere*, there are hardly any irregularities, and when there are, they are usually consistent with stem changes in the present. The best part is that the endings are the same for all three verb families. Just drop the final -*re* from the infinitive and add the endings in Table 21.6.

Table 21.6   Imperfect Endings

Singular	Plural
io -vo	noi -vamo
tu -vi	voi -vate
lui/lei/Lei -va	loro -vano

The verbs in Table 21.7 all share the same endings. Take a look at them.

Table 21.7 Imperfect Examples

Parlare (to Speak)	*Leggere* (to Read)	*Capire* (to Understand)
parlavo	leggevo	capivo
parlavi	leggevi	capivi
parlava	leggeva	capiva
parlavamo	leggevamo	capivamo
parlavate	leggevate	capivate
parlavano	leggevano	capivano

The only verb that completely changes form in the imperfect is the verb *essere*, shown in Table 21.8.

Table 21.8 Essere (to Be)

Singular	Plural
io ero	noi eravamo
tu eri	voi eravate
lui/lei/Lei era	loro erano

Fill in the Spazio

Take a look at these stem-changing verbs and fill in the rest of the chart using the endings you just learned.

	Dire (to Say)	*Fare* (to Do/Make)	*Bere* (to Drink)
io	_____	facevo	_____
tu	dicevi	_____	_____
lui/lei/Lei	_____	_____	beveva
noi	dicevamo	_____	_____
voi	_____	facevate	_____
loro	_____	_____	bevevano

As a Rule

You use the imperfect when you want to say that something happened regularly. The imperfect also describes states of being (mental, emotional, and physical) that occurred in the past and is used to express age, time, and weather.

Quando ero piccola...	When I was small...
Quando avevo cinque anni...	When I was five years old...
Mi sentivo bene.	I felt well.
Faceva freddo.	It was cold.
Erano le sei.	It was 6:00.

What's Done Is Done

It's awkward trying to speak in the present tense all the time. Turn the following paragraph into the past tense using the present perfect (review Chapter 19 if you need to) and the imperfect where appropriate:

Arriviamo il 21 settembre, il primo giorno d'autunno. Il sole brilla e fa bel tempo. Viaggiamo spesso ma questa è la nostra prima volta in Italia e vogliamo vedere molto. Prima andiamo a Roma dove ci aspettano il Vaticano, il Foro Romano e il Colosseo, poi andiamo a Firenze per una settimana. Mi piace la città ma mio marito preferisce stare in campagna—allora andiamo al sud dove stiamo in un albergo piccolo vicino al mare. Ogni notte beviamo vino, mangiamo al ristorante e guardiamo le stelle durante le belle serate. Non voglio tornare a casa.

The Least You Need to Know

➤ To tell someone that a certain part of your body doesn't feel well, use *Mi fa male...* plus the body part.

➤ Certain body parts are irregular in the plural.

➤ The imperfect tense is used to indicate something that occurred in the past over a period of time or something you did habitually. It is also used to talk about a mental, emotional, or physical condition that happened in the past.

➤ The present perfect is used to indicate an isolated event that occurred in the past.

Chapter 22

Earth to Mars: Can You Read Me?

In This Chapter

➤ Using the telephone

➤ Visiting the post office

➤ Writing a letter

➤ The future tense

Hello? Hello?

Think for a moment what life was like before the telephone, when letters were the only way to communicate over distance. Before a literate society, you had only word of mouth. The twentieth century has brought us to levels of communication that a Roman living during Virgilio's time could not fathom. Satellites are beaming down signals through space. You drop a package off today, and it clears the continent by tomorrow.

You've become accustomed to these services and may require them in Italy. This chapter shows you how to make a telephone call, send a fax, deal with the post office, and write a letter. You'll also take a look at what's to come in the future.

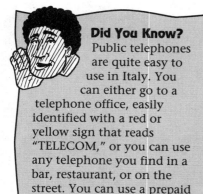

Il Telefono (The Telephone)

Most numbers in Italy start with 0 plus area code followed by the number. When calling outside Italy, you do not need to dial 0. To get an operator, you must dial 15; to get an international operator, dial 170. For an emergency or to get the *la polizia* dial 113, or for *i carabinieri* dial 112. It's always a good idea to find out any local numbers that you might need in a quandary.

Types of Phone Calls

When speaking to an international operator, you can probably speak in English. What happens if you're in a small village and need to call back home? The vocabulary in Table 22.1 should help you reach out and touch someone.

Table 22.1   Types of Calls

Type of Call	La Telefonata
collect call	una telefonata a carico del destinatario
credit-card call	una telefonata con carta di credito
long-distance call	una telefonata interurbana
intercontinental call	una telefonata intercontinentale
international call (Europe)	una telefonata internazionale
person-to-person call	una telefonata con preavviso
local call	una telefonata urbana

Before your fingers do any walking with the Yellow Pages (which is a handy reference for more than phone numbers—check it out for listings of museum hours, places to go, and things to do), familiarize yourself with the terms related to the telephone in Table 22.2.

Table 22.2   The Telephone

The Telephone	Il Telefono
800 number (free)	il numero verde
answering machine	la segreteria telefonica

The Telephone	Il Telefono
area code	il prefisso
booth	la cabina telefonica
cellular phone	il telefonino/il cellulare
coin return	la restituzione monete
cordless phone	il telefono senza fili
keypad	la tastiera
line	la linea
message	il messaggio
operator	l'operatore
phone card	la scheda telefonica
public phone	il telefono pubblico
receiver	il ricevitore/la cornetta
telephone book	l'elenco telefonico
telephone call	la telefonata
token	il gettone
touch-tone phone	il telefono a tastiera
Yellow Pages	le pagine gialle

Some useful verbs and expressions related to the telephone might come in handy. (Bonus: You've probably seen most of these verbs by now!)

Table 22.3   Phone Phrases and Verbs

The Verb	Il Verbo
to call back	richiamare
to dial	comporre il numero
to drop a line/to buzz someone	dare un colpo di telefono (idiomatico)
to hang up	riagganciare
to hold	attendere
to insert the card	introdurre la carta

continues

Table 22.3   Continued

The Verb	Il Verbo
to leave a message	lasciare un messaggio
to make a call	fare una telefonata
to pick up	alzare il ricevitore
to receive a call	ricevere una telefonata
to ring	suonare/squillare
to speak to an operator	parlare con un operatore
to telephone	telefonare

Say What?

Speaking on the telephone in a foreign language can be stressful because you don't have the added benefit of body language to help get your point across. Writing down what you want to say before you make a call will help you ask for whom or what you need. The words and phrases in Table 22.4 should help you get your point across.

Table 22.4   Ice Breakers

L'Italiano	English
Con chi parlo?	With whom do I speak?
Vorrei fare una telefonata.	I would like to make a phone call.
Vendete schede telefoniche?	Do you sell telephone cards?
Pronto!	Hello! (Used only on the telephone and literally meaning "Ready!")
C'è...?	Is...there?
Sono...(il tuo nome)	It's...(your name)
Vorrei parlare con...	I'd like to speak with...
Richiamo più tardi.	I'll call back later.

As a Rule

When spelling out words or names to an operator, Italians generally use the names of Italian cities. Be careful to enunciate your vowels correctly; the letter *i* in Italian sounds like "ee" in English. For letters that do not exist in Italian, like *w*, use a city like Washington.

Hello, Operator?

You can run into many problems when you're making a phone call. You may dial the wrong number or hear a recording telling you the number is no longer in service. The following are some phrases you might hear or want to say to an operator. They may be in the past tense, so keep an ear out for the auxiliary verbs and their participles.

What you might say:

Attendere.	Hold.
È caduta la linea.	The line was disconnected.
La linea è sempre occupata.	The line is always busy.
Mi scusi, ho sbagliato numero.	Excuse me, I dialed the wrong number.
Non posso prendere la linea.	I can't get a line.
Posso parlare con un operatore internazionale?	May I speak with an international operator?
Mi può mettere in communicazione con...?	Can you connect me with...?

What the operator might say:

Che numero ha fatto?	What number did you dial?
Non risponde.	No one is answering.
Questo (quel) numero di telefono è fuori servizio.	This (that) number is out of service.
Questo (quel) numero non funziona.	This (that) number does not work.
Siete pregati di attendere.	Please hold.

Who's Talking?

Barbara and her husband Steve are on their way to the small town of Pienza where they are to meet a friend of theirs at the Hotel Relais, an old convent. Barbara calls her friend Pamela to let her know when they are arriving. See how much you understand.

Hotel: Buona sera, Hotel Relais.

Barbara: Buona sera. Mi chiamo Barbara Peterson. Vorrei parlare con la Signora Pamela Ponsi, camera numero 103.

Hotel: Certamente, signora. Attenda un attimo.

***

Hotel: Signora, la linea è occupata. Vuole lasciare un messaggio?

Barbara: No, devo assolutamente parlarle. C'è possibilità di interrompere* la telefonata?

Hotel: No, signora. Ma come Le ho detto, può lasciare un messaggio.

Barbara: Ho capito. Va bene, riprovo fra qualche minuto.

Barbara aspetta. Poi, prova a telefonare la sua amica una seconda volta.

Hotel: Buona sera. Hotel Relais.

Barbara: Buona sera. Ho telefonato cinque minuti fa per la Signora Ponsi. È libera la linea adesso?

Hotel: Signora Peterson? Sì, gliela passo subito.

Barbara: Grazie.

***

Pamela: Pronto. Sei tu Barbara? Quando arrivi?

Barbara: Sì, sono io. Domani sera Steven e io arriviamo con l'autobus alle otto. Ci aspetti?

Pamela: Certo! Non vedo l'ora.**

Barbara: Anch'io. Ci vediamo domani.

*interrupt
**idiomatic meaning, "I can't wait."

Play Telephone

If you have a couple of friends, why not play telephone in Italian? Make a list of words that everyone can pronounce, or take an idiomatic expression from a previous chapter and see what happens by the time it gets to the last person. You'll probably have created an entirely new language.

Just the Fax

You might have some business to attend to while you are away or need directions to your next destination point. The terms in Table 22.5 all relate to sending messages electronically or through the telephone lines.

Table 22.5   Faxing Lingo

English	L'Italiano
fax/fax machine	il facsimile/il fax
fax number	il numero di fax
to send a fax	inviare un fax/"faxare"
fax modem	il fax modem
Internet	l'internet
e-mail	la posta elettronica
e-mail address	l'indirizzo elettronico/internet

Rain or Shine: The Post Office

A visit to the post office can bring the most sane person to the verge of insanity. All you want is a stamp, but you've got to wait in *la fila* (line) just like everyone else. If you want to send a *pacco*, you wait in one line only to find out you should have been on the other line. What to do? It helps to know how to ask for envelopes, stamps, paper for packages, and other items. Don't get frustrated if you're told to go to the other *sportello* (counter). Take a deep breath and remember: You're not just in the post office, you're in the post office in *Italy*. Things could be worse.

Table 22.6 The Post Office

English	L'Italiano
addressee	il recipiente
cardboard box	la scatola di cartone
counter/window	lo sportello
envelope	la busta
letter	la lettera
line	la fila
mail	la posta
mailbox	la cassetta della posta
mail carrier	il postino
money transfer	il vaglia postale, il vaglia telegrafico
package	il pacco
packing paper	la carta da pacchi
post office	l'ufficio postale
post office box	la casella postale
postage	la tariffa postale
extra postage	la soprattassa postale
postal worker	l'impiegato postale
postcard	la cartolina
receipt	la ricevuta
sender	il mittente
stamps	i francobolli
telegram	il telegramma
to send	spedire, mandare

There are many different ways to send something—some costing more, some taking longer than others. If you don't indicate how you want something to be shipped, chances are it will take the longest route. *Vorrei mandare questa lettera…* (I'd like to send this letter…)

Table 22.7 Letter Perfect

English	L'Italiano
by air mail	per posta aerea/per via aerea
by express mail	per espresso
registered mail	per posta raccomandata
by special delivery	per corriere speciale
for the United States	per gli Stati Uniti
by C.O.D.	con pagamento alla consegna

Getting Service

Do you need to communicate your postal needs quickly? The phrases in Table 22.8 should get you and your mail out the door as quickly as possible.

Table 22.8 Going Postal

English	L'Italiano
Where is the nearest...	Dov'è...
...post office?	...l'ufficio postale più vicino?
...mailbox?	...la buca da lettere più vicina?
What is the postal rate?	Qual è la tariffa postale?
I would like to send this letter...	Vorrei spedire questa lettera...
...by airmail	...per posta aerea
...by express mail	...per espresso
...registered mail	...per posta raccomandata
How much does this letter (package) weigh?	Quanto pesa questa lettera (questo pacco)?
When will it arrive?	Quando arriverà?

As a Rule

Remember that cities take the preposition *a*, whereas countries take the preposition *in*.

Remember to use the correct form of the demonstrative adjective (*questo/questa* and so on) before the noun you are using.

*Vorrei mandare questa lettera **a** Roma ma questo pacco va **in** Francia.*

Dear Gianni

Pick up some beautiful handmade marbleized paper from a *cartoleria*, and indulge in a fine *penna*. You don't have to write a lot; a couple of lines letting someone know you appreciate him or her goes a long way.

Table 22.9   La Lettera

La Lettera	Letter
Caro/a	Dear (informal)
Egregio/a	Dear (formal)
Affettuosamente	Affectionately
Cordialmente	Cordially (formal)
Il tuo/la tua	Yours (informal)
Sinceramente	Sincerely (formal)
Un abbraccio	A hug (informal)

A Review

You've seen these verbs before and should know them pretty well by now. Each verb has its participle in parentheses. Conjugate each verb in the present tense and then turn it into both the present perfect (simple past) and then the imperfect tense using the helping verb *avere*. Refer to Appendix B for more blank tables you can use to practice.

Scrivere (scritto)

Singular		Plural	
io _____		noi _____	
tu _____		voi _____	
lui/lei/Lei _____		loro _____	

Spedire (spedito)

Singular		Plural	
io _____		noi _____	
tu _____		voi _____	
lui/lei/Lei _____		loro _____	

Leggere (letto)

Singular		Plural	
io _____		noi _____	
tu _____		voi _____	
lui/lei/Lei _____		loro _____	

Mandare (mandato)

Singular		Plural	
io _____		noi _____	
tu _____		voi _____	
lui/lei/Lei _____		loro _____	

Che Sarà Sarà: The Future

The future tense is quite easy. It is used in Italian in exactly the same manner as English. Some irregular verbs may change their stem (such as *potere*, *fare*, and *andare*), but future endings are all the same for all three verb families.

The endings are added to the end of an infinitive minus its final *-e*. Regular *-are* verbs must also change the final *-a* of the future stem to *-e* except the verbs *dare*, *fare*, and *stare*.

Table 22.10   Future Endings

Singular	Plural
io -ò	noi -emo
tu -ai	voi -ete
lui/lei/Lei -à	loro -anno

Table 22.11 illustrates how the future works in all three verb families.

Table 22.11   Future Examples

Parlare (to speak)	*Leggere* (to read)	*Capire* (to understand)
parlerò	leggerò	capirò
parlerai	leggerai	capirai
parlerà	leggerà	capirà
parleremo	leggeremo	capiremo
parlerete	leggerete	capirete
parleranno	leggeranno	capiranno

Ti parlerò domani.	I'll speak to you tomorrow.
Quest'estate leggerò molti libri.	This summer I will read many books.

Will You Be Mine?

Table 22.12 shows you how to travel through time and be in the future.

Table 22.12   Essere (to Be)

Singular	Plural
io sarò	noi saremo
tu sarai	voi sarete
lui/lei/Lei sarà	loro saranno

Che sarà sarà.	What will be will be.
Saremo in città lunedì.	We will be in the city on Monday.

What Will You Have?

Table 22.13 shows how the verb *avere* is conjugated in the future.

Table 22.13 Avere (to Have)

Singular	Plural
io avrò	noi avremo
tu avrai	voi avrete
lui/lei/Lei avrà	loro avranno

Avrai tempo di vedermi la settimana prossima?	Will you have time to see me next week?
Sì, avrò tempo.	Yes, I will have time.

As a Rule

In Italian, you can express probability by using the future tense.

Dov'è Roberto?	Where is Robert?
Sarà in giro.	He must be around.

Look for the Pattern

Verbs that end in *-care* or *-gare* (such as *cercare, giocare,* and *pagare*) add an *-h* before the *-er* base in order to maintain the original sound of their infinitives. Verbs such as *cominciare, lasciare, mangiare,* and *noleggiare* that end in *-ciare, -giare,* and *-sciare* change *-ia* to *-e*.

car	→	cher	cercherò, chercherai…
gare	→	gher	pagherò, pagherai…
ciar	→	cer	lascerò, lascerai…
giare	→	ger	mangerò, mangerai…

As a Rule

Often it is not the endings that are irregular in the future tense, but the stems of the infinitives. Once you have memorized the stem, you will have no problem conjugating a verb into the future.

Irregular Stems

The following table shows a list of commonly used verbs with irregular future stems.

Verb	Stem	Future
andare (to go)	andr-	andrò, andrai…
bere (to drink)	berr-	berrò, berrai…
cercare (to search)	cercher-	cercherò, cercherai…
dare (to give)	dar-	darò, darai…
dovere (to have to)	dovr-	dovrò, dovrai…
fare (to do/make)	far-	farò, farai…
giocare (to play)	giocher-	giocherò, giocherai…
mangiare (to eat)	manger-	mangerò, mangerai…
pagare (to pay)	pagh-	pagherò, pagherai…
potere (to be able to)	potr-	potrò, potrai…
rimanere (to remain)	rimarr-	rimarrò, rimarrai…
sapere (to know)	sapr-	saprò, saprai…
stare (to stay)	star-	starò, starai…
tenere (to hold)	terr-	terrò, terrai…
vedere (to see)	vedr-	vedrò, vedrai…
venire (to come)	verr-	verrò, verrai…
volere (to want)	vorr-	vorrò, vorrai…

Ti darò i soldi fra una settimana.	I'll give you the money in a week.
Staremo in vacanza per dieci giorni.	We will be on vacation for ten days.

Back to the Future

Fill in the blanks with the proper future conjugation of the following verbs. Look at the stems to determine the rest:

	Andare	Dovere	Potere	Sapere	Vedere
io	andrò	dovrò	potrò	saprò	vedrò
tu	_____	_____	_____	_____	_____
lui/lei/Lei	_____	_____	potrà	_____	_____
noi	andremo	_____	_____	_____	_____
voi	_____	_____	_____	_____	vedrete
loro	_____	_____	_____	sapranno	_____

Verbs such as *bere, rimanere, tenere, venire,* and *volere* double the final *-r* before the endings. See if you can fill in the conjugation for them:

	Bere	Rimanere	Tenere	Venire	Volere
io	berrò	rimanerrò	terrò	verrò	vorrò
tu	berrai	_____	_____	_____	_____
lui/lei/Lei	_____	_____	_____	_____	_____
noi	_____	rimarremmo	_____	_____	_____
voi	_____	rimarrete	_____	_____	_____
loro	_____	_____	_____	verrano	_____

Now let's put it all together. Turn the following paragraph into the future by using the future tense:

> Domani ho molto da fare. Devo fare la spesa* per una cena. Prima devo comprare la frutta al mercato, poi compro il pane alla panetteria. Vado al supermercato per comprare la pasta e poi voglio passare alla pescheria per un bel filetto di sogliola. Probabilmente sono stanca; allora prendo l'autobus per tornare a casa. I miei amici arrivano alle otto.

> *In this case, la spesa refers to food shopping.*

The Future Perfect

When you have finished this book, you will have learned the Italian language. The future perfect indicates something that *will have happened* in the future before another future action. You form the future perfect by using either the auxiliary verb *avere* or *essere* in the future and the past participle of a verb.

Per l'anno prossimo avrò imparato l'italiano.	I will have learned Italian by next year.
Sarai tornato dal lavoro alle otto?	Will you have returned from work by 8:00?

The Least You Need to Know

➤ Italians use the names of Italian cities when spelling something out over the telephone.

➤ The future endings are the same for all three verb families.

➤ Many verbs have irregular stems in the future tense.

➤ The verbs *avere* and *essere* are irregular in the future and must be memorized.

casa
bene
casa

Benvenuto

Chapter 23

Home Sweet Home

In This Chapter

➤ Apartments and houses

➤ Rooms, furnishings, and amenities

➤ The conditional tense

Some people visit Italy and never leave. If you're one of the many who have fallen in love with the beautiful panoramas, wonderful food, and warm people, you may want to invest in a house or villa (or maybe even a castle!) nestled deeply within the Italian countryside. Should you decide to stay awhile, this chapter will help you make your fantasy come true. (If you're still only at the dream stage, you'll also learn about the conditional tense!)

Your Home Away from Home

You're interested in finding out how everyday life is in Italy, and you want to give it a test run before taking the plunge. Renting a villa, apartment, or farmhouse has become quite popular in recent years, and foreigners are generally welcomed with open arms. It's not as difficult as it may seem, once you've decided to begin looking for the perfect home. Pick up a local paper and comb through the real estate section. How many bedrooms does it have? Is there a balcony? Table 23.1 lists the various features people look for in a home. Use the expression *Ce l'ha...* (Does it have...) to ask if it has what you're looking for.

Table 23.1 Internal Affairs

English	L'Italiano
air conditioning	l'aria condizionata
apartment	l'appartamento
attic	la soffitta
backyard	il giardino
balcony	il balcone
basement	la cantina
bathroom	il bagno
bathtub	la vasca da bagno
bedroom	la camera da letto
building	il palazzo
cathedral ceiling	il soffitto a cattedrale
ceiling	il soffitto
condominium	il condominio
courtyard	il cortile
day room	il soggiorno
dining room	la sala da pranzo
entrance	l'ingresso
elevator	l'ascensore
fireplace	il camino
floor	il pavimento
floor (story)	il piano
garage	il garage
ground floor	il pianterreno
hallway	il corridoio
heating	il riscaldamento
…electric	…elettrico
…gas	…a gas
house	la casa
kitchen	la cucina

English	L'Italiano
laundry room	la lavanderia
lease	il contratto di locazione
living room	il soggiorno
maintenance	la manutenzione
owner	il padrone di casa
rent	l'affitto
roof	il tetto
room	la stanza, la camera
security deposit	il deposito cauzionale
shower	la doccia
stairs	le scale
storage room	la cantina
tenant	l'inquilino, l'affittuario
terrace	la terrazza
villa	la villa
window	la finestra

Inside Your Home

Is the house furnished, or do you have to provide your own bed? Is there an eat-in kitchen? Curtains for the windows? Clothes dryers are quite uncommon in Italy; you'll have to *stendere* your clothes on a line just like the Italians do. Table 23.2 gives you the names of the basics you need to live comfortably.

Table 23.2 Furniture and Accessories

Furniture	I Mobili
armchair	la poltrona
bed	il letto
bookcase	la libreria
carpet	il tappeto
chair	la sedia

continues

Table 23.2 Continued

Furniture	I Mobili
dishwasher	la lavapiatti
dresser	la cassettiera
freezer	il freezer
furniture	i mobili
lamp	la lampada
microwave oven	il forno a micro onde
mirror	lo specchio
oven	il forno
refrigerator	il frigorifero
sofa	il divano
stereo	lo stereo
stove	la macchina del gas
table	il tavolo
television	la televisione, il televisore
VCR	il videoregistratore
washing machine	la lavatrice

Buying or Renting

You'll have lots of questions for a real estate agent or management company. You don't want anyone to waste his (or your) time looking at things that aren't consistent with your vision. Being able to tell them what your *esigenze* (needs) are will help you get exactly what you want.

Did You Know?

Current rent laws in Italy make it quite difficult for a landlord to reclaim a property once he has a renter, regardless of the circumstances. Also, if a piece of land has not been used for a long period of time, that land becomes public domain and can be used for a variety of purposes, usually for agricultural or pastoral needs.

Table 23.3   Oh, Give Me a Home...

English	L'italiano
I am looking for…	Sto cercando…
I need…	Ho bisogno di…
Where can I find…?	Dove posso trovare…?
…the classified ads	…gli annunci (immobiliari)
…a real estate agency	…un'agenzia immobiliare
I'd like…	Vorrei…
…to lease	…noleggiare
…to rent	…affittare
…to buy	…comprare
Is this house available to rent?	È possibile affittare questa casa?
Is there rent control?	C'è l'equo cannone?
How much is the rent…	Quanto è l'affitto…
…per week?	…alla settimana?
…per month?	…al mese?
Does it include…	Include…
…heat?	…il riscaldamento?
…water?	…l'acqua?
…electric?	…la corrente?
Do I have to leave a deposit?	Devo lasciare un deposito?
How many square meters?	Quanti metri quadrati?

Useful Verbs

It's always good to know your verbs. Table 23.4 contains a few you might find useful when shopping around for a home.

Table 23.4   Verbs for Renting (or Buying)

Verb	Il Verbo
to buy	comprare
to lease	noleggiare

Table 23.4   Continued

Verb	Il Verbo
to move	cambiare casa
to rent	affittare/prendere in affitto
to sell	vendere
to share	condividere
to transfer	trasferirsi

Is your concern light or space? Do you want something modern or old? The adjectives in Table 23.5 can help you describe just what you're looking for.

Table 23.5   It Looks Like...

Adjective	L'Aggettivo
antique	antico
big	grande
bright	luminoso
luxurious	lussuoso
modern	moderno
modest	modesto
new	nuovo
noisy	rumoroso
old	vecchio
quiet	silenzioso
restored	ristrutturato, restaurato
small	piccolo

How's Your Italian?

Read the following *annunci* (ads) in the real estate section and see how much you understand. If you're staying for a couple of weeks somewhere, why not rent a room in someone's apartment? Usually there's a maximum stay of three weeks, but if an owner likes you, you may be able to stay longer. Many ads indicate when you should call: *Ore pasti* means during lunch and dinner hours. Other ads will tell you not to waste any time: *No perditempo*. Keep in mind that Italians use the metric system. *Metri quadrati* is square meters.

Trastevere
Appartamento in affitto. 40 mq. 2[dg] piano. Luminoso, ristrutturato. Referenze. No perditempo.
06-34-56-32

Testaccio
Palazzo in vendita. 4 piani, 8 appartamenti: da ristrutturare. No agenzie.
06-45-16-22

Via Flaminia
Casa in vendita o affitto. Totale mq. 180. Giardino mq. 1500 con alberi alto fusto. Migliore offerente. Dilazioni. Tel. ore pasti
06-78-53-10

Centro
Camera affittasi a turisti in ampio appartamento. Uso cucina. Massimo 3 settimane - 1 settimana di deposito.
06-99-45-12

That Would be Nice: The Conditional Tense

You already use the conditional tense of the verb *volere* every time you indicate *Vorrei* (I would like). There are other times you will want to use the conditional, especially when you're dreaming. Maybe you would prefer to live in a small village. Would you rather be in a big city? The conditional tense is used to express what would happen or what you would do under certain circumstances.

Forming the Conditional Tense

The conditional tense follows easy, idiot-proof rules that make it one of the easier tenses to learn. Verbs that are irregular in the present tense tend to be regular in the conditional. That said and done, there's *always* an exception to every rule, except this one. The good news is that the same stems you learned for the future tense apply here.

As you saw with the future tense, simply drop the final *-e* of the infinitive and add the endings.

What's What
What distinguishes a regular verb from an irregular verb is its stem. Regular verbs have stems that remain constant and consistent, like a Labrador Retriever. Irregular verbs have stems that change and are a little feisty in nature, like a monkey. Once the stem has been determined for a verb, it usually stays the same.

Regular *-are* verbs, except the verbs *dare*, *fare*, and *stare*, must again change the final *-a* of their base to *-e*.

The conditional tense is often used in conjunction with another tense, the subjunctive. You'll see how that works in the next chapter.

Table 23.6 Conditional Endings

Singular	Plural
io -ei	noi -emmo
tu -esti	voi -este
lui/lei/Lei -ebbe	loro -ebbero

The following examples in Table 23.7 illustrate how the conditional works.

Table 23.7 Conditional Examples

Parlare (to speak)	*Vendere* (to sell)	*Capire* (to understand)
parlerei	venderei	capirei
parleresti	venderesti	capiresti
parlerebbe	venderebbe	capirebbe
parleremmo	venderemmo	capiremmo
parlereste	vendereste	capireste
parlerebbero	venderebbero	capirebbero

Non gli parlerei per nessun motivo.	I wouldn't talk to him for any reason.
Per quattro soldi venderebbe anche sua madre.	For money, he would even sell his mother.

The verb *essere* maintains the same stem as it did for the future.

Table 23.8 Essere (to be)

Singular	Plural
io sarei	noi saremmo
tu saresti	voi sareste
lui/lei/Lei sarebbe	loro sarebbero

Andare in Italia sarebbe una buona idea.　　Going to Italy would be a good idea.

Sareste interessati a fare un viaggio?　　Would you be interested in taking a trip?

As a Rule

The conditional tense uses the same stems as the future. Once you have learned the stems, you simply add the appropriate conditional ending. Note that the first person plural in the future should not be confused with the conditional, which has an extra *-m*:

Future: *vorremo* (we will want)

Conditional: *vorremmo* (we would like)

Just like you saw in the future tense, verbs such as *cercare*, *giocare*, and *pagare* that end in *-care* or *-gare* add an *-h* before the *-er* base in order to maintain the original sound of their infinitives:

> **What's What**
> The conditional tense of the verbs *dovere*, *potere*, and *volere* express "should," "could," and "would like."

car	→	cher	cercherei, chercheresti…
gare	→	gher	pagherei, pagheresti…
ciar	→	cer	lascerei, lasceresti…
giare	→	ger	mangerei, mangeresti…

Let's look at some of those stem changing verbs again. Try finishing the conjugations.

Verb	Stem	Conditional
andare (to go)	andr-	andrei, andresti…
bere (to drink)	berr-	berrei, berresti…
cercare (to search)	cercher-	cercherei, cercheresti…
dare (to give)	dar-	darei, daresti…
fare (to do/make)	far-	farei, faresti…
giocare (to play)	giocher-	giocherei, giocheresti…
mangiare (to eat)	manger-	mangerei, mangeresti…
pagare (to pay)	pagh-	pagherei, pagheresti…

continues

continued

Verb	Stem	Conditional
rimanere (to remain)	rimarr-	rimarrei, rimarresti…
sapere (to know)	sapr-	saprei, sapresti…
stare (to stay)	star-	starei, staresti…
tenere (to hold)	terr-	terrei, terresti…
vedere (to see)	vedr-	vedrei, vedresti…
venire (to come)	verr-	verrei, verresti…

As a Rule

The verb *piacere* is used in the conditional to indicate that something would be pleasing to you and is used like the verb *volere*, as in "would like."

Ti piacerebbe andare al cinema?   Would you like to go to the movies?

Sì, mi piacerebbe andarci.   Yes, I'd like to go (there).

Coulda, Shoulda, Woulda

The verbs *dovere* (to have to), *potere* (to be able to), and *volere* (to want) are often used in the conditional tense. When you should do something, you use the verb *dovere*. When you could do something, use the verb *potere*. When you would like something, use *volere*. These verbs in the conditional are often used with the infinitive form of another verb.

Table 23.9   Dovere, Potere, and Volere

Dovere (to Have to)	*Potere* (to Be Able to)	*Volere* (to Want)
dovrei	potrei	vorrei
dovresti	potresti	vorresti
dovrebbe	potrebbe	vorrebbe
dovremmo	potremmo	vorremmo
dovreste	potreste	vorreste
dovrebbero	potrebbero	vorrebbero

Dovresti studiare di più.   You should study more.

Andare in Italia potrebbe essere una buona idea.   Going to Italy could be a good idea.

Vorresti bere un tè?   Would you like to drink a tea?

Practice Makes Perfetto

Translate the following sentences into Italian:

1. I'd like to go to Italy for the summer.

2. We should leave; it's getting late.

3. I could come later.

4. Would you like to see a film?

5. I'd like a big house in the country.

6. I would be rich with a million dollars.

The Least You Need to Know

➤ The conditional is formed by adding the conditional endings to the stem of the verbs.

➤ Many irregular stems are the same as used in the future tense.

➤ To express that you should, could, or would like, you must use the conditional form of the verbs *dovere*, *potere*, and *volere*.

➤ The verb *piacere* is used in the conditional to indicate that something would be pleasing to you and is used like the verb *volere*, as in "would like."

Chapter 24

Money Matters

In This Chapter

➤ Banking terms

➤ The subjunctive

➤ The past absolute

Money can't buy you love, but you sure can have fun spending it. For people doing business in Italy and for those fortunate enough to have the opportunity to stay in Italy for an extended period of time, this chapter gives you the terms you need to open a bank account, take out a mortgage, or make an investment. It also teaches you the subjunctive, a tense used most often when one is thinking about a hypothetical situation (such as, you guessed it, living in Italy).

Bank on It

Let's face it, banking terms are neither sexy nor fun, but they are absolutely necessary. You have probably learned quite a few terms by now because one tends to learn quickly when there is a need. Money talks, and so do you.

Did You Know?

Founded in 1472, Monte dei Paschi di Siena is one of the oldest banks in the world. The official currency used at the time was the *florin* (named after Florence) but credit as we know it today was an alien concept until the creation of the *cambiale*—the first example of an official document stating one's debt to another. In today's world, we call this a check.

Table 24.1 Mini Dictionary of Banking Terms

The Bank	La Banca
automated teller machine	Bancomat/lo sportello
balance	l'estratto conto
bank	la banca
bank account	il conto bancario
bill	la bolletta
branch	la filiale
cash	contanti
cashier	il cassiere
change	gli spiccioli
change (transaction)	il cambio
check	l'assegno
checkbook	il libretto degli assegni
checking account	il conto corrente
coins	le monete
credit	il credito
currency (foreign)	la valuta
customer	il cliente
debt	il debito
deposit	il deposito
down payment	l'anticipo
employee	l'impiegato
endorse	la girata
exchange rate	il tasso di scambio
final payment	il saldo

The Bank	La Banca
guarantee	la garanzia
holder	il titolare
installment plan	il piano di pagamento
interest	l'interesse
…compound	…composto
…rate	…tasso di
investment	l'investimento
loan	il prestito
long term	a lungo termine
monthly statement	l'estratto conto
mortgage	il mutuo
overdrawn check	l'assegno scoperto
payment	il pagamento
percentage	la percentuale
promissory note	la cambiale
quarter	il trimestre
rate	la rata
receipt	la ricevuta
revenue	i ricavi
safe	la cassaforte
sale	la vendita
savings account/savings book	il libretto di risparmio
short term	a breve termine
signature	la firma
stock	l'azione
sum	la somma
teller	l'impiegato di banca
to borrow	prendere in prestito
total	il totale
traveler's check	travel check
window	lo sportello

Do you need to cancel a check? Open an account? Take out a loan to continue your fabulous Italian vacation? You may need to know the verbs in Table 24.2.

Table 24.2   Banking Lingo

Verb	Il Verbo
to annul/cancel	annullare
to cash	incassare
to change money	cambiare i soldi
to close an account	chiudere il conto
to deposit	depositare
to endorse	girare
to fill out (a form)	riempire/compilare
to go to the bank	andare in banca
to invest	investire
to loan	prestare
to manage	occuparsi
to open an account	aprire un conto
to pay by check	pagare con assegno
to pay cash	pagare in contanti
to save	risparmiare
to sign	firmare
to take out a loan	prendere in prestito
to transfer	trasferire
to withdraw	ritirare

Transactions

You already have all the skills you need to express your needs at the bank, so let's practice a little. Use the conditional of *volere*, "Vorrei..." to tell the nice folks at the bank you would like to do the following:

1. Open a checking account.
2. Take out a loan.
3. Change some money.
4. Cash a check.
5. Make a deposit.
6. Make a withdrawal.

Everyone Has Needs: Il Congiuntivo (The Subjunctive)

Il congiuntivo is not pink eye; it's the subjunctive. The subjunctive is a mood, not a tense, and it expresses wishes, feelings, and doubt. It's the mood you use to express your hunches, your dreams, your musings. It is describes what might be and *not* what is.

You use the subjunctive every time you express your opinion or describe a hypothetical situation. When the fiddler on the roof starts singing, he uses the subjunctive mood in the imperfect tense: "If I *were* a rich man...."

Using the Subjunctive

The subjunctive is most often used in dependent clauses introduced by *che*, (meaning "that," as in "I think that..." or "It's important that...").

> *Penso che Marcello arrivi domani.*
> I think that Marcello is arriving tomorrow.
>
> *È importante che lui parli con un dottore.*
> It's important that he speak to a doctor.

What's What
The present subjunctive can be used to refer to either the present or the future. The past subjunctive talks about things you "wished had happened."

As a Rule

The subjunctive is used when

1. Two different clauses exist (dependent and independent) pertaining to two different subjects.

2. Those clauses are joined by *che.*

3. One of these clauses expresses need, emotion, doubt, or an opinion:

Need: *È necessario che lui vada da un dottore.* It's necessary for him to go to the doctor.

Doubt: *Dubito che vinca la nostra squadra.* I doubt our team will win.

Opinion: *Credo che tu sia la più bella donna del mondo.* I think that you are the most beautiful woman in the world.

Emotion: *Ho paura che sia troppo tardi per andarci.* I am afraid it's too late to go there.

The present subjunctive is formed by adding the following endings to the stem of the verb. Sorry, but many of the irregular stems used for the future and conditional don't apply to the subjunctive. The good news is the stems of most verbs used in the subjunctive don't change much from the infinitive.

The singular subjunctive endings are the same, requiring the use of the singular subject pronouns (*io, tu, lui/lei/Lei*) to avoid confusion. They are presented in Table 24.3 with *che* to familiarize you with this construction.

Table 24.3 Present Subjunctive Examples

Parlare	Vendere	Offrire	Capire
che io parli	che io venda	che io offra	che io capisca
che tu parli	che tu venda	che tu offra	che tu capisca
che lui (lei/Lei) parli	che lui (lei/Lei) venda	che lui (lei/Lei) offra	che lui (lei/Lei) capisca
che parliamo	che vendiamo	che offriamo	che capiamo
che parliate	che vendiate	che offriate	che capiate
che parlino	che vendano	che offrano	che capiscano

È difficile che lui venda la casa a quel prezzo.   It's difficult that he sell the house at that price.

Non penso che lui capisca.   I don't think that he understands.

The verbs *essere* and *avere* are both irregular.

Table 24.4 Essere (to Be)

Singular	Plural
che io sia	che siamo
che tu sia	che siate
che lui/lei/Lei sia	che siano

Penso che Luisa sia bella.   I think that Luisa is beautiful.

Credo che siano a casa.   I believe that they are at home.

Table 24.5 Avere (to Have)

Singular	Plural
che io abbia	che abbiamo
che tu abbia	che abbiate
che lui/lei/Lei abbia	che abbiano

Penso che Tiziana abbia ragione.   I think that Tiziana is right.

È un peccato che non abbiano il tempo di venire.   It's a shame that they don't have time to come.

Oh, So Moody

Oh, those irregularities. It should be no surprise at this point that there are several verbs with irregular subjunctive forms.

Table 24.6   Irregular Verbs in the Present Subjunctive

Verb	Irregular Present Subjunctive
andare	vada, vada, vada, andiamo, andiate, vadano
dare	dia, dia, dia, diamo, diate, diano
dire	dica, dica, dica, diciamo, diciate, dicano
dovere	debba, debba, debba, dobbiamo, dobbiate, debbano
fare	faccia, faccia, faccia, facciamo, facciate, facciano
mantenere	mantenga, mantenga, mantenga, manteniamo, manteniate, mantengano
piacere	piaccia, piaccia, piaccia, piacciamo, piacciate, piacciano
potere	possa, possa, possa, possiamo, possiate, possano
rimanere	rimanga, rimanga, rimanga, rimaniamo, rimanete, rimangano
salire	salga, salga, salga, saliamo, saliate, salgano
sapere	sappia, sappia, sappia, sappiamo, sappiate, sappiano
stare	stia, stia, stia, stiamo, stiate, stiano
tenere	tenga, tenga, tenga, teniamo, teniate, tengano
venire	venga, venga, venga, veniamo, veniate, vengano
volere	voglia, voglia, voglia, vogliamo, vogliate, vogliano

Dependent Clauses and the Subjunctive

The following expressions are all dependent clauses requiring the subjunctive mood. What makes a dependent clause? If a phrase cannot stand on its own, it is dependent. "I think that..." depends on the independent clause, "...it's raining." You use the subjunctive when you're not sure of something. It could be raining or not.

As a Rule

When negating a sentence, you must place the word *non* between the subject pronoun and the subjunctive:

È possibile che io non possa venire.   It's possible that I can't come.

Table 24.7 Express Yourself

L'Espressione	Expression
Expressions of Wishing, Emotion, Need, and Doubt	
Credo che…	I believe that…
Penso che…	I think that…
Dubito che…	I doubt that…
Immagino che…	I imagine that…
Desidero che…	I desire that…
Voglio che…	I want that…
Mi dispiace che…	I am sorry that…
Sono contento che…	I am happy that…
Impersonal Expressions and Conjunctions	
A meno che	Unless
Affinché	So that
Benché	Even though
Bisogna che…	It's necessary that…
È bene/male che…	It's good/bad that…
È difficile che…	It's difficult that…
È facile che…	It's easy that…
È importante che…	It's important that…
È incredibile che…	It's incredible that…
È possibile/impossibile che…	It's possible that…
È probabile che…	It's likely (probable) that…
È strano che…	It's strange that…
Finché non…	Until…
Nel caso che…	In case…
Non importa che…	It's not important that…
Prima che…	Before…
Purché…	Provided that…
Sebbene…	Although…
Sembra che…	It seems that…
Senza che…	Without…

Mi sembra che tu sia intelligente.	It seems to me that you are intelligent.
Sebbene io non possa suonare il violino, mi piace ascoltarlo.	Although I can't play the violin, I like listening to it.

Attenzione

You can avoid the subjunctive altogether when the subject is the same for both the dependent and the independent clauses by using *di* plus the infinitive:

Penso di andare al cinema.   I'm thinking of going to the movies.

Practice Makes Perfetto

Paola hopes she can go to Italy this summer to study the language. She wants her friend Silvia to join her on an excursion. Fill in the blanks with the appropriate form of the subjunctive.

> 1 aprile
> Caro Silvia:
> Spero che tu _____(stare) bene.
>
> Ho ricevuto la tua lettera. È probabile che
> io _____(andare) in italia quest'estate. Penso
> che _____(essere) una buona idea per imparare
> la lingua e voglio che tu _____(venire) con me in
> Sardegna. Mi dicono che l'isola _____(essere)
> molto bella. Che cosa pensi? Ti piace l'idea?
> Basta che tu mi _____(scrivere) la tua risposta.
> Immagino che tu non _____(avere) molto tempo
> ma mi piacerebbe vederti. Sono contenta che la
> tua famiglia _____(stare) bene.
> Scrivimi!
>
> Un'abbraccio forte,
> Paola

Silvia d'Argento
Via Flaminia 23
00100   Roma
Italia

The Past (Present Perfect) Subjunctive

To make the past subjunctive, use the present subjunctive form of the auxiliary verbs *avere* and *essere* with the past participle of your verb. Remember that verbs requiring *essere* as their auxiliary reflect gender and number in the participle. You use the past (or "perfect") subjunctive when the action expressed by the verb of the dependent clause occurred before the action expressed by the verb in the independent clause.

Table 24.8   Past Subjunctive

Avere + Telefonare	Essere + Andare
che io abbia telefonato	che io sia andato/a
che tu abbia telefonato	che tu sia andato/a
che lui/lei/Lei abbia telefonato	che lui/lei/Lei sia andato/a
che noi abbiamo telefonato	che siamo andati/e
che voi abbiate telefonato	che siate andati/e
che loro abbiano telefonato	che siano andati/e

Sono contenta che tu abbia telefonato.   I am happy that you telephoned.

Sembra che lui sia andato pazzo.   It seems that he has gone crazy.

Purely Speculation: The Imperfect Subjunctive

The imperfect subjunctive is most often used when someone is talking about what they *would* do *if*, as in "If I were rich, I would buy a villa," or "If I had more time, I would stay in better shape." This application will not be covered here. To learn more about the imperfect subjunctive, consult a good grammar book.

Il Passato Remoto (The Past Absolute)

Attenzione!
The *passato remoto* is used almost exclusively in the written language. You will occasionally hear it spoken in place of the *passato prossimo* as part of various dialects.

The *passato remoto* doesn't have an equivalent in English in that there is no separate tense used for events long past. It translates to the simple past, as in "I went." The past absolute therefore requires you to look at time in a different manner than you are accustomed. It is a past tense used to express an event that took place at a specific time in the past that is over and done with. It is highly irregular and used most often in the written language, particularly in literature, fables, and historical references. You don't need to use it in your daily speech, but a minimal understanding can be helpful for those of you attempting to read in Italian.

Table 24.9   Past Absolute Examples

Parlare (to Speak)	*Vendere* (to Sell)	*Capire* (to Understand)
parlai	vendei	capii
parlasti	vendesti	capisti

Parlare (to Speak)	*Vendere* (to Sell)	*Capire* (to Understand)
parlò	vendette	capì
parlammo	vendemmo	capimmo
parlaste	vendeste	capiste
parlarono	venderono	capirono

You may encounter these two familiar friends and not recognize them.

Table 24.10 Essere (to Be)

Singular	Plural
io fui	noi fummo
tu fosti	voi foste
lui/lei/Lei fu	loro furono

Table 24.11 Avere (to Have)

Singular	Plural
io ebbi	noi avemmo
tu avesti	voi aveste
lui/lei/Lei ebbe	loro ebbero

Dante scrisse La Divina Commedia nel 1307.	Dante wrote the Divine Commedy in 1307.
Cristoforo Colombo scoprì l'America nel 1492.	Christopher Columbus discovered America in 1492.

The Least You Need to Know

➤ The subjunctive is a mood and not a tense and is used to express opinions, thoughts, feelings, and desires.

➤ The absolute past is used primarily in the written language and is very irregular.

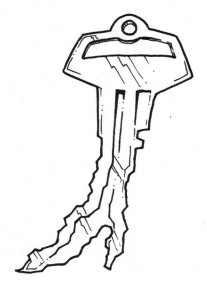

Answer Key

Chapter 2

Practice Makes Perfetto

1. dentro

2. stomaco

3. entro

4. informazioni riservate

5. L'interno

Chapter 4

Your Turn

1. Il dottore è elegante.

2. Il presidente è famoso.

3. La banca è ricca.

4. La violenza è terribile.

5. La discussione è importante.

6. L'idiota è intelligente.

A Piece of Cake

1. Italy is part of the continent of Europe.

2. The student studies mathematics and history.

3. The actor is very famous in the movies.

4. The mechanic repairs the automobile.

5. The cook prepares a salad and an appetizer.

6. The doctor converses with the patient.

7. The family desires a modern and big apartment.

8. The Japanese tourist visits the museum and the cathedral.

9. The president presents the program (the plan).

10. Robert prefers classical music.

What's Your Take?

1. La cioccolata è deliziosa.

2. Il ristorante è eccellente.

3. La città è splendida e magnificente.

4. Il profumo è elegante.

5. La conversazione è interessante.

6. Il dottore è sincero.

7. Lo studente è intelligente.

8. Il museo è importante.

9. Il balcon è alto.

10. Il treno è veloce.

Are You Well Read?

Dante—*The Divine Comedy*

Di Lampedusa—*The Leopard*

Eco—*The Name of the Rose*

Machiavelli—*The Prince*

Pirandello—*6 Characters in Search of an Author*

Chapter 5

An Idiomatic Workout

1. piano piano
2. addio
3. A più tardi
4. di mattina
5. a presto
6. a domani
7. nelle prime ore del pomeriggio
8. un'ora buona/un'oretta

Express Yourself

1. Ho fame.
2. Ho freddo.
3. Sono stanco/a; Ho sonno.
4. Sono contento/a.
5. Sono arrabbiato/a.

And the Forecast Is...

1. Nevica.
2. C'è il sole; Fa caldo.

3. C'è nebbia.

4. Fa brutto.

5. Fa caldo.

Chapter 6
Practice Makes Perfetto

1. la casa

2. il cane

3. l'albero

4. il piatto

5. la lezione

6. l'estate

7. la chiesa

8. lo straniero

9. la cattedrale

10. la pianeta

What Does It Mean?

1. aeroplani: masculine plural (airplanes)

2. bambini: masculine plural (children)

3. libro: masculine singular (book)

4. nome: masculine singular (name)

5. tavole: feminine plural (tables)

6. notte: feminine singular (night)

7. dollari: masculine plural (dollars)

8. birra: feminine singular (beer)

9. vacanza: feminine singular (vacation)

10. scuole: feminine plural (schools)

11. supermercato: masculine plural (supermarkets)

12. odore: masculine singular (odor)

13. viaggi: masculine singular (trip)

14. invenzione: feminine singular (invention)

15. ragazze: feminine plural (girls)

16. stranieri: masculine plural (foreigners)

Practice Those Plurals

1. Cerco le cartoline.

2. Cerco le riviste.

3. Cerco le collane.

4. Cerco i profumi.

5. Cerco le cravatte.

6. Cerco le penne.

What Have You Learned About Gender?

1. female: Searching for mature actress (40–50 years old) with the capacity to speak English and French to interpret the role of countess. Distinct look. Send resume with photo to Via Garibaldi 36, Roma.

2. male: Searching for strong actor, athletic, young with light hair to interpret the role of Caesar. Present yourself on June 25 at 9:00 at Superforte gym, second floor.

3. male and female: Searching for truly sexy men and women to appear nude in beach scene. No experience necessary. Telephone at 06/040357.

4. female: Tired housewife who falls in love with her neighbor while her husband travels. Please note that this is a very dramatic role. We're looking for a real star. Audition: July 5 at the Cinecitta studio.

Chapter 7

What's the Subject

1. The stars (they)

2. Jessica (she)

3. Leslie (she)

4. My mother (she)

5. Louis (he)

6. The food (it)

7. Italian (it)

8. Herby (he)

Cooking with Gas

1. Davide/lui; David takes the bus.

2. Io; I eat dinner.

3. Patrizia e Raffaella/loro; Patrizia and Raffaella study art.

4. L'insalata/lei; The salad is fresh.

5. La farmacia/lei; The pharmacy is open.

6. Lo studente/lui; The student converses with the professor.

7. Io e Gianni/noi; Gianni and I are going to Italy.

8. La ragazza/lei; The girl is going home.

Chapter 8
Practice Makes Perfetto I

1. lavora

2. aspettiamo

3. abiti

4. studio

5. passate

6. preparano

Practice Makes Perfetto II

1. spendono

2. scrivo

3. accendi

4. vediamo

5. risolve

6. prendete

Chapter 9
Making Progress

1. stiamo guardando

2. stai scrivendo

3. sta cucinando

4. stanno dormendo

5. stanno leggendo

6. sto pulendo

Chit Chat

1. stiamo

2. sono

3. sta

4. sono

5. è

6. è

Circle Marks the Spot

1. C'è

2. Ci sono

3. Ci sono

4. C'è

5. c'è

6. Ci sono

7. Ci sono

8. c'è

Ask Away

(Cinzia)
Come ti chiami? Dove abiti? Qual è la tua professione? Cosa studi? Come viaggi? Con chi viaggi? Quanto tempo passi in Italia? Dove vai? Quando ritorni?

(Il Signore Pesce)
Come si chiama? Qual è la sua professione? Parla l'inglese? Dove abita? Quanti figli ha? Come si chiamano i figli? Dove va?

Chapter 10

A Sense of Belonging

1. la sua casa

2. la mia scuola

3. i suoi libri

4. i suoi libri

5. il tuo amico

Using Avere

1. ho l'abitudine

2. ha l'intenzione di

3. ho fame

4. hanno la fortuna

5. hai sete

6. Avete bisogno

One Yellow Banana, Please

1. bianca; pulita (The white house is clean.)

2. vecchio (The Colosseo is very old.)

3. alte (The mountains in Switzerland are high.)

4. chiuso (The store is closed on Sundays.)

5. economico (This hotel is inexpensive.)

6. tirchio (The Scrooge is a very cheap man.)

Back to Your Roots

1. Olivier è francese e abita a Parigi.

2. Patrizia è cattolica e ha cinque sorelle.

3. Mia nonna è ebrea.

4. Massimo è di origine italiana.

5. Ci sono molti turisti giapponesi in Italia.

Chapter 11

In the Comfort Zone

Available to passengers on board are Italian and foreign magazines, blankets and pillows, medicine, stationery, toys for children, pens, postcards, cigarettes, Italian sparkling wines, wine, beer, and various beverages.

Going, Gone, Gone

1. vanno

2. vado

3. vai

4. andiamo

5. andate; vanno

Switcharoo

1. alla festa

2. in piazza

3. in macchina

4. nell'armadio

5. degli spaghetti

Tell Me What to Do

aiutare: Aiuta! Aiuti!

mangiare: Mangia! Mangi!

portare: Porta! Porti!

telefonare: Telefona! Telefoni!

Chapter 12

All Verbed Up

1. prendo

2. andiamo

3. prendono

4. vai

5. prendete

6. va

Tell Me Your Worries

1. una gomma a terra or una ruota bucata

2. La macchina

3. affitto

4. un cricco

5. gentile

Time Will Tell

1. Andiamo al cinema alle sei.

2. Il volo parte alle otto e venticinque.

3. La cena è alle sette.

4. C'è l'autobus per Verona a mezzogiorno.

5. Sono le quattro e quarantaquattro.

What to Do, What to Do

1. facciamo: Why don't we take a spin?

2. faccio: I am taking a nice shower when I arrive at the hotel.

3. fa: My throat hurts.

4. fa: He is asking a question at the information booth.

Chapter 13
Room Service Please

1. Mi serve della carta da lettera.

   Vorrei la carta de lettera.

2. Mi serve una chiave in più.

   Vorrei una chiave in più.

3. Mi serve un'asciugamano in più.

   Vorrei un asciugamano in più.

4. Mi serve la sveglia.

   Vorrei la sveglia.

5. Mi serve una saponetta in più.

   Vorrei una saponetta in più.

Practice Makes Perfetto

1. due coperte

2. cuscino

3. un' asciugacapelli

4. chiave

5. ristoranti

6. una camera

7. una bottiglia d'acqua minerale

Learning by Example

1. Avete bisogno di

2. Impari a

3. Continua a

4. Andiamo a

5. Smetto di

6. Finiscono di

Practice Makes Perfetto II

1. voglio

2. finisce di

3. aiutano di

4. credete di

5. hai bisogno di

6. fare

Chapter 14

Quale Festa?

Holidays in Italy are very important. *Ferragosto* is an opportunity to relax. When there is a holiday, all of the families eat, drink, and party together. Some families go to the sea, others go to the mountains, while others go abroad. Naturally, they hope to have a good time.

The Dating Game

1. Il mese scorso

2. L'anno scorso

3. L'anno prossimo

4. Fra dieci anni

5. La primavera scorsa

6. L'inverno prossimo

7. Sette anni fa

8. Ieri notte

9. Ieri sera

10. Stamattina

Chapter 15
Your Turn

trovo, trovi, trova, troviamo, trovate, trovano

vado, vai, va, andiamo, andate, vanno

passo, passi, passa, passiamo, passate, passano

faccio, fai, fa, facciamo, fate, fanno

ritorno, ritorni, ritorna, ritorniamo, ritornate, ritornano

Practice Makes Perfetto

1. Pasquale fa una passaggiata in piazza.

2. Vado a vedere un film.

3. Noi andiamo ad ascoltare l'opera.

4. Giuseppe e Marta fanno una foto del castello.

5. Fate un giro in macchina.

6. Prendi l'autobus.

A Refresher

1. Sono americano/a. Sono d'origine...

2. Sono francese. Sono d'origine francese.

3. Sono spagnolo/a. Sono d'origine spagnola.

4. Sono greco/a. Sono d'origine greco.

5. Sono irlandese. Sono d'origine irlandese.

Chapter 16
Who's Who

1. La mangiamo.
2. Dante e Boccaccio vogliono mangiarla.
3. Lo prendo.
4. Mario lo scrive.
5. Li vedo.
6. La bacia.
7. La comprate.
8. La capisce?

Who's Who II

1. Desideriamo parlarvi.
2. Mario e Giorgio ti danno un regalo.
3. Carlo la telefona.
4. Lo studente gli fa una domanda.
5. La offro un caffè.
6. Li danno una cioccolatina.
7. Gli offro una birra.
8. Ci augurano una buona notte.

Who's Who—Final Round

1. Lo guardate.
2. Lo regalo a Lorenzo.
3. La vede?
4. Gli regalo un mazzo di fiori.
5. Danno i libri a loro.
6. Lo conosco molto bene.
7. Li danno ai bambini.
8. Lo accettiamo volentieri.

Chapter 17

The Use of the Pronoun Ne

1. Sì, ne hanno. No, non ne hanno.

2. Sì, ne abbiamo. No, non ne abbiamo.

3. Sì, ne bevo. No, non ne bevo.

4. Sì, c'è ne. No, non c'è ne.

5. Sì, ne vogliamo comprare. No, non ne vogliamo.

Using the Verb Piacere

1. piace

2. piace

3. piacciono

4. piace

5. piacciono

6. piace

Using the Verb Piacere II

1. Ti piacciono i dolci?

   Sì, mi piacciono i dolci.

   No, non mi piacciono i dolci.

2. Ti piace la pasta?

   Sì, mi piace la pasta.

   No, non mi piace la pasta.

3. Ti piacciono gli spaghetti?

   Sì, mi piacciono gli spaghetti.

   No, non mi piacciono gli spaghetti.

4. Ti piacciono le acciughe?

   Sì, mi piacciono le acciughe.

   No, non mi piacciono le acciughe.

375

5. Ti piacciono i fichi?

   Sì, mi piacciono i fichi.

   No, non mi piacciono i fichi.

6. Ti piace il fegato?

   Sì, mi piace il fegato.

   No, non mi piace il fegato.

Test Your Reflexes

1. mi alzo

2. si conoscono

3. ti diverti

4. lavarsi

5. ti chiami

6. ci telefoniamo

7. si sente

8. si sposano

Chapter 19

Make a Date

1. Perché non ci incontriamo domani alle tre?

2. Ti va di nuotare?

3. Perché non andiamo in montagna la settimana prossima.

4. Perché non andiamo al museo?

5. Vuoi giocare a tennis con me?

The More Things Change

1. dolcemente

2. sinceramente

3. con intelligenza

4. necessariamente

5. velocemente

6. regolarmente

7. con difficoltà

8. probabilmente

9. solamente

10. gentilmente

Chapter 20

Stressful Exercise

1. te

2. se

3. me

4. lei

5. noi

6. me, lei

Go On and Brag a Little

1. Tu sei la più bella donna del mondo.

2. Il panorama è bellissimo.

3. Lui è tanto simpatico quanto bello.

4. Mi sento meglio, grazie.

5. Vai in Italia quest'anno? Sì, ci vado.

Chapter 21

Tell Me Where It Hurts

1. Mi fa male il ginocchio.

2. Mi fanno male le spalle.

3. Mi fanno male i piedi.

4. Mi fa male la gola.

5. Mi fa male il dente.

6. Mi fa male la caviglia.

Fill in the Spazio

dicevo, diceva, dicevate, dicevano

facevi, faceva, facevamo, facevano

bevevo, bevevi, bevevamo, bevevate

Chapter 22

Who's Talking

Hotel:	Good evening, Hotel Relais.
Barbara:	Good evening. My name is Barbara Peterson. I'd like to speak with Mrs. Pamela Ponsi, room number 103.
Hotel:	Certainly, Signora. Wait one moment.

***

Hotel:	Signora, the line is busy. Do you want to leave a message?
Barbara:	No, I must absolutely speak to her. Is there a possibility of interrupting the call?
Hotel:	No, Signora. But as I told you, you may leave a message.
Barbara:	Understood. Okay, I'll try again in five minutes.

Barbara waits. Then she tries calling her friend a second time.

Hotel:	Good evening, Hotel Relais.
Barbara:	Good evening. I called five minutes ago for Mrs. Ponsi. Is the line free now?
Hotel:	Mrs. Peterson? Yes, I'll pass you to her immediately.

A Review

scrivere: scrivo, scrivi, scrive, scriviamo, scrivete, scrivono

spedire: spedisco, spedisci, spedisco, spediamo, spedite, spediscomo

leggere: leggo, leggi, legge, leggiamo, leggete, leggono

mandare: mando, mandi, manda, mandiamo, mandate, mandanoBack to the Future

Back to the Future

andrai, andrà, andrate, andranno

dovrai, dovrà, dovremo, dovrete, dovranno

potrai, potremo, potrete, potranno

saprai, saprà, sapremo, saprete

vedrai, vedrà, vedremo, vedranno

berrai, berrà, berremo, berrete, berranno

rimanerai, rimanerà, rimarranno

terrai, terrà, terremo, terrete, terranno

verrai, verrà, verremo, verrete

vorrai, vorrà, vorremo, vorrete, vorrano

In the Future

Domani avrò molto da fare. Dovrò fare la spesa per una cena. Prima dovrò comprare la frutta al mercato, poi comprerò la pasta e poi vorrò passare alla pescheria per un bel filetto di sogliola. Probabilmente sarò stanca; allora prenderò l'autobus per tornare a casa. I miei amici arriveranno alle otto.

Chapter 23

How's Your Italian?

Trastevere. Apartment for rent. 40 square meters. 2nd floor. Lots of light, renovated. References required. Don't waste time.

Testaccio. Building for sale. 4 floors, 8 apartments: needs restoration. No agencies.

Via Flaminia. House for sale or rent. Total square meters 180. Shaded garden 1500 square meters. Best offer. Installment plan. Call during meal times.

Downtown. Room for rent for tourists in large apartment. Use of kitchen. Maximum stay 3 weeks—1 week deposit.

Practice Makes Perfetto

1. Vorrei andare in Italia quest'estate.

2. Dovremmo partire; fa tardi.

3. Potrei venire più tardi.

4. Vorresti vedere un film?

5. Vorrei una grande casa in campagna.

6. Sarei ricco con un milione di dollari.

Chapter 24

Transactions

1. Vorrei aprire un conto.

2. Vorrei prendere in prestito.

3. Vorrei cambiare i soldi.

4. Vorrei incassare un assegno.

5. Vorrei depositare i soldi.

6. Vorrei ritirare i soldi.

Practice Makes Perfetto

stia, vada, sia, venga, sia, scriva, abbia, stia

Verb Tables

Copy and use these work charts to practice conjugating verbs.

ESSERE: to be

	Singular		Plural
io	**sono**	noi	**siamo**
tu	**sei**	voi	**siete**
lui/lei/ Lei	**è**	loro	**sono**

AVERE: to have

	Singular		Plural
io	**ho**	noi	**abbiamo**
tu	**hai**	voi	**avete**
lui/lei/ Lei	**ha**	loro	**hanno**

	Singular		Plural
io		noi	
tu		voi	
lui/lei/ Lei		loro	

	Singular		Plural
io		noi	
tu		voi	
lui/lei/ Lei		loro	

	Singular		Plural
io		noi	
tu		voi	
lui/lei/ Lei		loro	

	Singular		Plural
io		noi	
tu		voi	
lui/lei/ Lei		loro	

	Singular		Plural
io		noi	
tu		voi	
lui/lei/ Lei		loro	

	Singular		Plural
io		noi	
tu		voi	
lui/lei/ Lei		loro	

	Singular		Plural
io		noi	
tu		voi	
lui/lei/ Lei		loro	

	Singular		Plural
io		noi	
tu		voi	
lui/lei/ Lei		loro	

	Singular		Plural
io		noi	
tu		voi	
lui/lei/ Lei		loro	

	Singular		Plural
io		noi	
tu		voi	
lui/lei/ Lei		loro	

Glossary

English to Italian

A

about circa

above sopra

abroad estero

abuse, to abusare

accompany, to accompagnare

add, to aggiungere

address indirizzo

admire, to ammirare

after dopo; poi

afternoon pomeriggio

again ancora

against contro

age età

agency agenzia; a. di viaggi (travel agency)

air aria

air conditioning aria condizionata

airplane aeroplano

airport aeroporto

alarm clock sveglia

already già

also anche

always sempre

ambitious ambizioso

American americano

and e

angry arrabbiato

animal animale

anniversary anniversario

announcement annuncio

answer risposta

anticipate, to anticipare

apartment appartamento

appetizer antipasto

apple mela

appointment appuntamento

apricot albicocca

April aprile

aquarium acquario

arch arco

architecture architettura

arm braccio (p. le braccia)

around attorno a

arrive, to arrivare

art arte; artista (artist)

artichoke carciofo

article articolo

as come

ascend, to salire

ashtray portacenere

ask, to chiedere

assist, to assistere

at a

atmosphere atmosfera

August agosto

August holidays ferragosto

aunt zia

autumn autunno

awaken, to svegliarsi

B

bad male; cattivo

bag bustina

bakery fornaio

balcony balcon

banana banana

bank; banker banca; bancario

barber barbiere

bathing suit costume da bagno

bathroom bagno

battery batteria

be, to essere; stare

be born, to nascere

beach spiaggia

beans fagioli

beard barba

beautiful bello

because perché

bed letto

bedroom camera da letto

beef manzo

beer birra

before davante

begin to cominciare

behind dietro a

believe, to credere

belt cintura; c. di sicurezza (seatbelt)

beneath sotto

besides; beyond oltre

better meglio

between fra; tra

bicycle bicicletta

big grande

billion milliardo

bird uccello

birth nascita

birthday compleanno

black nero

blanket coperta

blond biondo

blue blu

body corpo

boil, to bollire

book libro; libreria (book store)

boot stivale

boss padrone

bottle bottiglia

boy ragazzo

bra reggiseno

bread pane

break, to rompere

break-down guasto

breakfast colazione

breathe, to respirare

bring, to portare

brother fratello

brother-in-law cognato

brown castano

brunette bruno

building palazzo

bus autobus

business affare

but ma

butcher macellaio

buy, to comprare

C

café bar; caffè

cake torta

calculate, to calcolare

call, to chiamare

calm calmo; sereno

camera macchina fotografica

camping campeggio

can; to be able to potere

Canadian canadese

cancel, to cancellare

candy caramella

car automobile; macchina

car rental autonoleggio

carry, to portare

cash contanti

cash register cassa

cashier cassiere

castle castello

cat gatto

cathedral cattedrale

Catholic cattolico

celebrate, to festeggiare; celebrare

center centro

century secolo

chair sedia

change, to cambiare

change; coins spiccioli

check assegno; conto

cheese formaggio

cherry ciliegia

chicken pollo

Chinese cinese

chocolate cioccolata

choose, to scegliere

Christmas Natale

church chiesa

cinema cinema

citizen cittadino/a

city città

class classe

classical classico

clean pulito

clean, to pulire

clear chiaro

clever; sly furbo

climate clima

clock orologio

close, to chiudere

closed chiuso

clothing abbigliamento

cloud nuvola

coat giubbotto

coffee caffè

coin moneta

cold freddo

color colore

comb, to pettinare

come, to venire

communicate, to comunicare

concert concerto

conclude, to concludere

condition condizione

connection coincidenza

cook, to cucinare; cuocere

cool fresco

corn mais

correspond, to corrispondere

cosmetics
shop   profumeria

cost, to   costare

cotton   cotone

count, to   contare

counter;
window   sportello

country   campagna;
paese

courageous   coraggioso

courteous   cortese

cousin   cugino/a

cream   crema

create, to   creare

credit card   carta di
credito

cruise   crociera

cry, to   piangere

culture   cultura

cup   tazza

curiosity   curiosità

curious   curioso

customer   cliente

customs   dogana

cute   carino

D

dairy store   latteria

dance, to   ballare

dangerous   pericoloso

dark   buio

daughter   figlia

day   giorno

dear   caro

December   dicembre

decide, to   decidere

degree   laurea

delicious   delizioso

dentist   dentista

depart, to   partire

departure   partenza

descend, to   scendere

desire, to   desiderare

destination   destinazione

determine,
to   determinare

die, to   morire

diet   dieta

difficult   difficile

dirty   sporco

discotheque   discoteca

discount   sconto

discourteous   scortese

discuss, to   discutere

discussion   discussione

displeasing   spiacevole

divorced   divorziato

do, to   fare

doctor   dottore;
dottoressa

dollar   dollaro

doorman   portiere

double   doppio

down   giù

dream, to   sognare

dress   abito; vestito

dress, to   vestirsi

drink, to   bere

drive, to   guidare

driver's
license   patente

drug   droga

dry, to   asciugare

dry cleaner   tintoria

duck   anatra

E

each   ogni

ear   orecchio

early   anticipo (in);
presto

earth, dirt   terra

east   est

Easter (Happy
E.)   Pasqua (Buona P.)

easy facile

eat, to mangiare

eat breakfast, to fare colazione

eat dinner, to cenare

eat lunch, to pranzare

egg uovo (p. uova)

eggplant melanzana

elegant elegante

elevator ascensore

employee impiegato

empty vuoto

end fine

enemy nemico

enjoy oneself, to divertirsi

enough abbastanza

enter, to entrare

entrance entrata

envelope busta

evening sera

ever mai

everywhere dappertutto

exactly; precisely esaltamente

excellent eccellente

exchange, to scambiare

excursion gita

excuse, to scusare

exit uscita

expense spesa

expensive caro

experience esperienza

explain, to spiegare

expression espressione

eye glasses occhiali

eyes occhi

F

fabulous favoloso

face faccia

fact fatto

factory fabbrica

fall, to cadere

family famiglia

famous famoso

fantastic fantastico

far lontano

far-sighted presbite

farm fattoria

fat grasso

father padre

father-in-law suocero

fear paura

February febbraio

fiancé fidanzato/a

field campo

find, to trovare

finger il dito (p. le dita)

finish, to finire

fire fuoco

firefighter pompiere

firm azienda; ditta

first primo

first; before prima

first course primo piatto

fish pesce

flower fiore; fioraio (florist)

fly, to volare

fog nebbia

follow, to seguire

foot piede

for; in order to per

foreigner straniero/a

forget, to dimenticare

fork forchetta

fountain fontana

French francese

Friday venerdì

friend amico/a

from; by da

fruit   frutta

full   pieno

function,
to   funzionare

funny   buffo

G

garden   giardino

garlic   aglio

gas tank   serbatoio

gasoline   benzina

generous   generoso

get up, to   alzarsi

gift   regalo

girl   ragazza

give, to   dare

glass   bicchiere

gloves   guanti

go, to   andare

God   Dio

gold   oro

good   buono

good; capable   bravo

goodbye   ciao

gram   grammo

granddaughter   nipote

grandfather   nonno

grandmother   nonna

grandson   nipote

grapefruit   pompelmo

grapes   uva

Greek   greco

green   verde

group   gruppo

gum   gomma

gym   palestra

H

hair   capelli

hair
dryer   asciugacapelli

hairdresser   parrucchiere

half   mezzo

hand   mano

handsome   bello

happen, to   succedere

happy   allegro

hat   cappello

hate, to   odiare

have, to   avere

head   testa

headlight   faro

health   salute; sano
(healthy)

heart   cuore

heat   riscaldamento

heavy   pesante

help, to   aiutare

here   qui, qua

hide, to   nascondere

high school   liceo

highway   autostrada

hire, to   assumere

honest   onesto

hope, to   sperare

horrible   orribile

hospital   ospedale

hot   caldo

hotel   albergo

hour; now   ora

house   casa

how   come

how much   quanto

hug, to   abbracciare

humble   umile

humid   umido

hunger   fame (avere
fame)

husband   marito

I

ice   ghiaccio

ice cream   gelato;
gelateria (i. shop)

idea   idea

if   se

imagine, to immaginare

immediately subito

important importante

in in

in a hurry in fretta

in front of; before; ahead davanti

indicate, to indicare

inexpensive economico

infant bambino/a

infinitive infinito

inform/advise, to avvisare

information informazione

inside dentro

instead invece

intelligent intelligente

intense intenso

interesting interessante

invite, to invitare

island isola

Italian italiano

J

jacket giacca

January gennaio

Japanese giapponese

jealous geloso

Jesus Gesù

jewelry store gioielleria

July luglio

June giugno

K

key chiave

kill, to uccidere

kilogram chilo

kind (adj.) gentile; simpatico

kind (n.) tipo

kiss, to baciare

knife coltello

know, to (someone) conoscere

know, to (something) sapere

L

lace merletto/pizzo

lake lago

lamb agnello

language lingua

last scorso; ultimo

last name cognome

late ritardo (in), tardi

laugh, to ridere

laundry service lavanderia

lawyer avvocato

lazy pigro

leaf foglia

learn, to imparare

leather cuoio; pelle

leave (something), to lasciare

left sinistra

leg gamba

lemon limone

lend, to prestare

less meno

lesson lezione

letter lettera

light leggero (adj.); luce (n.)

light blue azzurro

light/turn on, to accendere

lightning flash lampo

line fila

list lista

liter litro

little piccolo (size); poco (adj.)

live, to abitare; vivere

liver fegato

local   locale

long   lungo

look, to   guardare

lose, to   perdere

love, to   amare; amore (n.)

lucky   fortunato

lunch   pranzo

M

magazine   rivista

magnificent   magnifico

maid   cameriera

mail   posta; cassetta delle lettere (m. box); postino (m. man)

make, to   fare

man   uomo; signore

manager   amministratore

March   marzo

market   mercato

marry, to   sposare; sposato (married)

marvelous   meraviglioso

masterpiece   capolavoro

match   fiammifero

mathematics   matematica

May   maggio

maybe   forse; puo darsi

meal   il pasto

measure, size   misura

meat   carne; polpette (m. balls)

mechanic   meccanico

medicine   medicina

meet, to   incontrare; conoscere

merchant   commerciante

Middle Ages   Medioevo

midnight   mezzanotte

milk   latte

minute   minuto

mirror   specchio

Miss   signorina

miss, to   perdere (un treno…)

modern   moderno

moment   momento

Monday   lunedì

money   soldi; denaro

money exchange   scambio

month   mese

moon   luna

morning   mattina

mother   madre; suocera (mother-in-law)

motor   motore

mountain   montagna

mouth   bocca

move, to   muovere

movie   film; cinema

Mr., sir   signore; (abb.) sig.

Mrs., Ms.   signora; (abb.) sig.ra

much   molto

museum   museo

mushroom   fungo

music   musica; musicista (musician)

must, to have to   dovere

N

name   nome

napkin   tovagliolo

nation   nazione

near   vicino

necessary   necessario; bisogna (it is necessary); avere bisogno di (to need)

nephew   nipote

nervous   nervoso

never   mai

new   nuovo

news notizia

newspaper giornale

next prossimo

nice simpatico

niece nipote

night notte

no one; nobody nessuno

noise rumore

noon mezzogiorno

normal normale

north nord

nose naso

not non

notebook quaderno

noun nome

November novembre

now adesso

number numero

nurse infermiera

O

ocean oceano

October ottobre

odor odore

of; from; about di

offend, to offendere

offer, to offrire

office ufficio

often spesso

oil olio

old vecchio

olive oliva

on top of; on; up su

onion cipolla

open, to aprire; aperto (open)

opera opera

operate, to operare

or o

orange arancia

order, to ordinare

original originale

other altro

outside fuori

overcoat cappotto

owner proprietario

P

package pacco

pain dolore

paint, to dipingere; pittore (painter); quadro (painting)

painting pittura

pair paio

pants pantaloni

paper carta; c. igenica (toilet p.)

paradise paradiso

parent genitore

park parco

parking lot parcheggio

party festa; partito (political p.)

pass, to passare

passport passaporto

pasta pasta

pastry pasta; pasticceria (p. shop)

path via

pay, to pagare; pagamento (payment)

pen penna

pencil matita

pension pensione

people gente

pepper pepe

percentage percentuale

perfect perfetto

perfume profumo

person persona

pharmacy farmacia

phrase frase

piece pezzo

393

pillow cuscino

pink; rose rosa

plate piatto

play, to giocare (play. a game); suonare (play an instrument)

please per favore

pleasing piacevole

police officer poliziotto

politics politica

pool piscina

poor povero

Pope il Papa

pork maiale

possibility possibilità

post office ufficio postale

postage stamp francobollo

postcard cartolina

potato patate

prepare, to preparare

prescription prescrizione

present, to presentare

price prezzo

private privato

probability probabilità

problem problema

profession professione

professor professore/ essa

pronounce, to pronunziare

protect, to proteggere

proud orgolioso

purse borsa

put, to mettere

Q

question, to domandare

quickly, early presto

R

race corsa; razza (nationalità)

radiator radiatore

railway track binario

rain pioggia

rain, to piovere

rainbow arcobaleno

raise, to alzare

rapid rapido

read, to leggere

ready pronto

receive, to ricevere; ricevuta (receipt)

recipe ricetta

recommend, to raccomandare

red rosso

region regione

relative parente

relax, to rilassarsi

religion religione

remember, to ricordare

Renaissance Rinascimento

rent, to affittare; noleggiare

repair, to riparare

repeat, to ripetere

represent, to rappresentare

reserve, to prenotare; prenotazione (n.)

resolve, to risolvere

respect, to rispettare

respond, to rispondere

restaurant ristorante

return, to ritornare

rice riso

rich ricco

ridiculous ridicolo

right destra

river fiume

romantic romantico

room stanza; camera

rude maleducato

run, to correre

S

sad triste

safe/sure sicuro

saint santo

salad insalata

salami salame

salary salario

sale svendita; commesso (sales clerk)

salt sale

satisfy, to soddisfare

Saturday sabato

say, to dire

scarf sciarpa

schedule orario

school scuola

sculpture scultura

sea mare

search, to cercare

season stagione

seat posto; sedile

second secondo

secretary secretaria

see, to vedere

sell, to vendere

send, to mandare

sensitive sensibile

September settembre

serious serio

serve, to servire

service servizio

sew, to cucire

shadow ombra

shampoo shampoo

sheet of paper foglio

ship nave

shirt camicia

shoe scarpa; calzoleria (s. store)

shop bottega; negozio; fare le spese (to shop)

short basso; corto

shower doccia

shrimp gambero

side dish contorno

sign cartello

silk seta

sincere sincero

sing, to cantare

single celibe (m.); nubile (f.) singola (una camera s.)

sister sorella; cognata (sister-in-law)

size taglia

sketch schizzo

skin pelle

skirt gonna

sky cielo

sleep, to dormire

slow lento

slowly piano

small piccolo

smile, to sorridere

smoke, to fumare

snow neve

soap sapone

soft morbido (adj.) piano (adv.)

some alcune, qualche; qualcuno (s. one); qualche volta (s. times)

son figlio

song canzone

soon subito

south sud

Spanish spagnolo

sparkling wine spumante

speak, to parlare

special speciale

spend, to spendere

splendid splendido

spoon cucchiaio

spring primavera

square, plaza piazza

squid calamari

stadium stadio

staircase scala

station stazione; s. ferroviaria (train station)

stationery store cartoleria

stay, to stare

steak bistecca

steal, to rubare

stingy (slang) tirchio

stomach stomaco

stop fermata

store negozio

storm tempesta

strange strano

street strada

stroll, to passeggiare

strong forte

student studente/essa

study, to studiare

stupendous stupendo

stupid stupido

subway metro

sugar zucchero

suit vestito

summer estate

sun sole; alba (sunrise); tramonto (sunset)

Sunday domenica

supermarket supermercato

surname cognome

sweater magliome

swim, to nuotare; piscina (s. pool)

symbol simbolo

T

table tavola

take, to prendere

tall alto

taste, to assaggiare

tax tassa

taxi tassì

tea tè

teacher insegnante

telephone telefonare; telefono (n.); telefonata (t. call); interurbana (long distance c.)

television televisione

tell, to dire; raccontare

temperature temperatura

terrace terazzo

terrible terribile

thank you grazie

that che; quello; quella

the il, lo, la, l' (s.) i, gli, le (pl.)

theatre teatro

then allora; poi

there ci, là, lì

thin magro

think, to pensare

this questo; questa

Thursday giovedì

ticket biglietto, b. di andata e ritorno (R/T ticket); biglietteria (t. counter)

tight stretto

till; as far as fino a

time ora; tempo; volta

tire ruota

tissue fazzoletto

to a; in

tobacco shop tabaccaio

today oggi

together insieme

toilet toilette

tomato pomodoro

tomorrow domani

too troppo; anche

tooth dente; spazzolino (t. brush); dentifricio (t. paste)

total totale

touch, to toccare

tour giro

tourist turista

towel asciugamano

town città

train treno

transportation trasporti

travel, to viaggiare

tree albero

trip viaggio

tropical tropicale

true, real vero

try (on), to provare

Tuesday martedì

type; kind tipo

U

ugly brutto

umbrella ombrello

uncle zio

understand, to comprendere

underwear mutande (n.); mutandine (f.)

unhealthy; sick malato

use, to usare

usually di solito

V

vacation vacanza

vegetables verdura

very molto (adv.)

vinegar aceto

violence violenza (n.); violento (adj.)

visit, to visitare

visual arts visive arti

vocabulary vocabolario

vote, to votare

W

wait, to aspettare; sala d'aspetto (w. room)

waiter; waitress cameriere

walk, to camminare

wallet portafoglio

wash, to lavare

watch orologio

water, acqua; acqua. minerale (mineral w.)

weak debole

weather tempo

Wednesday mercoledì

week settimana

weigh, to pesare; ingrassare (to gain w.); dimagrire (to lose w.)

well bene; benvenuto (welcome)

west ovest

what che cosa; che

when quando

where dove

which quale

while mentre

white bianco

who, whom chi

why perché

widow vedovo/a

wife moglie

win, to vincere

wind vento

window finestra

wine vino; enoteca (w. bar)

wise saggio

with con; senza (without)

woman donna, signora

wool lana

work, to lavorare; lavoro (n.); operaio (worker)

write, to scrivere

Y

year anno

yellow giallo

yes sì

yesterday ieri

yet ancora

you're welcome prego

young giovane

Z

zone zona

zoo zoo

Italian to English

A

a to; at

abbastanza enough

abbigliamento clothing

abbracciare to hug

abitare to live

abito dress

abusare to abuse

accanto a beside

accendere to light; turn on

accompagnare to accompany

aceto vinegar

acqua water

acquario aquarium

adesso now

aeroplano airplane

aeroporto airport

affittare to rent

agenzia agency

aggiungere to add

aglio garlic

agnello lamb

agosto August

aiutare to help

alba sunrise

albergo hotel

albero tree

allegro happy

allora then

alto tall

altro other

alzarsi to awaken

amare to love

ambizioso ambitious

americano American

amico/a friend

amministratore manager

anche also

ancora still; again; yet

andare to go

animale animal

anniversario anniversary

anno year

annoiarsi to be bored

annuncio announcement; ad

anticipare to anticipate; wait

anticipo (in) early

antipasto appetizer

aperto open

appartamento apartment

appuntamento appointment; date

appunto exactly; precisely

aprile April

aprire to open

arancia orange

architettura architecture

arco arch

arcobaleno rainbow

aria air

arrabbiato angry

arrivare to arrive

arte art; artist

articolo article

ascensore elevator

asciugacapelli hair dryer

asciugamano towel

asciugare to dry

aspettare to wait; expect

assaggiare to taste

assegno check

assistere to assist

assumere to hire

atmosfera atmosphere

attendere to attend; to wait for

attorno a around

autobus bus

automobile car

autonoleggio car rental

autostrada highway

autunno autumn

avanti in front of; before; ahead

avere to have

avvocato lawyer

azienda firm

azzurro light blue

B

baciare to kiss

bagno bathroom

balcon balcony

ballare to dance

bambino/a infant

banana banana

banca bank

barba beard

barbiere barber

basso short

batteria battery

bello beautiful; handsome

bene well

benvenuto welcome

benzina gasoline

bere to drink

bianco white

bicchiere glass

bicicletta bicycle

biglietteria ticket counter

biglietto ticket

binario railway track

biondo blond

birra beer

bistecca steak

blu blue

bocca mouth

bollire to boil

borsa purse

bottega shop

bottiglia bottle

bravo good; capable

bruno brunette

brutto ugly

buffo funny

buio dark

buono good

busta envelope

bustina bag

C

cadere to fall

caffè coffee

calamari squid

calcolare to calculate

caldo hot

calmo calm

calzoleria shoe store

cambiare to change

cameriera maid

cameriere waiter; waitress

camicia shirt

camminare to walk

campagna country

campeggio camping

campo field

canadese Canadian

cancellare to cancel

candela spark plug

cantare to sing

capelli hair

capolavoro masterpiece

cappello hat

cappotto overcoat

caramella candy

carciofo artichoke

carino cute; pretty

carne meat

caro dear; expensive

carta paper

carta di credito credit card

cartoleria stationery store

cartolina postcard

casa house; home

cassa cash register

cassetta delle lettere mail box

cassiere cashier

castano brown

castello castle

cattedrale cathedral

cattivo bad; evil

cattolico Catholic

celebrare to celebrate

cenare to dine; to have dinner

centro center

cercare to look for something; to search

che what; that; which

chi who; whom

chiamare to call

chiave key

chiedere to ask

chiesa church

chilo kilogram

chiudere; chiuso to close; closed

ci there

cielo sky

ciliegia cherry

cinema cinema

cinese Chinese

cintura belt

cioccolata chocolate

cipolla onion

circa about; around

cittadino/a citizen

città city

classe class

classico classical

cliente customer

clima climate

cognata sister-in-law

cognato brother-in-law

cognome last name

coincidenza connection

colazione breakfast

colore color

coltello knife

come how

cominciare to begin

commerciante merchant

commesso sales clerk

compleanno birthday

comprare to buy

comprendere to understand

comunicare to communicate

con with

concludere to conclude

condizione condition

conoscere to know someone

contanti cash

contare to count

conto check

contorno side dish

contro against; opposite to

coperta blanket

coraggioso courageous

corpo body

correre to run

corrispondere to correspond

corsa race

cortese courteous

corto short

costare to cost

costume da bagno bathing suit

cotone cotton

creare to create

credere to believe

crema cream

crociera cruise

cucchiaio spoon

cucinare to cook

cucire to sew

cugino/a cousin

cultura culture

cuocere to cook

cuoco cook

cuoio leather

cuore heart

curiosità curiosity

curioso curious

cuscino pillow

D

da from; by

dappertutto everywhere

dare to give

davanti in front of

debole weak

decidere to decide

delizioso delicious

dente tooth

dentifricio toothbrush

dentista dentist

dentro inside

desiderare to desire

destinazione destination

destra right

determinare to determine

di of; from; about

di solito usually

dicembre December

dieta diet

dietro behind

difficile difficult

dimenticare to forget

Dio God

dire to say

direttore director

discoteca discotheque

discussione discussion

discutere to discuss

dito (p. le dita) finger; toe

ditta company

divertirsi to enjoy oneself

divorziato divorced

doccia shower

dogana customs

dollaro dollar

dolore pain

domandare to question

domani tomorrow

domenica Sunday

donna woman

dopo after

doppio double

dormire to sleep

dottore/ dottoressa doctor

dove where

dovere to have to; must

droga drug

E

e and

eccellente excellent

economico inexpensive

elegante elegant

enoteca wine bar

entrare; entrata to enter; entrance

esperienza experience

espressione expression

essere to be

est east

estate summer

estero abroad

età age

F

fabbrica factory

faccia face

facile easy

fagioli beans

fame hunger

famiglia family

famoso famous

fantastico fantastic

fare to do; make

farmacia pharmacy

faro headlight

fatto fact

fattoria farm

favoloso fabulous

fazzoletto tissue

febbraio February

fegato liver

fermata stop

ferragosto August holidays

festa party

festeggiare to celebrate

fiammifero match

fidanzato/a fiancé

figlio/a son; daughter

fila line

finestra window

finire to finish

fino a till; as far as

fiore; fioraio flower; florist

firmare to sign

fiume river

foglia leaf

foglio sheet of paper

fontana fountain

forchetta fork

formaggio cheese

fornaio bakery

forse maybe

forte strong

fortunato lucky

fra/tra between; among

francese French

francobollo postage stamp

frase phrase

fratello brother

freddo cold

frutta fruit

fumare to smoke

fungo mushroom

funzionare to function

fuoco fire

fuori outside

furbo clever; sly (slang)

G

gabinetto toilet

gamba leg

gambero shrimp

gatto cat

gelato; gelateria ice cream; i. shop

geloso jealous

generoso generous

genitore parent

gennaio January

gente people

gentile kind; polite

Gesù Jesus

ghiaccio ice

già already

giacca jacket

giallo yellow

giapponese Japanese

giardino garden

giocare to play a game

gioielleria jewelry store

giornale newspaper

giorno day

giovane young

giovedì Thursday

giro tour

gita excursion

giù down

giubbotto coat

giugno June

gomma gum

gonna skirt

grammo gram

grande big

grasso fat

grazie thank you

greco Greek

gruppo group

guanti gloves

guardare to look at something

guasto break-down; spoiled

guidare to drive

I

idea idea

ieri yesterday

immaginare to imagine

imparare to learn

impiegato employee

importante important

in in; to; at

in fretta in a hurry

incontrare to meet

indicare to indicate

indirizzo address

infermiera nurse

infinito infinitive

informazione information

insalata salad

insegnante teacher

insieme together

intelligente intelligent

intenso intense

interessante interesting

interurbana long distance call

invece instead

inverno fall

invitare to invite

isola island

italiano Italian

L

là, lì there

lago lake

lampo lightning flash

lana wool

lasciare to leave something

latte milk

latteria dairy store

laurea degree

lavanderia laundry service

lavare to wash

lavorare to work

leggere to read

leggero light

lento slow

lettera letter

letto bed

lezione lesson

libreria book store

libro book

liceo high school

limone lemon

lingua tongue; language

lista list

litro liter

locale local

lontano far

luce light

luglio July

luna moon

lunedì Monday

lungo long

M

ma but

macchina car

macchina fotografica camera

macellaio butcher

madre mother

maggio May

magliome sweater

magnifico magnificent

magro thin

mai never

maiale pork

mais corn

malato unhealthy; sick

male bad

maleducato rude

mandare to send

mangiare to eat

mano hand

manzo beef

mare sea

marito husband

martedì Tuesday

marzo March

matematica mathematics

matita pencil

mattina morning

meccanico mechanic

medicina medicine

Medioevo Middle Ages

meglio better

mela apple

melanzana eggplant

meno less

mentre while

meraviglioso marvelous

mercato market

mercoledì Wednesday

merletto lace

mese month

metro subway

mettere to put; place; set

mezzanotte midnight

mezzo half

mezzogiorno noon

miliardo billion

minuto minute

misura measure; size

moderno modern

moglie wife

molto a lot; much; very

momento moment

moneta coin

montagna mountain

morbido soft

motore motor

muovere to move

museo museum

musica;
musicista music;
musician

N

nascere; nascita to be born; birth

nascondere to hide

naso nose

Natale (Buon N.) Christmas (Merry C.)

nave ship

nazione nation

nebbia fog

necessario necessary

negozio store

nemico enemy

nero black

nervoso nervous

nessuno no one; nobody

neve snow

nipote granddaughter; grandson; nephew; niece

nome name; noun

non not

nonna grandmother

nonno grandfather

nord north

normale normal

notizia news

notte night

novembre November

numero number

nuotare to swim

nuovo new

nuvola cloud

O

occhi eyes

occhiali glasses

oceano ocean

odiare to hate

odore odor

offendere to offend

offrire to offer

oggi today

ogni each

olio oil

oliva olive

oltre besides; beyond

ombra shadow

ombrello umbrella

onesto honest

opera opera

opera d'arte work of art

operaio worker

operare to operate

ora hour; now

orario schedule

ordinare to order

orecchio ear

orgolioso proud

originale original

oro gold

orologio watch; clock

orribile horrible

ospedale hospital

ottobre October

ovest west

P

pacco package

padre father

padrone boss

paese country; town

pagamento payment

pagare to pay

paio pair

palazzo building; palace

palestra gym

pantaloni pants

Papa pope

paradiso paradise

parcheggio parking lot

parco park

parente relative

parlare to speak

parrucchiere hairdresser

partenza departure

partire to depart

Pasqua (Buona P.) Easter (Happy E.)

passaporto passport

passare to pass

passeggiare to stroll

pasta pasta; pastry

pasticceria pastry shop

pasto meal

patate potato

patente driver's license

paura fear

pelle skin; leather

penna pen

pensare to think

pensione pension

pepe pepper

per for; in order to

per favore please

percentuale percentage

perché why; because

perdere to lose

perfetto perfect

pericoloso dangerous

persona person

pesante heavy

pesare to weigh

pesce fish

pettinare to comb

pezzo piece

piacevole pleasing

piangere to cry

piano softly; slowly

piatto dinner plate

piazza square; plaza

piccolo small

piede foot

pieno full

pigro lazy

pioggia rain

piscina swimming pool

pittore painter

pittura painting

più more

poco not very much; little (adj./adv.)

poi after

politica politics

pollo chicken

polpette meat balls

pomeriggio afternoon

pomodoro tomato

pompelmo grapefruit

pompiere firefighter

portacenere ashtray

portafoglio wallet

portare to bring; carry; wear

portiere doorman

possibilità possibility

posta mail

posto seat; place

povero poor

pranzare; pranzo to eat lunch; lunch

prego you're welcome

prendere to take

prenotare to make a reservation

preparare to prepare

prescrizione prescription

presentare to present

prestare to lend

presto quickly; early

prezzo price

primavera spring

primo first; before

privato private

probabilità probability

problema problem

professione profession

professore/essa professor

profumeria cosmetics shop

profumo perfume

pronto ready

pronunziare to pronounce

proprietario owner

prosciutto smoked ham

prossimo next

proteggere to protect

provare to try

pulire; pulito to clean; clean (adj.)

Q

quaderno notebook

quadro painting

quale which

quando when

quanto how much

quello/quella that

questo/questa this

qui/qua here

R

raccomandare to recommend

raccontare to tell

radiatore radiator

ragazzo/a boy; girl

rapido rapid

rappresentare to represent

regalo gift

reggiseno bra

regione region

regista movie director

religione religion

rendere to render; give back

resistere to resist

respirare to breathe

ricco rich

ricetta recipe

ricevere to receive

ricevuta receipt

ricordare to remember

ridere to laugh

ridicolo ridiculous

rilassarsi to relax

Rinascimento the Renaissance

riparare to repair; fix

ripetere to repeat

riscaldamento heat

riservare to reserve; put aside

riso rice

risolvere to resolve

rispettare to respect

rispondere to respond

risposta answer; response

ristorante restaurant

ritardo (in) late

ritornare to return

rivista magazine

romantico romantic

rompere to break

rosa pink; rose

rosso red

s

rubare to steal

rumore noise

ruota tire

sabato Saturday

saggio wise

sala d'aspetto waiting room

salame salami

salario salary

sale salt

salire to go up; get on

salute health

sano healthy

santo saint

sapere to know something

sapone soap

scala staircase

scambiare to exchange

scambio money exchange

scarpe shoes

scendere to descend; to go down

schizzo sketch

sciarpa scarf

sconto discount

scorso last

scortese discourteous

scrittore/ scrittrice writer

scrivere to write

scultura sculpture

scuola school

scusarsi to excuse

se if

secco dry

secolo century

secondo second

secretaria secretary

sedia chair

seguire to follow

semplice simple

sempre always

sensibile sensitive

senza without

sera evening

serbatoio gas tank

sereno calm

serio serious

servire to serve

servizio service

seta silk

settembre September

settimana week

shampoo shampoo

sicuro safe; sure

signora Mrs.; Ms. woman

signore Mr. ; sir; man

signorina Miss.

simbolo symbol

simpatico nice; kind

sincero sincere

sinistra left

soddisfare to satisfy

sognare to dream

soldi money

sole sun

sopra above; on

sorella sister

sorridere to smile

sotto beneath

spagnolo Spanish

spazzolino toothbrush

specchio mirror

speciale special

spendere to spend

sperare to hope

spesa expense

spesso often

spiacevole displeasing

spiaggia beach

spiccioli change; coins

spiegare to explain

splendido splendid

sporco dirty

sportello counter; window

sposare; sposato to marry; married

spumante sparkling wine

stadio stadium

stagione season

stanza room

stare to be; stay

stasera this evening

stazione station

stazione ferroviaria train station

stivali boots

stomaco stomach

strada street

straniero foreigner

strano strange

stretto tight

studente student

studentessa student

studiare to study

stupendo stupendous

stupido stupid

su on top of; on; up

subito soon; immediately

succedere to happen

sud south

suocera mother-in-law

suocero father-in-law

suonare to play an instrument

supermercato supermarket

sveglia alarm clock

svegliarsi to awaken

svendita sale

T

tabaccaio tobacco shop

taglia size

tardi late

tassì taxi

tavola table

tazza cup

tè tea

teatro theater

telefonare to telephone

telefono telephone

televisione television

temperatura temperature

tempesta storm

tempo weather; time

terra earth; dirt

terrazzo terrace

terribile terrible

testa head

tintoria dry cleaner

tipo type; kind

tirchio stingy

toccare to touch

toilette toilet

totale total

tovagliolo napkin

tramonto sunset

trasporti transportation

treno train

triste sad

tropicale tropical

troppo too

trovare to find

turista tourist

U

uccello bird

uccidere to kill

ufficio; u. postale office; post office

ultimo last

umido humid

umile humble

uomo man

uovo (p. uova) egg

usare to use

uscita exit

uva grapes

V

vacanza vacation

vecchio old

vedere to see

vedovo/a widow

vendere to sell

venerdì Friday

venire to come

vento wind

verde green

verdura vegetables

vero true; real

vestito suit

via path

viaggiare to travel

viaggio trip

vicino near

vigile police officer

vincere to win

vino wine

violento violent

violenza violence

visitare to visit

visive arti visual arts

vivere to live

vocabolario vocabulary

volare to fly

volta time

votare to vote

vuoto empty

Z

zia aunt

zio uncle

zoo zoo

zucchero sugar

Map of Italy

0   100 m
160 km

VAL D'AOSTA
Courmayeur
Aosta
Alps
Merano
TRENTINO-ALTO ADIGE
Novara
Lake Maggiore
Bolzano
Turin
Como
Lake Como
Trent
Cortina d'Ampezzo
Asti
Vercelli
Milan
LOMBARDY
Bergamo
FRIULI-VENEZIA GIULIA
PIEDMONT
Brescia
Belluno
Cuneo
Cremona
Lake Garda
VENETO
Udine
Savona
Parma
Verona
Vicenza
Genoa
Mantua
Padua
Treviso
LIGURIA
Rapallo
Modena
Venice
San Remo
La Spezia
Ferrara
Trieste
Gulf of Genoa
EMILIA-ROMAGNA
Gulf of Venice
Ligurian Sea
Bologna
Pisa
Ravenna
Northern Appennine
Livorno
Florence
Rimini
SAN MARINO
Siena
Pesaro
Elba
TUSCANY
Perugia
Macerata
Ancona
Assisi
Viterbo
UMBRIA
THE MARCHES
Adriatic Sea
Orvieto
Spoleto
Civitavecchia
Terni
Teramo
ROME
L'Aquila
Pescara
VATICAN CITY
Chieti
LATIUM
ABRUZZI
Campobasso
MOLISE
Caserta
Gulf of Gaeta
Benevento
Foggia
Naples
Avellino
Íschia
Pompeii
Mt. Vesuvius
APULIA
Capri
Amalfi
Bari
Sorrento
Salerno
Paestum
CAMPANIA
Potenza
BASILICATA
Brindisi
Southern Appennine
Taranto
CALABRIA
Gulf of Taranto
Lecce
Cosenza
Trapani
Lipari Islands
Marsala
Palermo
Catanzaro
Selinunte
SICILY
Messina
Enna
Taormina
Agrigento
Mt. Etna
Reggio di Calabria
Catania
Ragusa
Syracuse
Mediterranean Sea
Tyrrhenian Sea
Ionian Sea

SARDINIA
Sassari
Ólbia
Nuoro
Cagliari

Index

P

W - Z